A Practitioner's
to Trusts

A Practitioner's Guide to Trusts

Fifth edition

by

John Thurston LLB, TEP
Solicitor

Tottel
publishing

Tottel Publishing Ltd, Maxwelton House, 41–43 Boltro Road, Haywards Heath, West Sussex, RH16 1BJ

© John Thurston

Crown copyright material is reproduced with the permission of the Controller of HMSO and the Queen's Printer for Scotland. Any European material in this work which has been reproduced from EUR-lex, the official European Communities legislation website, is European Communities copyright.

A CIP Catalogue record for this book is available from the British Library.

ISBN 13   978 1 84592 117 0

ISBN 10   1 84592 117 8

Typeset by Kerrypress Ltd, Luton, Beds

Printed and bound in Great Britain by Athenaeum, Gateshead, Tyne and Wear

Preface

Trusts are very important. They often affect a person from birth to death. When a child is born, parents may become trustees of money or assets for the child. When the child is an adult, the child may purchase a house with a spouse or partner. A trust will then arise. The child may become a member of a pension fund, and again usually a trust will be created. The child may be involved with a charity, and again trust law will be involved. The child may create a settlement in his or her lifetime, and again this will involve the creation of a trust. On death, a trust frequently arises.

This book was originally written as a guide for busy practitioners, be they solicitors or accountants or legal executives or anyone with an interest in the law of trusts. It proved to be very popular, and the original format, which was intended to be more useful to practitioners than the traditional format adopted by books on trusts, has been maintained in this edition. However, some parts have been rewritten, in particular chapter 13 to take account of the changes to the taxation of trusts in the Finance Act 2006. Recent cases of interest to the practitioner have also been included.

Of necessity, the treatment of some areas is in outline only; this will be obvious from the text.

I acknowledge Crown copyright for the Acts of Parliament, statutory instruments, orders and rules quoted in the text.

John Thurston
September 2006

Contents

Contents

Contents

Table of statutes

Table of Statutory Instruments

Table of Cases

Part I

Matters Common To All Trusts

Chapter 1

THE ESSENTIAL ELEMENTS OF A TRUST AND FORMALITIES

The three certainties

1.1   In *Knight v Knight (1840) Beav 148* at page 173 Lord Langdale stated that the requirements for a valid trust were as follows:

> 'First, if the words are so used, that upon the whole, they ought to be construed as imperative; Secondly, if the subject of the recommendation or wish be certain; and Thirdly, if the objects or persons intended to have the benefit of the recommendation or wish be also certain.'

Thus the requirements for a valid trust are:

(a)   certainty of words or intention;

(b)   certainty of subject matter;

(c)   certainty of objects.

It is also essential that the beneficial interest should be clearly defined in a fixed interest trust.

Certainty of words or intention

1.2   There are no particular words which have to be used in order to create a trust. What is important is the intention of the donor. Sometimes it will be clear that the donor intended to create a trust, but other times it will be unclear, for example if the donor uses precatory words – words which request the donor to do something, but do not expressly impose a trust.

In *Re Adams and the Kensington Vestry (1884) 27 Ch D 394* the testator gave all property to the absolute use of his wife in full confidence that she would do what was right as to its disposal between his children. It was held that no trust had been created. Cotton LJ said at page 409:

> 'The motive of the gift is, in my opinion, not a trust imposed upon her by the gift in the will.'

In *Comiskey and others v Bowring-Hanbury and another [1905] AC 84* the property was given to the testator's wife 'in full confidence that she will make such use of it as I should have made myself and that at her death she will devise it to such one or more of my nieces as she may think fit.'

It was held that a trust had been created. Lord Davey said at page 89:

> 'The words which have been so much commented upon "in full confidence", are, in my opinion, neutral. I think it would be impossible to regard them as technical words in any sense. They are words which may or may not create a trust, and whether they do so or not must be determined by the context of the particular will in which you find them. In the present case, I do not think it necessary to determine any such question.'

A trust can be created even though precatory words are used as well. In *Re Steele's Will Trust [1948] Ch 603* a will included the following bequest:

> 'I give my diamond necklace to my son to go and be held as an heirloom by him and by his eldest son on his decease and to go and descend to the eldest son of such eldest son and so on to the eldest son of his descendants as far as the rules of law and equity will permit (and I request my said son to do all in his power by his will or otherwise to give effect to this my wish).'

It was held that a trust had been created.

In *Re Kayford [1975] 1 All ER 604* a company carrying on a mail order business paid money received from customers into a deposit account so that if the company was forced into liquidation, those sums could be returned to the customers who had sent them. It was held that a trust had been created. Megarry J said at page 607:

> 'As for the requisite certainty of words, it is well settled that a trust can be created without using the words "trust" or "confidence" or the like: the question is whether in substance a sufficient intention to create a trust has been manifested.'

Certainty of subject matter

1.3   It must be possible to identity the subject matter of the gift with a reasonable degree of certainty. In *Bromley and Others v Tryon and Others [1952] AC 265* a clause in a will was expressed to operate if the issue of B became entitled to a specified settled estate 'or the bulk thereof'. The House of Lords held that the clause was not void for uncertainty. It meant anything over half. In *Hunter v Moss [1994] 3 All ER 215* a company had an issued share capital of 1,000 shares. It had been held that the defendant, who was the registered holder of 950 shares, had made a binding declaration of trust with regard to 50 shares. In this case it was argued that there was no certainty of subject matter as it was not possible to identify the actual shares as the subject of the declaration of the trust, but this argument was rejected. The requirement of certainty was satisfied if immediately after the purported declaration, the court could have made an order for the execution of the trust.

Certainty of objects

1.4   With fixed trusts, it must be possible to list all the beneficiaries exactly; otherwise the trust will be void. With discretionary trusts, a different test is applicable. In *IRC v Broadway Cottages Trusts [1955] Ch 20* the trustees had power to apply the income for the benefit of all or any of a class of beneficiaries specified in a schedule as the trustees in their absolute discretion thought fit. It was held that the trust was void because it was not possible to list all the possible beneficiaries. However, in *McPhail v Doulton [1971] AC 424, IRC v Broadway Cottages Trusts* was overruled by the House of Lords. The test is now whether it is possible to say that a person comes within the class of beneficiaries; it is no longer essential to be able to list all possible beneficiaries. Lord Wilberforce said at page 56:

'... the trust is valid if it can be said with certainty that any individual is or is not a member of the class'.

This was the test which had been applied to powers by the House of Lords in *Re Gulbenkian's Settlement [1970] AC 508*. (An example of a power is where a parent is given power to nominate which of his or her children should be entitled to property.)

Lord Wilberforce in *McPhail v Doulton* also referred to linguistic or semantic uncertainty and evidential uncertainty. He said at page 457:

'I desire to emphasise the distinction clearly made and explained by Lord Upjohn [1970] AC 508, 524 between linguistic and semantic uncertainty which, if unresolved by the court, renders the gift void, and the difficulty of ascertaining the existence or whereabouts of members of the class, a matter with which the court can appropriately deal on an application for directions.'

If it is unclear from the words used who is to benefit, the trust will fail. But if there is no doubt from the words used who is to benefit, the trust will not fail. It is then a question of evidence as to whether someone comes within the class of those entitled to benefit.

Evidential uncertainty will never defeat a trust, but administrative unworkability may render it void. A discretionary trust for everyone owning a bicycle in a small village might be valid, but not if it was for everyone in the world owning a bicycle.

If there is likely to be any doubt with regard to certainty of objects, it seems that it will be valid if a third party has the right to decide if a beneficiary qualifies (*Re Tuck's Settlement Trusts [1978] Ch 49*). This facility can be useful if a will or a settlement gives a surviving spouse or cohabitee the right to continue living in a house, but the right terminates if the surviving spouse or cohabitee remarries or cohabits. As there is no definition of cohabitation, then the trustees can be empowered to decide if there is cohabitation so that the right of the surviving spouse or cohabitee to live in the house terminates.

It should be noted that there is no requirement of certainty of objects for a charitable trust; charities are discussed in more detail in chapter 14.

Certainty of beneficial interest

1.5 It may be that there is uncertainty as to the beneficial interest. In *Re Golay [1965] 2 All ER 660* a will directed that a beneficiary should be entitled to receive a reasonable income from some properties. This was held to be valid. Ungoed-Thomas J said at page 662:

> 'In this case, however, the yardstick indicated by the testator is not what he or any other specified person subjectively considers to be reasonable but what he identifies objectively as "reasonable income". The court is constantly involved in making such objective assessments of what is reasonable and it is not to be deterred from doing so because subjective influences can never be wholly excluded. In my view the testator intended by reasonable income the yardstick which the court could and would apply in quantifying the amount so that the direction in the will is not in my view defeated by uncertainty.'

The trustees can be empowered to decide what is a reasonable income.

FORMALITIES

Wills

1.6 A will which creates a trust must comply with s 9 of the Wills Act 1837 as amended. It must be in writing, and must be signed by the testator in the presence of two witnesses, who must then sign the will in the presence of the testator. The witnesses and the testator can both acknowledge their signatures.

Inter vivos

1.7   Section 53(1)(a) of the Law of Property Act 1925 provides that no interest in land can be created or disposed of except by writing signed by the person creating or conveying the same, or by his agent thereunto lawfully authorised in writing, or by will, or by operation of law.

Section 53(1)(b) provides that a declaration of trust respecting any land or any interest therein must be manifested and proved by some writing signed by some person who is able to declare such trust or by his will.

Thus a declaration of trust relating to land must be evidenced in writing, although no formalities are required if the trust is of personalty.

Section 53(1)(c) provides that a disposition of an equitable interest or trust subsisting at the time of the disposition, must be in writing signed by the person disposing of the same, or by his agent thereunto lawfully authorised in writing or by will.

On the face of it, it is clear that any disposition of an equitable interest must be in writing. However, the subsection has caused problems, particularly in the *Vandervell* saga (*Vandervell v IRC [1967] 2 AC 291, Re Vandervell's Trusts (No 2) [1974] Ch 269*). It is clear that if the legal interest is transferred, there is no need to comply with s 53(1)(c). As Lord Upjohn said in the first *Vandervell* case:

> '[s 53(1)(c)] is, in my opinion directed to cases where dealings with the equitable estate are divorced from the legal estate ...'.

In order to eliminate any difficulties, practitioners should ensure that all transfers of equitable interests are in writing.

Employees who are members of pensions schemes may be able to nominate persons to receive benefits; it seems that such nominations need not comply with s 53(1)(c) and are not wills (*In re Danish Bacon Co Ltd Staff Pension Fund Trusts [1971] 1 WLR 248*).

Equity will not permit a statute to be used as an instrument of fraud, and in that situation will enforce a trust even if there has been non-compliance with the Law of Property Act (*Rochefoucald v Boustead [1897] 1 Ch 196*).

In *Grey v IRC [1960] AC 1* nominees, who were also the trustees of settlements, held the legal title to some shares. The true owner orally told the nominees to hold the shares on the settlement trusts. Subsequently the nominees executed declarations of trust in writing. It was held that there had been a disposal of an equitable interest, and that stamp duty was payable on the written declarations of trust.

Section 53 does not apply to resulting, implied or constructive trusts (s 53(2)).

SUMMARY

1.8

- Clear words must be used to create a trust.

- It must be possible to identify the subject matter of the trust with a reasonable degree of certainty.

- If it is a fixed trust, it must be possible to ascertain all the beneficiaries.

- If it is a discretionary trust, all that is required is that it should be possible for the trustees to say if a beneficiary comes within the class of beneficiaries.

- There must also be certainty as to the beneficial interests.

- A declaration of trust relating to land must be evidenced in writing.

- A disposition of an equitable interest must also be in writing.

Chapter 2

Powers of trustees

2.1   Certain powers are conferred on trustees and personal representatives; these powers will be examined in detail, and amendments suggested. Most of these powers apply to both trustees and personal representatives, and of course personal representatives frequently become trustees once they have completed the administration of the estate of a deceased person.

ADVANCEMENT

2.2   Section 32 of the Trustee Act 1925 empowers trustees to advance capital to a beneficiary.

When does the power of advancement arise?

2.3   Section 32(2) of the Trustee Act, as amended by the Trusts of Land and Appointment of Trustees Act 1996, provides that the section does not apply to capital money arising under the Settled Land Act 1925. Thus the trustees of a strict settlement have no power to advance capital to a beneficiary under s 32.

Section 32(1) gives the trustees wide powers to apply the capital for the advancement or benefit of a beneficiary. The beneficiary may be absolutely or contingently entitled, and if contingently entitled, the contingency can be attaining a specified age or some other contingency, for example a gift may be contingent on the beneficiary attaining the age of 25. It is immaterial that the interest of the beneficiary is liable to be defeated by the exercise of a power of appointment or revocation, or to be diminished by the increase of the class to which he belongs.

There is a proviso to s 32(1) limiting the powers of the trustees. Only one-half of the presumptive share of a beneficiary can be advanced, and when the beneficiary becomes absolutely and indefeasibly entitled, the advancement must be brought into account. In addition, if there is a beneficiary with a prior or life interest, an advancement cannot be made without the consent of that person in writing.

What is meant by 'advancement or benefit'?

2.4   This phrase has been given a wide meaning. In *Pilkington v IRC [1964] AC 612* Lord Radcliffe at page 635 said that it meant 'any use of money which will improve the material situation of the beneficiary'. It has been held to include even the payment of a donation to a charity (*Re Clore's Settlement Trust [1966] 2 All ER 272*), and also payments to a beneficiary which will result in a saving in tax (*Re Moxon's Will Trust [1958] 1 All ER 386*).

It is also possible to exercise the power of advancement in order to resettle trust funds. Furthermore, there is no objection to the exercise of the power if other persons benefit incidentally (*Pilkington v IRC [1964] AC 612*).

It is possible that a resettlement may infringe the equitable rule that trustees must not delegate (of course statute has now conferred some powers of delegation). However, in *Pilkington's* case, Viscount Radcliffe said at pages 638–639:

> 'I am unconvinced by this argument that the trustees would be improperly delegating their trust by allowing the money raised to pass over to new trustees under a settlement conferring new powers on the latter. In fact I think the whole issue of delegation is here beside the mark. The law is not that trustees cannot delegate; it is that trustees cannot delegate unless they have authority to do so. If the power of advancement which they possess is so read as to allow them to raise money for the purpose of having it settled then they do have the necessary authority to let the money pass out of the old settlement into the new trusts. No question of delegation of their powers or trusts arises. If, on the other hand, their power of advancement is read so as to exclude settled advances, *cadit quaestio*.'

The statutory power in s 32 is wide enough to permit the resettlement of trust funds, but a discretionary trust may not be permissible (see *Modern Law of Trusts*, 7th edition, by Parker and Mellows (Sweet & Maxwell) at pages 623–624).

Resettlements can fall foul of the perpetuity rules, but with settlements coming into existence after 15 July 1964 the 'wait and see' rule will apply so that the resettlement will only be invalid if it becomes clear that the perpetuity rules will be infringed. It should be noted that for perpetuity purposes the resettlement is treated as being contained in the original settlement.

Prior interests

2.5   An advancement cannot be made unless the person with a prior interest consents. Thus if there is a life tenant, no advance can be made to the remainderman unless the life tenant consents.

What is the position of discretionary beneficiaries? It is clear that they do not have any prior interest within the meaning of the section, and so their consent to an advancement is not necessary (*Re Harris' Settlement (1940) 162 LT 358*). However, a beneficiary with a protected interest does have a prior interest, and will not forfeit it by giving consent (*Re Hastings-Bass [1975] Ch 25, Re Shaw's Settlement [1951] Ch 833*). It should be noted that the court has no power to dispense with the consent required by s 32.

In *Henley v Wardell [1988] The Times 29 January*, a power of advancement was subject to an uncontrolled discretion, but it was still necessary to obtain the consent of the life tenant before it could be exercised.

It should be noted that there is no power to advance capital to a life tenant under s 32.

Money advanced for a particular purpose

2.6   If trustees advance money for a particular purpose, it will not be necessary for the trustees to ensure that it is applied for that particular purpose if they have grounds for thinking that this will be done. However, if money has been advanced in previous years for a particular purpose, and the trustees are aware that it was not applied for that particular purpose, the trustees must then ensure that any further advance is so applied (*Re Pauling's Settlement Trust [1964] Ch 303*).

Common alterations

2.7   It is common to include variations which:

(a)   permit the personal representatives to advance the whole of the capital;

(b)   dispense with the requirement that the advance should be brought into account, or give the trustees a discretion as to whether the advance should be brought into account;

(c)   dispense with consents of beneficiaries with prior interests;

(d)   if there is a life interest, advance capital to the life tenant.

APPROPRIATION

2.8   Section 41 of the Administration of Estates Act 1925 authorises personal representatives to appropriate any part of the real or personal estate, including things in action, of the deceased in the actual state or condition or state of investment thereof at the time of appropriation in or towards satisfaction of any legacy bequeathed by the deceased. Thus if a beneficiary has a legacy of £10,000, the personal representatives can satisfy that legacy by transferring shares worth £10,000 to the beneficiary.

Note that the section applies whether the deceased died intestate or not (s 41(9)).

If the asset is worth more than the legacy, it is probable that personal representatives cannot use s 41. Instead, they can sell the asset to the beneficiary.

There are various limitations on the power of appropriation. An appropriation must not be made so as to affect prejudicially any specific devise or bequest (s 41(1)(i)). If the beneficiary is absolutely entitled, the appropriation can only be made with the consent of that beneficiary. If the legacy is settled, the appropriation can only be made with the consent of the trustees, or the person for the time being entitled to the income (s 41(1)(ii)).

If the person whose consent is required cannot give it because he is an infant, or incapable of managing his own affairs by reason of mental disorder within the meaning of the Mental Health Act 1983, the consent can be given by his parents or parent, testamentary or other guardian, or receiver, or, if, in the case of an infant, there is no such parent or guardian, by the court on the application of his next friend. It is not necessary to obtain consent on behalf of a person who may come into existence after the time of appropriation, or who cannot be found or ascertained at that time (s 41(1)(iii)). However, s 41(5) provides that the personal representatives in making the appropriation shall have regard to the rights of any person who may thereafter come into existence, or who cannot be found or ascertained at the time of appropriation, and of any other person whose consent is not required by the section. Furthermore, if there is no receiver acting for a person suffering from mental disorder, and the appropriation is of an investment authorised by law or by the will, if any, of the deceased for the investment of money subject to the trust, no consent is required on behalf of the person suffering from mental disorder (s 41(1)(iv)). In similar circumstances, no consent is required if there is no trustee of a settled legacy, and there is no person of full age entitled to the income (s 41(1)(v)).

An appropriation made under s 41 binds all persons interested in the property whose consent is not required by the section (s 41(4)).

Assume that a beneficiary has a legacy of £20,000. The personal representatives can satisfy that legacy by transferring to the beneficiary land to the value of £20,000. If the land is worth more than the legacy, this cannot be done. Instead, the personal representatives can sell the asset to the beneficiary.

If the asset is the subject of a specific devise, appropriation cannot be made. If the residuary beneficiaries are entitled to the land, they are bound by any appropriation made by the personal representatives.

Valuation

2.9   Section 41(3) provides that the personal representatives may ascertain and fix the value of the respective parts of the real and personal estate and the liabilities of the deceased as they may think fit, and shall for that purpose employ a duly qualified valuer where necessary. Thus an executrix cannot value shares in an unquoted company herself, and then appropriate them in her favour at that valuation (*Re Bythway (1911) 104 LT 411*).

The date for the valuation of the assets could be very important in a volatile market. The Act does not provide any guidance, but the question was decided in the case of *Re Collins [1975] 1 WLR 309*, where it was held that the relevant date was the date of appropriation, and not the date of death. Thus if prices are rising, the beneficiary will want the appropriation to be made as soon as possible, whereas if they are dropping, the beneficiary will want the appropriation to be delayed.

Appropriation by the personal representatives in their own favour

2.10   There is some doubt as to whether a personal representative who is also a beneficiary can make use of s 41 of the Administration of Estates Act 1925. The general rule is that personal representatives and trustees cannot make use of the estate they are administering for their own benefit, and it is arguable that if personal representatives appropriate assets in their own favour they are infringing this rule.

The issue has recently been considered in *Kane v Radley-Kane [1998] 3 All ER 753*. James Radley-Kane died intestate in May 1994 leaving a widow, the first defendant, and three sons. The widow was, in fact, the stepmother of the three sons. The deceased owned 36 per cent of the ordinary shares in a company called Shiredean Limited and the shares were valued for probate purposes at £50,000. The net value of the deceased's estate was £93,000. Letters of administration were granted to the widow and she regarded herself as entitled to the whole estate under the intestacy rules. However, in January 1997 the shares in Shiredean were sold for £1,131,438. The plaintiff, one of the sons, issued proceedings claiming that the appropriation of the shares by the widow in her own favour was invalid. It was held that this was the case. However, the judge stated that if the assets had been the equivalent of cash, for example government stock, then the appropriation would have been valid.

This case is clear authority that executors and administrators cannot make use of s 41 to vest assets of the deceased in their own name if the value cannot be ascertained easily. It is in order, however, if the assets are equivalent to cash, e.g.

government stock or quoted securities. It may be that the decision would have been different if the widow had obtained a valuation just before she appropriated the shares in her favour, and this had confirmed that the value was £50,000.

In a will, appropriation under s 41 should be extended so that personal representatives can appropriate in their own favour. It may also be desirable to prescribe the procedure for fixing the value of any property appropriated – the certificate of an accountant or chartered surveyor is to be conclusive.

If the deceased died intestate leaving assets which cannot be easily valued, then it seems that an administrator cannot use s 41 to appropriate these assets in his or her favour. This raises the question of what the widow in the *Radley-Kane* case should have done. She could have renounced her right to the grant – the sons would then have been entitled to the grant, and they might not have agreed to the appropriation. She could have asked the sons to agree to the appropriation, but they might have refused. She could also have asked the court to agree to the appropriation.

Personal representatives exercising a power of appropriation under the Intestates' Estates Act 1952 with regard to the matrimonial home should ensure that they comply with s 41(3) of the Administration of Estates Act 1952, and employ a qualified valuer. If there is likely to be any subsequent challenge, for example by the children of a first marriage, it may be prudent to ask them to agree to the valuation.

Trustees and powers of appropriation

2.11   Section 41 applies only to personal representatives, and does not apply to trustees, who have the following powers of appropriation:

(a)   If there are separate trusts of separate property, the trustees can appropriate assets to the value of the separate amounts given.

(b)   If there is a trust for sale, and there is nothing in the trust instrument to indicate that an appropriation should not be made, the trustees may make an appropriation.

Normally any adult beneficiaries must agree.

For a fuller discussion see *Modern Law of Trusts*, 8th edition, by Parker and Mellows (Sweet & Maxwell) at page 709–710.

Stamp duty land tax

2.12   Stamp duty land tax is not payable on an assent whether or not the property which is the subject of the assent is subject to a charge. Instead, the beneficiary must self-certify the transaction using SDLT 60.

It is therefore clear that where a person takes a property under the will or intestacy of a deceased person, stamp duty land tax is not payable whether or not the property is subject to a charge. In such a case, the application for registration must be accompanied by a SDLT 60.

It is also clear that no stamp duty land tax is payable if a surviving joint tenant is absolutely entitled to a property which is not subject to any charge. However, the position if the property is subject to a charge is not clear. Schedule 4, paragraph 8 of the Finance Act 2003 provides that the assumption of existing debt by a purchaser is chargeable consideration, and it could be argued that a surviving joint tenant is a purchaser assuming an existing debt and that therefore stamp duty land tax is payable. However, in the view of the writer, stamp duty land tax is not payable as the vesting occurs by operation of law and, as far as joint tenants who are absolutely entitled are concerned, the survivor is already liable on the charge, and is not assuming any further debt.

If property vests in surviving trustees, or new trustees are appointed, stamp duty land tax is not payable if the property is free of charge. If the property is subject to a charge and vests in surviving trustees, in the opinion of the writer stamp duty land tax is not payable for the reasons given in the preceding paragraph. The position is not clear if new trustees are appointed and the property is subject to a charge.

A surviving spouse has certain rights with regard to the matrimonial home on the intestacy of the other spouse. As these rights give the surviving spouse the power to enforce a transfer of the matrimonial home, there is no element of sale, and so no stamp duty and tax is payable.

Stamp duty

2.13   Stock transfers are subject to stamp duty, but since the Stamp Duty (Exempt Instruments) Regulations 1987, stamp duty is not payable in respect of an instrument giving effect to an appropriation in or towards satisfaction of a general legacy, provided that the instrument is certified as coming within the appropriate category of the schedule to the regulations.

Suggested alterations

2.14
- To permit personal representatives to appropriate in their own favour.
- A mechanism for valuing assets which are difficult to value.

BUSINESSES

Sole traders

2.15   The personal representatives can continue the business, but only for the purpose of selling it, and only for a year. The personal representatives are personally liable for debts they incur, but there is a right of indemnity from the estate. This right takes priority over the rights of the creditors if the business is being run in order to sell it. However, if the business is being run under a power in the will, the personal representatives have right of indemnity in preference to the beneficiaries but not the creditors.

The personal representatives can only use the assets employed in the business at the date of death; these could prove to be insufficient.

Common variations

2.16   It is common to include clauses which provide for the following:

(a)   to run the business as long as the personal representatives like;

(b)   to use other assets;

(c)   to appoint a manager;

(d)   indemnity.

Partnerships

2.17   The death of a partner automatically dissolves a partnership;, unless the partnership agreement provides that on the death of a partner the partnership continues.

There is no need to give the personal representatives of a partner extra powers to run the business, but it should be done in the case of a small partnership as all the other partners may die or retire leaving the client as a sole trader.

Companies

2.18   The testator may have shares in a company which will pass to the personal representatives. The company will continue to trade as before, and so there is no need for any extra powers, apart perhaps from empowering the personal representatives to give warranties on a sale.

CHARGING CLAUSES

2.19   The traditional rule is that trustees are not entitled to profit from a trust and are entitled only to reasonable expenses. However, the Trustee Act 2000 has substantially changed the law. Section 29 contains provisions entitling a trustee who is a trust corporation, or acts in a professional capacity, to remuneration. Section 29(1) provides that a trustee who:

(a)   is a trust corporation, but

(b)   is not a trustee of a charitable trust,

is entitled to receive reasonable remuneration out of the trust funds for any services that the trust corporation provides on behalf of the trust.

A professional trustee is similarly entitled. Section 29(2) provides that a trustee who:

(a)   acts in a professional capacity, but

(b)   is not a trust corporation, a trustee of a charitable trust or a sole trustee,

is entitled to receive reasonable remuneration out of the trust funds for any services that he provides on behalf of the trust. All the other trustees must agree in writing that he may be remunerated for the services. Note that a sole trustee cannot charge.

Section 28(5) defines what is meant by acting in a professional capacity. A trustee acts in a professional capacity if he acts in the course of a profession or business which consists of or includes the provision of services in connection with:

(a)   the management or administration of trusts generally or a particular kind of trust, or

(b)   any particular aspect of the management or administration of trusts generally or a particular kind of trust,

and the services he provides to or on behalf of the trust fall within that description.

Section 29(3) defines reasonable remuneration. In relation to the provision of services by a trustee, it means such remuneration as is reasonable in the circumstances for the provision of those services on behalf of that trust by that trustee. If the trustee in an authorised institution under the Banking Act 1987, and provides the services in that capacity, reasonable remuneration is the institution's reasonable charges for the provision of such services. Section 29(4) provides that a trustee is entitled to remuneration even if the services in question are capable of being provided by a lay trustee.

A trustee who has been appointed as an agent of the trustees, or nominee or custodian under the powers conferred by Part IV (see 2.25 below) or the trust instrument is also entitled to remuneration under s 29 (s 29(6)).

Section 29(5) provides that a trustee is not entitled to remuneration under s 29 if any provision about his entitlement to remuneration has been made:

(a)   by the trust instrument, or

(b)   by any enactment or any provision of subordinate legislation.

It has always been the case that trustees were entitled to the reimbursement of expenses. Section 31(1) confirms this position by providing that a trustee is entitled to be reimbursed out of the trust funds or may pay out of the trust fund expenses properly incurred when acting on behalf of the trust. Section 31(2) provides that the section applies to a trustee who has been authorised under a power conferred by Part IV or the trust instrument:

(a)   to exercise functions as an agent of the trustees, or

(b)   to act as a nominee or custodian,

as it applies to any other trustee.

Section 28 contains provisions dealing with the situation where there is a charging clause. Section 28(1) provides that subsections (2) to (4) apply to a trustee if:

(a)   there is a provision in the trust instrument entitling him to receive payment out of trust funds in respect of services provided by him on behalf of the trust, and

(b)   the trustee is a trust corporation or is acting in a professional capacity.

Section 28(2) provides that the trustee is to be treated as entitled under the trust instrument to receive payment in respect of services even if they are services which are capable of being provided by a lay trustee. Section 28(6) provides that a person acts as a lay trustee if he:–

(a)   is not a trust corporation; and

(b)   does not act in a professional capacity.

Section 15 of the Wills Act 1837 provides that a gift to an attesting witness or the spouse of an attesting witness is void. Section 28(4) provides that any payments to which the trustee is entitled in respect of services are to be treated as remuneration for services and not as a gift for the purposes of s 15 of the 1837 Act. This means that a trustee or a trustee's spouse who are not beneficiaries can safely witness the will.

Section 34(3) of the Administration of Estates Act 1925 lays down the order in which the assets are to be applied in payment of the debts of the deceased. Again, s 28(4) applies so that any payments to which the trustee is entitled in respect of services are to be treated as remuneration for services and not as a gift.

Section 33(2) provides that nothing in ss 28 or 29 is to be treated as affecting the operation of:

(a)   section 15 of the Wills Act 1837, or

(b)   section 34(3) of the Administration of Estates Act 1925,

in relation to any death occurring before the commencement of ss 28 or 29.

Section 30 deals with the remuneration of trustees of charitable trusts. Section 30(1) provides that the Secretary of State may make regulations for the remuneration of trustees of charitable trusts who are trust corporations or act in a professional capacity. Section 30(2) provides that the power under sub-s (1) includes power to make provision for the remuneration of a trustee who has been authorised under a power conferred by Part IV or the trust instrument:

(a)   to exercise functions as an agent of the trustees, or

(b)   to act as a nominee or custodian.

Section 30(3) provides that regulations under the section may:

(a)   make different provisions for different cases;

(b)   contain such supplemental, incidental, consequential and transitional conditions as the Secretary of State considers appropriate.

Section 30(4) provides that the power to make regulations under the section is exercisable by statutory instrument which will be subject to annulment in pursuance of a resolution of either House of Parliament. At the time of writing, no such regulations have been made.

If there is an express charging clause, a trustee of a charitable trust who is not a trust corporation is only entitled to receive payment for services which are capable of being provided by a lay trustee:

(a)   if he is not a sole trustee, and

(b) to the extent that a majority of the other trustees have agreed that it should apply to him (s 28(3)).

Section 33(1) provides that ss 28, 29, 31 and 32 apply in relation to services provided or (as the case may be) expenses incurred on or after their coming into force on behalf of a trust whenever created.

Application to personal representatives

2.20 These provisions also apply to personal representatives (s 35(1) and (2) of the Trustee Act 2000). Remuneration to which a personal representative would be entitled under ss 28 or 29 is to be treated as an administration expense for the purposes of s 34(3) of the Administration of Estates Act 1925. It is also to be treated as an administration expense for the purposes of any provision giving reasonable administration expenses priority over the preferential debts listed in Sch 6 to the Insolvency Act 1986 (s 35(3)). Section 35(4) provides that nothing in sub-s (3) is to be treated as affecting the operation of the provisions mentioned in paragraphs (a) and (b) of that subsection in relation to any death occurring before the commencement of s 35.

It is now in order for a professional executor or the spouse of a professional executor to witness a will containing a charging clause. This also has retrospective effect; if a will was made before the Trustee Act 2000 came into force, and a professional executor witnessed the will, the professional executor will be able to charge under the clause if the testator died after the Act came into force (1 February 2001). If, however, the professional executor receives some other benefit under the will, for example a legacy, then he should not witness the will as the legacy will fail if he does so.

Should an express charging clause be inserted in wills and trust deeds?

2.21 Notwithstanding the Act, it is still desirable to insert an express charging clause in a trust instrument or will for two reasons:

(a) there is no right to charge if there is no other executor or trustee;

(b) even if there are other executors and trustees, it is possible they might not agree to the professional executor or trustee charging.

COMPOUNDING LIABILITIES

2.22 Section 15 of the Trustee Act 1925 empowers personal representatives or two or more trustees to, *inter alia*, 'compromise, compound, abandon, submit to arbitration, or otherwise settle any debt, account, claim, or thing whatever relating to the testator's or intestate's estate or to the trust'.

This is a very wide power, but it is tempered by the duties of trustees to act in the best interests of the trust. This means that the trustees must ensure that they have attained the best settlement that can be achieved taking all factors into account.

THE POWER TO DELEGATE

2.23   Before 1925 there was no doubt that a trustee could delegate his powers. In *Speight v Gaunt (1883) 22 Ch D 727* Jessel MR said at pages 739–740:

> 'It seems to me that on general principles a trustee ought to conduct the business of the trust in the same manner that an ordinary prudent man of business would conduct his own, and that beyond there is no liability or obligation on the trustee … . If the investment is an investment made on the Stock Exchange through a stockbroker, the ordinary course of business is for the investor to select a stockbroker in good credit and in a good position, having regard to the sum to be invested, and to direct him to make the investment – that is, to purchase on the Stock Exchange of a jobber or another broker the investment required.'

The Trustee Act 1925 contained various provisions concerning delegation by trustees.

The Trustee Act 2000 substantially changed the law. Sections 21, 23 and 30 of the Trustee Act 1925 were repealed. Instead, Part IV of the 2000 Act contains a comprehensive code dealing with the appointment of agents, nominees and custodians.

The Trustee Act 2000 is based on the recommendations of the Law Commission. Traditionally, the law has permitted trustees to delegate administrative decisions, but not fiduciary duties. The Law Commission considered that this distinction was out of date, and that the distinction ought to be between the administrative and distributive powers. It will be possible to delegate administrative powers, it will not be possible to delegate distributive powers.

Section 11(1) provides that trustees may authorise any person to exercise any or all of their delegable functions as their agent. Section 11(2) defines the trustees' delegable functions. These are any function other than:

(a)   any function relating to whether or in what way any assets of the trust should be distributed;

(b)   any power to decide whether any fees or other payment due to be made out of the trust funds should be made out of income or capital (this is a decision about the distribution of assets);

(c)   any power to appoint a person to be a trustee of the trust; or

(d)   any power conferred by any other enactment or the trust instrument which permits the trustees to delegate any of their functions or to appoint a person to act as nominee or custodian. (The agent cannot delegate again.)

Assume that there is the following gift in a will:

'I give my residuary estate to my trustees to apply the income and capital for such of my children and grandchildren as they shall in their absolute discretion think fit.'

(a)   The decision about which of A's children or grandchildren should benefit is a non-delegable decision.

(b)   If there is a life interest trust, whether the expenses come out of income or capital is an important decision as far as the life tenant and remainderman are concerned. It is clearly a decision about the distribution of the assets. If they are paid out of income, the life tenant will suffer; if they are paid out of capital, the remainderman will suffer.

Note that trustees may have no discretion as to whether the expenses are borne by the life tenant or the remainderman. If no discretion is conferred on the trustees, then so far as the expenses relate to income, they come out of income. As far as they relate to capital, they come out of capital. However, some wills or settlements will give the trustees a discretion as to whether they come out of capital or income.

(c)   This could be a decision about the distribution of the assets. If there is a discretionary trust, it will be the trustees who decide which beneficiary gets what. Clearly, the choice of trustee could affect who gets what in the discretionary trust.

(d)   It is merely saying that one delegation is enough. The agent cannot delegate again.

However, everything else is delegable – asset management functions, deciding whether assets should be sold and deciding whether the price is right.

Section 11(2) does not apply to charitable trustees. Instead, s 11(3) provides that in the case of a charitable trust, the trustees' delegable functions are:

(a)   any function consisting of carrying out a decision that the trustees have taken;

(b)   any function relating to the investment of assets subject to the trust (including, in the case of land acquired as an investment, managing the land and creating or disposing of an interest in the land);

(c)   any function relating to the raising of funds for the trust otherwise than by means of profits of a trade which is an integral part of the carrying out of the trust's charitable purpose;

(d)   any other function prescribed by an order made by the Secretary of State.

Section 11(4) provides that, for the purposes of sub-s (3)(c), a trade is an integral part of carrying out a trust's charitable purpose if, whether carried on in the United Kingdom or elsewhere, the profits are applied solely to the purposes of the trust and either:

(a)   the trade is exercised in the course of the actual carrying out of a primary purpose of the trust, or

(b)   the work in connection with the trade is mainly carried out by beneficiaries of the trust.

Section 12 of the Act deals with the question of who may be appointed as an agent. The trustees can appoint one of their number, but they cannot appoint a beneficiary, even if the beneficiary is a trustee. If two or more persons are appointed as agents, they must exercise their functions jointly. A person may be appointed to act as the agent of the trustees even though he is also appointed to act as the nominee or custodian of the trustees.

Section 13 of the Act deals with linked functions. Section 13(1) provides that a person who is authorised under s 11 to exercise a function is subject to any specific duties or restrictions attached to the function. The Act then goes on to provide as an example: a person who is authorised under s 11 to exercise a general power of investment is subject to the duties under s 4 in relation to that part. This applies whatever the terms of the agency. Section 13(2) provides that a person who is authorised under s 11 to exercise a power which is subject to a requirement to obtain advice is not subject to the requirement if he is the kind of person from whom it would have been proper for the trustees, in compliance with the requirement, to obtain advice. Thus if the trustees delegate the power of investment to a person who would normally give advice about investments, that person need not himself obtain further advice.

Section 11(1) of the Trusts of Land and Appointment of Trustees Act 1996 imposes a duty on trustees to consult beneficiaries and give effect to their wishes. Section 13(3) of the Trustee Act 2000 provides that sub-ss (4) and (5) apply to a trust to which s 11(1) of the 1996 Act applies. Subsection (4) provides that the trustees may not under s 11 authorise a person to exercise any of their functions on terms that prevent them from complying with s 11(1) of the 1996

Act. Subsection (5) provides that a person who is authorised under s 11 to exercise any function relating to land subject to the trust is not subject to s 11(1) of the 1996 Act. Thus trustees must still consult and give effect to the wishes of the beneficiaries even if they do delegate their powers.

Section 14(1) provides that the trustees may authorise a person to exercise functions as their agent on such terms as to remuneration and other matters as they may determine. This gives the trustees a wide discretion about the terms on which an agent is employed, but it is subject to various limitations. Section 14(2) provides that the trustees may not authorise a person to exercise functions as their agent on any of the terms mentioned in sub-s (3) unless it is reasonably necessary for them to do so. The terms mentioned in sub-s (3) are:

(a)   a term permitting the agent to appoint a substitute;

(b)   a term restricting the liability of the agent or his substitute to the trustees or any beneficiary;

(c)   a term permitting the agent to act in circumstances capable of giving rise to a conflict of interest.

With regard to (a) above it is the general principle that once there has been a delegation, there cannot be a further delegation.

With regard to (b), this term seeks to restrict exemption clauses. In any event the courts are unlikely to look favourably on an exemption clause.

With regard to (c), clearly it would be inappropriate for the agent to act if there is a conflict of interest. For example, if the trustees appoint an agent to sell some land, it would clearly be inappropriate if the agent bought the land himself.

Practitioners should be wary of standard conditions of contract which may contain terms which are encompassed by s 14(3). The section is not prohibiting these clauses completely; trustees can agree to them if it is reasonably necessary for them to do so. When might it be reasonably necessary for trustees to agree to such terms? Clearly it would be necessary if it was common practice for agents engaged in that type of business to include exemption clauses in their standard conditions of contract.

Delegation of asset management functions

2.24   Section 15 deals with asset management. Section 15(1) provides that the trustees may not authorise a person to exercise any of their asset management functions as their agent except by an agreement which is in, or is evidenced in, writing.

Section 15(2) provides that the trustees may not authorise a person to exercise any of their asset management functions as their agent unless:

(a) they have prepared a statement (known as a policy statement) that gives guidance as to how a function should be exercised; and

(b) the agreement under which the agent is to act includes a term to the effect that he will secure compliance with:

    (i) the policy statement, or

    (ii) if the policy statement is revised or replaced under s 22, the revised or replacement policy statement.

Section 15(3) provides that the trustees must formulate any guidance given in the policy statement with a view to ensuring that the functions will be exercised in the best interests of the trust.

Section 15(4) provides that the policy statement must be in, or evidenced in, writing.

Section 15(5) provides that the asset management functions of trustees are their functions relating to:

(a) the investment of assets subject to the trust,

(b) the acquisition of property which is to be subject to the trust, and

(c) managing property which is subject to the trust and disposing of, or creating or disposing of an interest in, such property.

Trustees are under a duty to review the performance of the agent under s 22(1) (see 2.27 below). If they have authorised an agent to exercise asset management functions, the duty under s 22(1) includes, in particular:

(a) a duty to consider whether there is any need to revise or replace the policy statement made for the purposes of s 15;

(b) if they consider that there is a need to revise or replace a policy statement, a duty to do so; and

(c) a duty to assess whether the terms of the policy statement are being complied with.

Section 22(3) provides that s 15(3) and (4) apply to the revision or replacement of a policy statement under s 22 as they apply to the making of a policy statement under that section.

Most brokers and independent financial advisers have specimen policy statements. There is also a precedent in the Autumn 2001 newsletter of the Society of Trust and Estate Practitioners.

2.25 *Powers of trustees*

Many settlements created before the Trustee Act 2000 contain express powers to delegate asset management functions. It is debatable whether, as a matter of law, a policy statement is required if the trustees are exercising an express power of delegation, but whatever the legal position it would seem desirable to prepare one.

It should be noted that trustees do not have to delegate asset management functions if they do not want to do so. It is always open to trustees to reserve the ultimate decision to themselves, although they may have to take advice about the trust investments (see 2.34). One example of a trust where it may be appropriate to delegate asset management functions is where the investments are such that it may be necessary to make decisions very quickly about what should be done.

Appointment of nominees and custodians

2.25   Section 16(1) of the Trustee Act 2000 provides that the trustees of a trust may:

(a)   appoint a person to act as their nominee in relation to such of the assets of the trust as they determine; and

(b)   take such steps as are necessary to secure that those assets are vested in a person so appointed.

An appointment under the section must be in, or evidenced in, writing, and the section does not apply to any trust having a custodian trustee or in relation to any assets vested in the official custodian for charities (s 16(2) and (3)).

Section 17 confers on trustees the power to appoint custodians. Section 17(1) provides that the trustees of a trust may appoint a person to act as a custodian in relation to such assets of the trust as they have determined. Section 17(2) provides that a person is the custodian in relation to assets if he undertakes safe custody of the assets or of any documents or records concerning the assets. Section 17(3) provides that an appointment under the section must be in, or evidenced in, writing. Section 17(4) provides that the section does not apply to any trust having a custodian trustee or in relation to any assets vested in the official custodian for charities. Section 39(1) provides that 'custodian trustee' has the same meaning as in the Public Trustee Act 1906.

Section 18 deals with investments in bearer securities. Section 18(1) provides that if trustees retain or invest in securities payable to bearer, they must appoint a person to act as a custodian of the securities. This does not apply if the trust instrument contains a provision which permits the trustees to retain or invest in securities payable to bearer without appointing a person to act as a custodian (s 18(2)). Section 18(3) provides that an appointment under the section must be in, or evidenced in, writing. Section 18(4) provides that the section does not apply to any trust having a custodian trustee or in relation to any securities vested in the official custodian for charities. Note that 25(2) provides that s 18 does not impose a duty on a sole trustee if that trustee is a trust corporation. It is believed that there are very few trusts in existence where the trustees hold bearer securities.

Section 19(1) deals with the question of who may be appointed as nominees or custodians. Section 19(1) provides that a person may not be appointed under ss 16, 17 or 18 as a nominee or custodian unless one of the relevant conditions is satisfied. Section 19(2) provides that the relevant conditions are that:

(a)   the person carries on business which consists of or includes acting as a nominee or custodian; or

(b)   the person is a body corporate which is controlled by the trustees; or

(c)   the person is a body corporate recognised under s 9 of the Administration of Justice Act 1985 (this is concerned with the incorporation of solicitors' practices).

Section 19(3) provides that the question whether a body corporate is controlled by trustees is to be determined in accordance with s 840 of the Income and Corporation Taxes Act 1988.

Section 19(4) provides that the trustees of a charitable trust which is not an exempt charity must act in accordance with any guidance given by the Charity Commission concerning the selection of a person for appointment as a nominee or custodian under ss 16, 17 or 18. The Commission have issued this guidance; it is available in printed form, or on the Charity Commission's website.

Section 19(5) provides that subject to sub-ss (1) and (4), the persons whom the trustees may appoint as a nominee or custodian under ss 16, 17 or 18 include:

(a)   one of their number, if that one is a trust corporation; or

(b)   two (or more) of their number, if they are to act as joint nominees or joint custodians.

It is arguable that the subsection does not permit the appointment as custodian of a solicitor or accountant who is a trustee as custodian on their own. Presumably the appointment of a partner who is not a trustee would comply with the Act.

It will be recalled that s 16 deals with the power of trustees to appoint nominees. Section 19(6) provides that the trustees may under s 16 appoint a person to act as their nominee even though he is also:

(a) appointed to act as their custodian (under ss 17 or 18 or any other power), or

(b) authorised to exercise functions as their agent under s 11 or any other power.

As already mentioned, s 17 deals with the power of trustees to appoint custodians, whilst s 18 deals with the power of trustees to retain or invest in securities payable to the bearer. Section 19(7) provides that the trustees may under those sections appoint a person to act as their custodian even though he is also:

(a) appointed to act as their nominee (under s 16 or any other power); or

(b) authorised to exercise functions as their agent (under s 11 or any other power).

Section 20 deals with the terms of appointment of nominees and custodians. Section 20(1) provides that the trustees may appoint a person to act as a nominee or custodian on such terms as to remuneration and other matters as they may determine.

Section 20(2) provides that the trustees may not appoint a person to act as a nominee or custodian on any of the terms mentioned in sub-s (3) unless it is reasonably necessary for them to do so. The terms mentioned in sub-s (3) are:

(a) a term permitting the nominee or custodian to appoint a substitute;

(b) a term restricting the liability of the nominee or custodian or his substitute to the trustees or to any beneficiary;

(c) a term permitting the nominee or custodian to act in circumstances capable of giving rise to a conflict of interest.

Section 20 is subject to ss 29–32.

Remuneration of agent, nominee or custodian

2.26   Section 29 contains further provisions dealing with the remuneration of a trustee who has been appointed as agent, nominee or custodian (see 2.19 above). Section 32(1) applies if a person other than a trustee has been:

(a) authorised to exercise functions as an agent of the trustees; or

(b) appointed to act as a nominee or custodian.

Section 32(2) provides that the trustees may remunerate the agent, nominee or custodian out of the trust funds for services if:

(a)   he is engaged on terms entitling him to be remunerated for those services; and

(b)   the amount does not exceed such remuneration as is reasonable in the circumstances for the provision of the services by him on behalf of that trust.

Section 32(3) provides that the trustees may reimburse the agent, nominee or custodian out of the trust funds for any expenses properly incurred by him in exercising functions as an agent, nominee or custodian.

Review and liability for defaults of agent

2.27   For the whole of the time that the agent, nominee or custodian continues to act for the trust, the trustees must keep under review the arrangements under which the agent, nominee or custodian acts, and how those arrangements are being put into effect. If circumstances make it appropriate to do so, the trustees must consider whether there is a need to exercise any power of intervention that they have, and if they consider there is a need to exercise such a power, they must do so (s 22(1) of the Trustee Act 2000).

Section 22(4) provides that a power of intervention includes:

(a)   a power to give directions to the agent, nominee or custodian; and

(b)   a power to revoke the authorisation or appointment.

If the trustees have authorised an agent to exercise asset management functions, the duty under s 22(1) includes, in particular:

(a)   a duty to consider whether there is any need to revise or replace the policy statement made for the purposes of s 15;

(b)   if they consider that there is a need to revise or replace a policy statement, a duty to do so; and

(c)   a duty to assess whether the terms of the policy statement are being complied with.

Section 22(3) provides that s 15(3) and (4) apply to the revision or replacement of a policy statement under s 22 as they apply to the making of a policy statement under that section. Section 15(3) requires that the trustees must formulate any guidance given in the policy statement with a view to ensuring that the functions will be exercised in the best interests of the trust. Section 15(4) provides that the policy statement must be in, or evidenced in, writing.

2.27   *Powers of trustees*

Section 23(1) provides that a trustee is not liable for any act or default of the agent, nominee or custodian unless he has failed to comply with the duty of care applicable to him, under para 3 of Sch 1:

(a)   when entering into the arrangement under which the person acts as agent, nominee or custodian; or

(b)   when carrying out his duties under s 22.

The duty of care is defined in s 1. A trustee must exercise such care and skill as is reasonable in the circumstances, having regard in particular:

(a)   to any special knowledge or experience that he has or holds himself out as having; and

(b)   if he acts as trustee in the course of a business or profession, to any special knowledge or experience that it is reasonable to expect of a person acting in the course of that kind of business or profession.

Paragraph 3(1) of Sch 1 provides that the duty of care applies to a trustee:

(a)   when entering into arrangements under which a person is authorised under s 11 to exercise functions as an agent;

(b)   when entering into arrangements under which a person is appointed under s 16 to act as a nominee;

(c)   when entering into arrangements under which a person is appointed under ss 17 or 18 to act as a custodian;

(d)   when entering into arrangements under which, under any power conferred by the trust instrument, a person is authorised to exercise functions as an agent or is appointed to act as a nominee or custodian;

(e)   when carrying out his duties under s 22.

Paragraph 3(2) provides that for the purposes of para 3(1), entry into arrangements under which a person is authorised to exercise functions or is appointed to act as a nominee or custodian includes, in particular:

(a)   selecting a person to act;

(b)   determining any terms on which he is to act; and

(c)   if a person is being authorised to exercise asset management functions, the preparation of a policy statement under s 15.

Section 23(2) provides that if a trustee has agreed a term under which the agent, nominee or custodian is permitted to appoint a substitute, the trustee is not liable for any act or default of the substitute unless he has failed to comply with the duty of care applicable to him, under para 3 of Sch 1:

(a)   when agreeing that term; or

(b)   when carrying out his duties under s 22 in so far as they relate to the use of the substitute.

General

2.28   Section 24 of the Trustee Act 2000 deals with the effect of trustees exceeding their powers. If trustees exceed their powers in authorising a person to exercise a function of theirs as an agent, or in appointing a person to act as a nominee or custodian, the authorisation or appointment is still valid.

Section 25(1) provides that a sole trustee can exercise all the powers described above.

Section 26 provides that the powers conferred by the Act on trustees to appoint agents, nominees and custodians are in addition to powers conferred on trustees otherwise than by the Act. However, powers can be restricted or excluded by the trust instrument or by any enactment or any provision of subordinate legislation. It is debatable whether the powers under the Act can be extended as s 26 only refers to restricting or excluding the powers; in the opinion of the author, it should be possible to extend them in the absence of a specific prohibition on extensions.

It is provided by s 27 that the provisions about appointing agents, nominees and custodians apply in relation to trusts whether created before or after the commencement of the Act.

Delegation by individual trustee

2.29   Section 5 of the Trustee Delegation Act 1999 has substituted a new s 25 in the Trustee Act 1925. Section 25(1) provides that, notwithstanding any rule of law to the contrary, a trustee may, by power of attorney, delegate the execution or exercise of all or any of the trusts, powers and discretions vested in him as trustee either alone or jointly with another person or persons. Thus individual trustees can delegate their powers by making use of this section.

A delegation under s 25(1) commences with the date of execution of the power if the instrument makes no provision as to the commencement of the delegation, and lasts for 12 months or any shorter period specified by the instrument creating the power (s 25(2)).

Section 25(3) provides that the persons who may be donees of a power of attorney under the section include a trust corporation.

Section 25(6) sets out a form which can be used. If a donor uses this form, or a form to the like effect but expressed to be made under s 25(5), it operates to delegate to the person identified in the form as the donee of the power the execution and exercise of all the trusts, powers and discretions vested in the donor as trustee (either alone or jointly with any other person or persons) under the trust so identified.

The donor must give written notice of the giving of the power to:

(a)   each person (other than himself), if any, who under any instrument creating the trust has power (whether alone or jointly) to appoint a new trustee; and

(b)   each of the other trustees, if any.

The written notice must specify:

(a)   the date on which the power comes into operation;

(b)   its duration;

(c)   the donee of the power;

(d)   the reason why the power is given; and

(e)   where some only are delegated, the trusts, powers and discretions delegated.

The notice must be given within seven days of the giving of the power (s 25(4)).

Failure to comply with sub-s (4) does not invalidate any act done or instrument executed by the donee in favour of a person dealing with the donee of the power.

What happens if the donee of the power commits a breach of trust? Section 25(7) provides that the donor of the power is liable for the acts or defaults of the donee in the same manner as if they were the acts or defaults of the donor.

Section 25(8) provides that for the purpose of executing or exercising the trusts or powers delegated to him, the donee may exercise any of the powers conferred on the donor as trustee by statute or by the instrument creating the trust. This includes the power, for the purpose of the transfer of any inscribed stock, himself to delegate to an attorney power to transfer, but not including the power of delegation conferred by this section.

Section 25(9) provides that the fact that it appears from any power of attorney given under s 25, or from any evidence required for the purposes of any such power of attorney or otherwise, that in dealing with any stock the donee of the power is acting in the execution of a trust shall not be deemed for any purpose to affect any person in whose books the stock is inscribed or registered with any notice of the trust.

Section 25(10) provides that s 25 applies to a personal representative, tenant for life and statutory owner as it applies to a trustee. However, the written notice as required by s 25(4) must be given:

(a)   in the case of a personal representative, to each of the other personal representatives, if any, except any executor who has renounced probate;

(b)   in the case of a tenant for life, to the trustees of the settlement and to each person, if any, who together with the person giving the notice constitutes the tenant for life; and

(c)   in the case of a statutory owner, to each of the persons, if any, who together with the person giving the notice constitute the statutory owner and, in the case of a statutory owner by virtue of s 23(1)(a) of the Settled Land Act 1925, to the trustees of the settlement.

Readers are reminded that s 7 of the Trustee Delegation Act 1999 preserves the two trustees rule so that if land is to be sold, delegation to a sole co-trustee does not mean that the sole co-trustee can give a valid receipt for capital money. Thus if spouses are holding the legal estate on trust for themselves, and one grants a power of attorney under s 25 to the other, the donee of the power cannot give a valid receipt for capital money.

Delegation to beneficiary with an interest in possession

2.30   Section 9 of the Trusts of Land and Appointment of Trustees Act 1996 has extended the powers of trustees to delegate, although it is a limited power.

Section 9(1) provides that trustees of land can delegate any of their functions by power of attorney. The attorney must be a beneficiary of full age, and must also be entitled to an interest in possession in land subject to the trust. The power must be given by all the trustees jointly, and may be revoked by one or more of them, unless expressed to be irrevocable and to be given by way of security. If another person is appointed trustee, the power is revoked, although the death of any of the original appointors will not cause a revocation. Similarly, if an appointor ceases to be a trustee for any reason, the power will not be revoked (s 9(3)).

The delegation can be for any period or can be indefinite (s 9(5)), but an enduring power cannot be used (s 9(6)) for the purposes of delegation of their functions under s 9(1).

Section 9(4) provides that if the attorney ceases to be a person beneficially entitled to an interest in possession in land, and is the sole attorney, the power is revoked. If there is more than one attorney, the power is still exercisable by the other beneficiaries, provided that the functions delegated to them are specified to be exercised by them jointly and not separately, and they continue to be beneficially entitled to an interest in possession in the land in question. If, however, the functions have been delegated to the attorney and to other beneficiaries to be exercised by them separately or either separately and jointly, the power is revoked in so far as it relates to the attorney who ceases to be beneficially entitled to an interest in possession of the land.

Section 9(7) provides that the beneficiaries to whom functions have been delegated under s 9(1) are in the same position as trustees with the same duties and liabilities. However, they are not regarded as trustees for any other purpose, including in particular any enactment permitting the delegation of functions by trustees or imposing requirements relating to the payment of capital money. The effect of this subsection is that trustees cannot delegate the power of sale to the life tenant.

The Trustee Act 2000 has inserted s 9A into the Trusts of Land and Appointment of Trustees Act 1996. This provides that the duty of care under s 1 of the Trustee Act 2000 applies to trustees of land in deciding whether to delegate any of their functions under s 9. If the trustees of land delegate any of their functions under s 9, and the delegation is not irrevocable, while the delegation continues, the trustees:

(a)   must keep the delegation under review;

(b)   if circumstances make it appropriate to do so, must consider whether there is a need to exercise any power of intervention that they have; and

(c)   if they consider that there is a need to exercise such a power, must do so.

(s 9A(3)).

Section 9A(5) provides that the duty of care under s 1 of the Trustee Act 2000 applies to the carrying out of any of these duties by trustees. 'Power of intervention' includes:

(a)   a power to give directions to the beneficiary; and

(b)   a power to revoke the delegation.

Section 9A(6) provides that a trustee of land is not liable for any act or default of the beneficiary, or beneficiaries, unless the trustee fails to comply with the duty of care in deciding to delegate any of the trustees' functions under s 9 or in carrying out any duty under sub-s (3).

Section 9(2) provides protection for persons dealing with the attorney. It provides that if a person deals with the attorney in good faith, the attorney shall be presumed to have been a person to whom the function could be delegated unless that other person has knowledge at the time of the transaction that he was not such a person.

There is a presumption in favour of any purchaser whose interest depends on the validity of that transaction that that other person dealt in good faith and did not have such knowledge if that other person makes a statutory declaration to that effect, before or within three months after the completion of the purchase.

The section applies to trusts where a beneficiary has a life interest, and also to co-ownership, but there is little point in using it where the trustees and beneficiaries are the same. In the great majority of co-ownership situations the beneficiaries and trustees will be the same person.

Delegation by trustee who is also beneficially interested

2.31   Section 1(1) of the Trustee Delegation Act 1999 provides that the donee of an ordinary or an enduring power of attorney can exercise the trustee functions of the donor in relation to:

(a)   land;

(b)   capital proceeds of a conveyance of land; or

(c)   income from land.

It is immaterial whether the donor is a sole trustee or a joint trustee (s 1(2)(b)). However, the donor must have a beneficial interest in the land, proceeds or income when the act is done.

Thus if spouses hold land on trust for themselves as joint tenants, and one executes a power of attorney in favour of a child, that child will be able to exercise the trustee functions of the parent, and will be able to give a valid receipt for capital money if the land is sold in conjunction with the other spouse. Note that s 7 preserves the two trustee rule so that if one spouse grants a power of attorney to the other, that spouse cannot give a valid receipt for capital money.

Section 1(1) can be excluded by the instrument which created the power of attorney, and has effect subject to the terms of that instrument (s 1(3)).

What is the position if the donee of the power does an act which would be a breach of trust if committed by the donor? Section 1(4) provides that the donor will be liable in this situation. However, the donor is not liable by reason only that the function is exercised by the donee. Section 1(4) is subject to any contrary intention expressed in the trust instrument, and has effect subject to the terms of such an instrument (s 1(5)).

Section 1(6) provides that the fact that it appears that, in dealing with any shares or stock, the donee of a power of attorney is exercising a function by virtue of s 1(1) does not affect with any notice of any trust a person in whose books the shares are, or stock is, registered or inscribed.

If the donee of a power of attorney is acting under (a) a statutory provision or (b) a provision in the instrument (if any) creating a trust, under which the donor of the power is expressly authorised to delegate the exercise of all or any of his trustee functions by power of attorney, he is acting under a trustee delegation power, and is not to be regarded as exercising a trustee function by virtue of s 1(1). Thus the attorney cannot usually delegate again.

Section 1 applies only if the donor of the power has a beneficial interest in the land. How can a purchaser from the attorney be certain that this is the case? Section 2 provides that an appropriate statement is, in favour of a purchaser, conclusive evidence that the donor of the power had a beneficial interest in the property at the time of doing the act. An 'appropriate statement' means a signed statement made by the donee:

(a)   when doing the act in question, or

(b)   at any other time within the period of three months beginning with the day on which the act is done,

that the donor has a beneficial interest in the property at the time of the donee doing the act (s 2(3)). If the appropriate statement is false, the donee is liable in the same way as he would be if the statement were contained in a statutory declaration.

Section 10(2) of the Powers of Attorney Act 1971 provides that a general power of attorney in the form set out in Sch 1 to that Act, or a similar form, does not confer on the donee of the power any authority to exercise functions of the donor as trustee. Section 3 of the Trustee Delegation Act 1999 provides that s 10 of the 1971 Act is now subject to s 1 of the 1999 Act.

Thus spouses can grant each other enduring powers of attorney. If one becomes mentally incapable, the other cannot give a valid receipt for capital by signing a transfer as attorney and in her personal capacity. However, it is possible to appoint another trustee under s 36 of the Trustees Act 1925 as amended.

(These issues are more fully discussed in the author's book *A Practitioner's Guide to Powers of Attorney*, published by Tottel Publishing.)

INSURANCE

2.32   Section 19 of the Trustee Act 1925 conferred on trustees a power to insure the trust property. The Trustee Act 2000 has replaced the original s 19 with a new section. The substituted s 19 provides that a trustee may insure any property which is subject to the trust against risk of loss or damage due to any event. The premiums may be paid out of the trust funds (s 19(1)). Section 19(5) provides that 'trust funds' means any income or capital funds of the trust.

Special rules apply to property held on a bare trust. Section 19(3) provides that property is held on a bare trust if it is held on trusts for:

(a)   a beneficiary who is of full age and capacity and absolutely entitled to the property which is subject to the trust; or

(b)   beneficiaries each of whom is of full age and capacity and who (taken together) are absolutely entitled to the property subject to the trust.

If property is held on a bare trust, the beneficiary or each of the beneficiaries may direct that any property specified in the direction is not to be insured, or that it is only to be insured on such conditions as may be specified (s 19(2)). If such a direction is given, the power to insure ceases to be a delegable function for the purposes of s 11 of the Trustee Act 2000 (power to employ agents).

Section 34(3) provides that the amendments made by the section apply in relation to trusts whether created before or after the commencement of the Act.

Section 20 deals with the application of any trust money. It is to be regarded as capital money, and under s 20(4) it may be applied by the trustees in rebuilding, reinstating, replacing or repairing the property lost or damaged, but any such application by the trustees shall be subject to the consent of any person whose consent is required – by the instrument, if any, creating the trust – to the investment of money subject to the trust. If it is a settlement within the Settled Land Act, any such application of the money is subject to the provisions of that Act.

Section 20(5) preserves the rights of third parties to require the insurance money to be applied in rebuilding, reinstating, replacing or repairing the property lost or damaged. Mortgagees, lessors and lessees may have the right to insist on rebuilding or reinstatement.

Possible amendments

2.33   It is common to make the following variations to the power:

(a)   Section 19 does not impose any duty on the trustees to insure; such a duty could be imposed. The imposition of a duty may not be desirable as it is sometimes not possible to obtain insurance if, for example, the house is situated in an area prone to flooding. If trustees fail to insure when they could have done so, such failure will probably be a breach of the duty of care.

(b)   The trustees may be given an express discretion as to whether insurance money should be used to reinstate the settled property.

INVESTMENT

2.34   The Trustee Act 2000 has substantially amended the law with regard to investment. It has repealed most of the Trustee Investments Act 1961 which most practitioners considered too restrictive. However, in view of what has happened to the stock market recently, it may be that the approach adopted by the 1961 Act of requiring trust funds to be split into two, and a proportion invested in narrower range securities, had much to commend it.

Section 3(1) of the Trustee Act 2000 provides that, subject to the provisions of Part II of the Act, a trustee may make any kind of investment that he could make if he were absolutely entitled to the assets of the trust. Subsection (2) provides that the power under sub-s (1) is called 'the general power of investment'. Section 3(3) provides that the general power of investment does not permit a trustee to make investments in land other than in loans secured on land. However, s 8 does contain a power to invest in land. Section 8 is discussed at 2.35 below. Section 3(4) provides that a person invests in a loan secured on land if he has rights under any contract under which:

(a)   one person provides another with credits; and

(b)   the obligation of the borrower to repay is secured on land.

'Credit' is given a wide meaning in s 3(5),where it is defined as including any cash loan or other financial accommodation. Section 3(6) provides that cash includes money in any form.

It should be noted that whilst the Act has provisions dealing with loans secured on land, there is nothing in the Act dealing with unsecured loans. Presumably these are permissible if they can be classed as an investment. In any event, it might be a breach of the duty of care for a trustee to make an unsecured loan if it proves to be irrecoverable.

The general power of investment is subject to various restrictions. Section 4 lays down the standard investment criteria. Section 4(1) provides that in exercising any power of investment, a trustee must have regard to the standard investment criteria. This duty applies whether or not the powers under the Act are being exercised, and so it applies to trustees who invest under an express investment clause in a will or settlement. Section 4(2) provides that a trustee must from time to time review the investments of the trust and consider whether, having regard to the standard investment criteria, they should be varied. Section 4(3) provides that the standard investment criteria, in relation to a trust, are:

(a)   the suitability to the trust of investments of the same kind as any particular investment proposed to be made or retained and of that particular investment as an investment of that kind; and

(b)   the need for diversification of investments of the trust in so far as is appropriate to the circumstances of the trust.

It should be noted that these standard investment criteria apply to trustees exercising express powers of investment just as they apply to trustees exercising the powers conferred by the Act.

The criteria in (a) above means that trustees must first consider in what areas they wish to invest. Having decided that they wish to invest in a particular area, they must then decide in which companies they are going to invest in within that area.

With regard to (b) above it would clearly be wrong to invest a large sum of money in one company. A prudent trustee will invest in different types of assets. The need for diversification, however, may be difficult or impossible to satisfy if there is only one asset comprised in the trust, the matrimonial home, or the family farm, or shares in the family company. In this situation, the trustees may be justified in not diversifying on the basis that it is 'not appropriate to the circumstances of the trust'.

A trustee is also under a duty to obtain advice, whether investing under the Act or exercising an express power of investment. Section 5(1) provides that, before exercising any power of investment, a trustee must obtain and consider proper advice about the way in which, having regard to the standard investment criteria, the power should be exercised. The duty to obtain and consider advice also applies when trustees are reviewing the investments of the trust. Section 5(2) provides that a trustee must obtain and consider proper advice about whether, having regard to the standard investment criteria, the investments should be varied. The Act is silent about how frequently the investments should be reviewed or advice sought. Presumably the interval should not be longer than a year, and there might be circumstances (as at the time of writing!) in which the interval should be much shorter, for example, if the trust has many investments.

Section 5(3) provides that a trustee need not obtain such advice if he reasonably concludes that, in all the circumstances, it is unnecessary or inappropriate do so. If the trust fund is large, trustees cannot reasonably claim it is inappropriate. On the other hand, if the trust fund is under £100 it would be reasonable for a trustee to conclude that it was unnecessary and inappropriate. 'Proper advice' is defined in s 5(4) as the advice of a person who is reasonably believed by the trustee to be qualified to give it by his ability and practical experience of financial and other matters relating to the proposed investment.

It is quite common for wills to contain gifts or legacies to children, grandchildren, nephews and nieces and godchildren of relatively small amounts of money: £500, £1,000, £5,000, £10,000. Such beneficiaries will not be able to give a valid receipt for capital money whilst they are under 18, and it may be that the gift will be contingent on attaining a greater age. Until the beneficiary attains a vested interest, the money will be held in trust, and must be invested. As there is an element of doubt about the level beneath which advice is not required, it may be that a specific direction should be included in the will as to how the legacy is to be invested. A direction that the money should be paid to the parents of the child merely means that the parents become trustees.

Anyone advising trustees must be authorised under the Financial Services and Markets Act 2000. Trustees can choose between various types of advisers; usually the choice will be between brokers or independent financial advisers.

The general power of investment is in addition to powers conferred on trustees otherwise than by the Act, but it is subject to any restriction or exclusion imposed by the trust instrument or by any enactment or any provision of subordinate legislation (s 6(1)). Section 6(2) provides that for the purposes of the Act, an enactment or a provision of subordinate legislation is not to be regarded as being, or as being part of, a trust instrument.

What effect do ss 3, 4, 5 and 6 have on existing trusts? Section 7(1) provides that they apply to trusts whether created before or after the commencement of the Act. However, there are various exceptions to this provision.

Section 7(2) provides that no provision relating to the powers of a trustee contained in a trust instrument made before 3 August 1961 is to be treated (for the purposes of s 6(1)(b)) as restricting or excluding the general power of investment. This means that trustees of a trust made before 3 August 1961 have the general power of investment.

Section 7(3) provides that a provision contained in a trust instrument made before the commencement of Part II which:

(a)   has effect under s 3(2) of the Trustee Investments Act 1961 as a power to invest under that Act, or

(b)   confers power to invest under that Act;

is to be treated as conferring the general power of investment on a trustee.

This means that if trustees are authorised to invest under the Trustee Investments Act 1961, they now have the general powers of investment as a trustee.

It should be noted that Part 2 of Sch 2 to the Act contains provisions dealing with the investment of the proceeds of sale of settled land.

Acquisition of land

2.35   Part III of the Act contains default powers for trustees to acquire freehold and leasehold land.

Section 8(1) provides that a trustee may acquire freehold or leasehold land in the United Kingdom:

(a)   as an investment;

(b)   for occupation by a beneficiary; or

(c)   for any other reason.

Section 8(2) provides that 'freehold or leasehold land' means:

(a)   in relation to England and Wales, a legal estate in land,

(b)   in relation to Scotland:

    (i)   the estate or interest of the proprietor of the *dominium utile* or, in the case of land not held on feudal tenure, the estate or interest of the owner, or

    (ii)   a tenancy, and

(c)   in relation to Northern Ireland, a legal estate in land, including land held under a fee farm grant.

Thus, there is power to acquire a leasehold interest. The Act does not impose any requirement as to the length of lease which must remain unexpired, although a lease which has little time left to run will not be a good buy. In addition, before trustees can invest in land, the trustees must comply with duties imposed on trustees before making any investment. The trustees must take advice from someone qualified to advise about the acquisition of land, and take advice periodically about whether the land should be retained or sold.

Note that there is no power to acquire land situated abroad, or equitable interests in land. If either of these situations is likely, then the trustees should include express powers in the will or settlement authorising them to hold land abroad or equitable interests.

41

2.35 *Powers of trustees*

Generally, the Act applies to personal representatives administering an estate according to the law as it applies to a trustee carrying out a trust for beneficiaries (s 35(1)). However, the definition of a beneficiary under s 8(1)(b) is to be read as a reference to the person who under the will of the deceased or under the law relating to intestacy is beneficially interested in the estate. This provision is necessary as otherwise a creditor might come within the definition of a beneficiary.

Section 9(a) provides that the powers conferred by Part III are in addition to powers conferred on trustees otherwise than by that part. This means that if the trustees already have power to invest in land under the will or settlement, they do not need to make use of the powers contained in the Act. However, if the will or settlement specifically prohibits the trustees from investing in land, then they cannot do so. Section 9(b) provides that the powers conferred by the Act are subject to any restriction or exclusion imposed by the trust instrument or by any enactment or any provision of subordinate legislation.

Section 10 contains provisions dealing with existing trusts. Section 10(1) provides that Part III of the Act does not apply in relation to a trust of property which consists of or includes land which is settled land (despite s 2 of the Trusts of Land and Appointment of Trustees Act 1996). Nor does it apply to a trust to which the Universities and Colleges Estates Act 1925 applies.

Subject to this, Part III applies to trusts whether created before or after its commencement (s 10(2)).

Section 8(3) provides that for the purpose of exercising his functions as a trustee, a trustee who acquires land under this section has all the powers of an absolute owner in relation to the land.

Section 6(3) of the Trusts of Land and Appointment of Trustees Act 1996 provides that trustees of land have the power to acquire land under the power conferred by s 8 of the Trustee Act 2000.

Section 6(5) provides that in exercising the powers conferred by the section, the trustees must have regard to the rights of the beneficiaries. Section 6(6) provides that the powers conferred by the section shall not be exercised in contravention of, or of any order made in pursuance of, any other enactment or any rule of law or equity. Section 6(7) states that the reference to an order in sub-s (6) includes an order of any court or of the Charity commissioners. Section 6(8) provides that where any enactment other than s 6 confers on trustees authority to act subject to any restriction, limitation or condition, trustees of land may not exercise the powers conferred by s 6 to do any act which they are prevented from doing under the other enactment by reason of the restriction, limitation or condition. Section 6(9) (inserted by the Trustee Act 2000) provides that the duty of care under s 1 of the Trustee Act 2000 applies to trustees of land when exercising the powers conferred by this section.

General duties with regard to investment

2.36   The duty of care applies to a trustee:

(a)   when exercising the general power of investment conferred on him by the trust instrument;

(b)   when carrying out a duty to which he is subject under ss 4 or 5 (duties relating to the exercise of a power of investment or to the review of investments) (Sch 1 para 1).

Section 1 defines the duty of care. A trustee must exercise such care and skill as is reasonable in the circumstances, having regard in particular:

(a)   to any special knowledge or experience that he has or holds himself out as having; and

(b)   if he acts as trustee in the course of a business or profession, to any special knowledge or experience that it is reasonable to expect of a person acting in the course of that kind of business or occupation.

Pre-Trustee Act 2000 cases may still be relevant in deciding whether or not there has been a breach of this duty. Lindley MR in *Re Whiteley (1886) Ch D 347* at page 355 said:

'The duty of a trustee is not to take such care only as a prudent man would take if he had only himself to consider; the duty rather is to take such care as an ordinary prudent man would take if he were minded to make an investment for the benefit of other people for whom he felt morally bound to provide.'

A prudent man might be prepared to take a chance on an investment if he was only acting for himself, but if he was aiming to provide for his children, he might think twice before making a hazardous investment. The duty is thus higher than merely acting prudently.

More recently the duty of trustees with regard to investment was considered in *Nestle v National Westminster Bank plc [1993] 1 WLR 1260* where the action against the bank failed. Leggatt LJ said at page 1282:

'The essence of the bank's duty was to take such steps as a prudent businessman would have taken to maintain and increase the value of the trust fund. Unless it failed to do so, it was not in breach of trust.

A breach of duty will not be actionable, and therefore will be immaterial, if it does not cause loss. I would endorse the concession by Mr. Nugee for the bank that "loss" will be incurred by a trust fund when it makes a gain less than would have been made by a prudent businessman. A claimant will therefore fail who cannot prove a loss in this sense caused by breach of duty. So here in order to make a case for an inquiry, the plaintiff must show that loss was caused by breach of duty on the part of the bank.'

It was held that the plaintiff had not proved that she had suffered loss as a result of the breaches of trust by the bank.

In *Cowan v Scargill [1985] Ch 270* there was a dispute about the investment policies of the mineworkers' pension fund. Megarry V-C said at pages 287–288:

'The assertion that trustees could not be criticised for failing to make a particular investment for social or political reasons is one that I would not accept in its full width. If the investment in fact made is equally beneficial to the beneficiaries, then criticism would be difficult to sustain in practice, whatever the position in theory ... .

In considering what investments to make trustees must put on one side their own personal interest and views ... .

... if the only actual or potential beneficiaries of a trust are all adults with very strict views on moral and social matters, condemning all forms of alcohol, tobacco and popular entertainment, as well as armaments, I can well understand that it might not be for the "benefit" of such beneficiaries to know that they are obtaining rather larger financial returns under the trust by reason of investments in those activities than they would have received if the trustees had invested the trust funds in other investments.'

Express powers of investment

2.37   Most, if not all, professionally drawn wills and settlements contain an express investment clause; frequently these will authorise the trustees to invest the trust funds as if they were the absolute owners. It has now been established that this means what it says – trustees can invest in appropriate investments (*Re Harari's Settlement Trusts [1949] 1 All ER 430*).

There is also some doubt about the meaning of the word 'invest'. Is it confined to assets which yield income, or does it include assets which are purchased in the hope that they will show large capital gains? There are some old cases where it has been held that assets purchased in the hope that they will increase in value are not 'investments'. However, in *Marson v Morton [1986] 1 WLR 1343*, a tax case, at page 1350 Sir Nicolas Browne-Wilkinson said 'But in my judgment in 1986 it is not any longer self-evident that unless land is producing income it cannot be an investment'. The Law Commission, on whose report the Trustee Act 2000 is based, was of the view that trustees could invest either for capital growth or income or both.

Even though trustees may have wide powers of investment, it should be remembered that trustees are still subject to s 4 of the Trustee Act 2000, and the general duties imposed on trustees with regard to investment.

Express power to lend money on mortgage

2.38   Express investment powers frequently include a power to lend money to a beneficiary. The trustees may also be empowered not to charge any interest, and to make the loan without any security. Even though the express power may be very wide, the trustees must still have regard to the duties imposed by s 4 of the Trustee Act 2000. Thus it would normally be wrong for trustees to lend all the trust money on mortgage, although there may be exceptional circumstances where this is justified. Furthermore, trustees are under a duty to hold the balance fairly between the life tenant and the remainderman, and whilst a mortgage may satisfy the needs of a life tenant for income, there will be little capital appreciation to satisfy the needs of the remainderman. A mortgage where the amount of capital to be repaid and the rate of interest are both linked to other currencies as in *Multiservice Bookbinding v Marden [1979] Ch 84* may satisfy both the remainderman and the life tenant, but equally could disappoint depending on currency movements – unless carefully drafted, such a mortgage may not be permitted.

An unsecured loan to a beneficiary may be unfair to the remainderman as it may never be repaid. On the other hand, an interest-free loan to the remainderman, or a loan at a low rate of interest to a beneficiary, may be unfair to the life tenant.

Express powers to lend money will also be found in wills creating nil rate band discretionary trusts, and giving the trustees power to accept an IOU from the surviving spouse for the amount of the IOU. When the surviving spouse dies, the IOU is deductible from his or her estate thereby preserving the nil rate band of the first spouse to die. The trustees of the nil rate band discretionary trust are making a loan to the surviving spouse.

For a more detailed discussion of nil rate band discretionary trusts, and other schemes designed to save inheritance tax, please see 'Estate Planning for the Middle Income Client', Tottel Publishing by the author.

THE POWER OF MAINTENANCE

2.39   Section 31 of the Trustee Act 1925 contains a power of maintenance. This authorises the trustees to apply the whole of the income of a trust fund for the maintenance, education or benefit of a beneficiary.

When does s 31 apply?

2.40   Section 31 clearly applies to vested gifts, where the beneficiary will be entitled to the income, but in the case of a contingent interest s 31(3) states that it applies to a contingent interest only if the limitation or trust carries the intermediate income of the property.

Which contingent gifts carry the intermediate income? The law in this area is quite complicated, but the following gifts will carry the intermediate income:

(a)   A contingent or future specific devise or bequest of real or personal property – 'I give Blackacre to A if he becomes a doctor', or 'I give Blackacre to A after B has qualified as a doctor'.

(b)   A contingent residuary devise of freehold land.

(c)   A specific or residuary devise of freehold land to trustees upon trust for persons whose interests are contingent or executory.

(s 175 of the Law of Property Act 1925.)

(d)   A contingent bequest of residuary personality (*Re Adams [1893] 1 Ch 329*).

A contingent pecuniary legacy – 'I give £10,000 to A if he qualifies as a doctor' – does not normally carry interest until the time when it is payable. However, in the following situations, the gift will carry the intermediate income:

(i)   If the donor has shown an intention that the income should be applied for the maintenance of the beneficiary.

(ii)   If the testator is the parent of the beneficiary, or stands *in loco parentis* to the beneficiary, the testator has not made any other provision for the beneficiary, the gift is directly to the beneficiary, and the condition to be satisfied is attaining an age no greater than 18.

(iii) If the testator has directed that the legacy should be set aside for the benefit of a beneficiary.

Section 31(3) provides that the section also applies to a future or contingent legacy by the parent of, or by a person standing *in loco parentis* to, the legatee, if and for such period as, under the general law, the legacy carries interest for the maintenance of the legatee. This is very similar to (ii) above.

How is the power exercisable?

2.41   Section 31(1) provides that the trustees may, at their sole discretion, pay to the beneficiary's parent or guardian, if any, or otherwise apply for his benefit or towards his maintenance, education or benefit, the whole or such part, if any, of the income of that property as may, in all the circumstances, be reasonable, whether or not there is:

(a)   any other fund applicable for the same purpose; or

(b)   any person bound by law to provide for his maintenance or education.

What factors should the trustees take into account in deciding whether or not to exercise their discretion?

2.42   There is a proviso to s 31 which requires trustees to have regard to the following matters in deciding whether or not to apply the income for the maintenance, education or benefit of a beneficiary. These are as follows:

(a)   the age of the infant;

(b)   the requirements of the infant;

(c)   the circumstances of the case;

(d)   other income applicable for the same purpose;

(e)   if the income of more than one fund is applicable for the maintenance, education or benefit of the infant, a proportionate part only of the income of each fund shall be so paid or applied.

The effect of that proviso is to impose an objective test on the trustees, and to remove some of their discretion.

Entitlement at 18

2.43   A beneficiary who does not attain a vested interest at 18 is entitled to the income until he either attains a vested interest or dies, or until the failure of his interest (s 31(1)(ii)).

Thus if there is a gift to a beneficiary contingent on the beneficiary attaining 30, the beneficiary will be entitled to the income at the age of 18, although he will not be entitled to the capital until the age of 30.

What happens to any income which is not applied for the benefit of the beneficiaries?

2.44   If any of the income is not applied for the maintenance, education or benefit of the beneficiary, it must be accumulated and invested. It must then be paid to a beneficiary who:

(a)   attains the age of 18 years, or marries or forms a civil partnership under that age, and his interest in such income during his infancy or until his marriage or the formation of a civil partnership is a vested interest; or

(b)   on attaining the age of 18 years or on marriage or the formation of a civil partnership under that age becomes entitled to the property from which such income arose in fee simple, absolute or determinable, or absolutely, or for an entailed interest (s 31(2)).

Note that under (b) a beneficiary must become absolutely entitled to personalty, or have an entailed interest; a beneficiary with a conditional or determinable interest in personalty will not be entitled to the accumulated income on attaining 18 or marriage or the formation of a civil partnership. The position is different if the subject matter of the gift is land. 'Absolute' means complete beneficial ownership and dominion over property. It does not include an interest which can be destroyed at any time by the exercise of a power or the fulfilment of a condition with the consequence that the property must be retained by the trustees until the power or condition is spent (*Re Sharp's Settlement Trust [1972] 3 WLR 765* at page 769).

Section 31(2)(ii) provides that in any other case the trustees shall, notwithstanding that such person had a vested interest in such income, hold the accumulations as an accretion to the capital of the property from which such accumulations arose, and as one fund with such capital for all purposes. If such property is settled land, such accumulations are to be held upon the same trusts as if the same were capital money arising from the settled land.

The receipt of a married infant is a good discharge.

Class gifts

2.45   If there is a contingent class gift, the trustees are entitled to treat the share of each potential beneficiary separately, and to apply the income of each potential beneficiary's share for the maintenance of that beneficiary even if one or more beneficiary has satisfied the contingency (*Re Holford [1894] 3 Ch 30*). If a beneficiary dies without satisfying the contingency, any accumulated income accrues to the other beneficiaries as capital.

Express power of maintenance and prohibition on benefiting settlor

2.46   In *Fuller v Evans and others [2000] 1 All ER 636* the settlor created an accumulation and maintenance settlement for the benefit of his children. The trustees had power to provide for the maintenance and education of the children. Clause 12 of the settlement prohibited the trustees from exercising their power in such manner that the settlor would or might become entitled either directly or indirectly to any benefit in any manner or in any circumstances whatsoever. There was a divorce, and the settlor agreed to pay for the children's maintenance and school fees. The trustees were concerned that if they exercised their power of maintenance, they would indirectly benefit the settlor, and would infringe clause 12 of the settlement. It was held that if the trustees did exercise their power of maintenance, they would not infringe clause 12.

Common variations

2.47   It is common to make the following variations to the statutory power of maintenance:

(a)   The trustees are given a complete discretion as to whether the income should be applied for the maintenance, education or benefit of a beneficiary.

(b)   The entitlement to income may be postponed to an age greater than 18.

Powers with regard to minors

2.48   Personal representatives and trustees cannot pay the income or hand the capital to a minor, but there are various exceptions to this rule. They are:

(a)   Under s 21 of the Law of Property Act 1925 a married infant has power to give a valid receipt for all income but not capital. As an infant has to be 16 years of age to marry, this is a very limited exception as it can only apply for two years.

(b)   Section 31 of the Trustee Act 1925 authorises trustees to apply income for the maintenance of an infant beneficiary. Such payments are to be made to the parent or guardian of the child. Section 32 authorises the advancement of a maximum of one-half of the capital.

(c) *Payment into court.* Section 63(1) of the Trustee Act 1925 provides that trustees, or the majority of trustees, having in their hands or under their control money or securities belonging to a trust, may pay the same into court. Section 63(2) provides that the receipt of the proper officer shall be a sufficient discharge to trustees for the money or securities so paid into court.

(d) The will or trust instrument may authorise payment to the infant or to the guardian or parent of the child.

(e) Section 42 of the Administration of Estates Act 1925 applies where the will does not appoint trustees, and the infant is absolutely entitled; the personal representatives can then appoint a trust corporation or two or more individuals not exceeding four (whether or not including the personal representatives) to be trustees. Note that s 42 only applies if the will does not appoint trustees, and the infant must be absolutely entitled.

(f) Section 41 of the Administration of Estates Act 1925 enables personal representatives to appropriate any asset in satisfaction of any legacy if the beneficiaries agree; in the case of an infant beneficiary, the consent can be given by the parent or guardian of the infant.

Power of trustees to give receipts

2.49   Section 14(1) of the Trustee Act 1925 provides that the receipt in writing of a trustee for any money, securities, investments or other personal property or effects payable, transferable, or deliverable to him under any trust or power shall be a sufficient discharge to the person paying, transferring, or delivering the same and shall effectually exonerate him.

Section 14(2) provides that the section does not, except where the trustee is a trust corporation, enable a sole trustee to give a valid receipt for:

(a) the proceeds of sale or other capital money arising under a trust of land;

(b) capital money arising under the Settled Land Act 1925.

It is not possible to displace this section by a provision in the trust deed.

SALE

The powers

2.50   Trustees have extensive powers to sell trust property. If the trust property consists of land, it will be a Settled Land Act settlement, or a trust for sale, or a trust of land. As a result of the Trusts of Land and Appointment of Trustees Act 1996, it has not been possible since 1 January 1997 to create Settled Land Act settlements, although those created before that date remain in existence. If it is a Settled Land Act settlement, the tenant for life can sell the property (s 38(1) of the Settled Land Act 1925), although the purchase price will have to be paid to at least two trustees or a trust corporation (s 94(1) of the Settled Land Act). If it is a trust of land or trust for sale, the trustees have the power to sell the trust property (s 6(1) of the Trusts of Land and Appointment of Trustees Act 1996), although again the trustees have to pay the purchase price to at least two trustees or a trust corporation (s 27(2) of the Law of Property Act 1925).

Section 8(1) of the Trusts of Land and Appointment of Trustees Act 1996 provides that s 6 of the 1996 Act can be excluded, and s 8(2) provides that if any consent is required for the exercise of the power, the power may not be exercised without that consent. Section 10(1) of the 1996 Act provides that if the consent of more than two persons is required for the exercise by the trustees of any function relating to land, a purchaser need only satisfy himself that the consent of any two has been obtained. However, purchasers dealing with trustees of land held on charitable, ecclesiastical or public trusts must ensure that all appropriate consents have been obtained (s 10(2)).

It should be noted that the provisions of the 1996 Act apply to all trusts whenever created, apart from land which is settled land or land to which the Universities and Colleges Estates Act 1925 applies (s 1 of the Trusts of Land and Appointment of Trustees Act 1996).

The 1996 Act provides that trustees are also under a duty to consult the beneficiaries of full age and beneficially entitled to an interest in possession in the land so far as practicable (s 11(1)). They must give effect to the wishes of those beneficiaries so far as consistent with the general interest of the trust; if there is a dispute, the views of the majority by value prevail (s 11(1)). The duty to consult can be excluded, and will not normally apply to a trust created before the Trusts of Land and Appointment of Trustees Act 1996 came into force (1 January 1997), or to a trust created or arising under a will made before 1 January 1997 (s 11(2)), or in the case of a transfer to all the beneficiaries if they are of full age and capacity and absolutely entitled.

Suppose that T1 and T2 are the trustees of a settlement under which A is the life tenant. T1 and T2 are under a duty to consult A about the operation of the trust. If A wants any land in the trust to be sold, T1 and T2 must give effect to those wishes unless advised by a valuer that it would be best not to sell the land until the next year.

It is common to exclude the duty to consult beneficiaries in wills and settle-ments.

Section 18(1) of the Trusts of Land and Appointment of Trustees Act 1996 provides that ss 10 and 11 of the Act do not apply to personal representatives.

Chattels may also be subject to an express trust with a power of sale, or it may be implied – for example under s 33 of the Administration of Estates Act 1925 when a person dies intestate. In the case of other property, for example stocks and shares, it is probable that there is an implied power of sale.

Section 16 of the Trustee Act 1925 provides that where trustees are authorised by the trust instrument or by law to pay capital money subject to the trust, they can raise such money by the sale or mortgage of all or any part of the trust property for the time being in possession.

Section 212 of the Inheritance Tax Act 1984 provides that a person liable for IHT other than the transferor or the transferor's spouse has power to sell the property for the purpose of paying the IHT.

Method of sale

2.51   Section 12 of the Trustee Act 1925 confers a wide discretion on the trustees as to the mode of sale. It provides that where a trustee has a duty or power to sell property, he may sell or concur with any other person in selling all or any part of the property, either subject to prior charges or not, and either together or in lots, by public auction or by private contract, subject to any such conditions respecting title or evidence of title or other matter as the trustee thinks fit, with power to vary any contract for sale, and to buy in at any auction, or to rescind any contract for resale and to resell, without being answerable for any loss.

Section 12(2) provides that a trust or power to sell or dispose of land includes a trust or power to sell or dispose of part thereof, whether the division is horizontal, vertical, or made in any other way.

Duty of trustees

2.52   It is the duty of trustees to obtain the best possible price for trust property (*Buttle v Saunders [1950] 2 All ER 193*). Thus although trustees have a wide discretion as to the mode of sale, they should choose the method which is likely to yield the best price.

Protection of purchasers of land

2.53   Section 16 of the Trusts of Land and Appointment of Trustees Act 1996 contains provisions for the protection of purchasers. It does not apply if the title is registered.

Section 16(1) provides that a purchaser of land which is or has been subject to a trust need not be concerned to see that any requirement imposed on the trustees by s 6(5), 7(3) or 11(1) has been complied with. Section 6(5) provides that, in exercising the powers conferred by the section, the trustees must have regard to the rights of the beneficiaries. Section 7 is concerned with the partition of the land subject to a trust, and provides that, before exercising their powers, the trustees must obtain the consent of the beneficiaries. Section 11(1) imposes a duty on trustees to consult the beneficiaries.

Section 16(2) provides that if trustees convey land and contravene s 6(6) or (8), but the purchaser from the trustees has no actual notice of contravention, the contravention does not invalidate the conveyance. Section 6(6) provides that the powers conferred by s 6 must not be exercised in contravention of, or of any order made in pursuance of, any enactment or any rule of law or equity. Section 6(8) provides that where any enactment other than s 6 confers on the trustees authority to act subject to any restriction, limitation or condition, trustees of land may not exercise the powers conferred by s 6 to do any act which they are prevented from doing under the other enactment by reason of the restriction, limitation or condition.

Section 16(3) provides that where the powers of the trustees of land are limited:

(a)   the trustees must take all reasonable steps to bring the limitation to the notice of any purchaser of the land from them; but

(b)   the limitation does not invalidate any conveyance by the trustees to a purchaser who has no actual notice of the limitation.

Section 16(2) and (3) do not apply to land held on charitable, ecclesiastical or public trusts.

Section 16(4) provides that where land which is subject to the trust is conveyed by the trustees to persons who are believed by them to be beneficiaries absolutely entitled to the land and of full age and capacity, the trustees must execute a deed declaring that they are discharged from the trust in relation to the land. If they fail to do so, the court may make an order requiring them to do so. Section 16(5) provides that a purchaser of land to which a deed under sub-s (4) relates is entitled to assume that, as from the date of the deed, the land is not subject to the trust unless he has actual notice that the trustees were mistaken in their belief that the land was conveyed to beneficiaries absolutely entitled to the land under the trust and of full age and capacity.

POWER TO CONVEY THE LAND TO BENEFICIARIES

2.54   Section 6(2) of the Trusts of Land and Appointment of Trustees Act 1996 permits the trustees to convey the land to the beneficiaries if they are all of full age and capacity, even if the beneficiaries have not required the trustees to do so. The beneficiaries must do whatever is necessary to ensure that the land vests in them; for example, they must get themselves registered as proprietors of the land. If the beneficiaries fail to do so, the court may make an order requiring them to do so.

POWER TO PARTITION LAND

2.55   The trustees have power to partition the land under s 7 where the beneficiaries (i) are of full age and absolutely entitled in undivided shares to land subject to the trust, and (ii) agree to the partition. The trustees may provide for the payment of any equality money by way of mortgage or otherwise.

Where a share in the land is affected by an incumbrance, the trustees may either give effect to it, or provide for its discharge from the property allotted to that share as they think fit (s 7(4)).

If a share in land is absolutely vested in a minor, the provisions of s 7 apply as if he were of full age, except that the trustees may act on his behalf and retain land or other property representing his share in trust for him (s 7(5)).

SUMMARY

2.56
- *Advancement*: it is common to permit the trustees to advance the whole of the capital, to modify the requirement that any advancement should be brought into account, to dispense with the requirement that any beneficiary with a prior interest must consent and to confer power to advance capital to a life tenant.

- *Appropriation*: it is common to dispense with the requirement of consent, and to permit personal representatives to appropriate in their own favour. It may be appropriate to include a mechanism for valuing assets where the value cannot be easily ascertained. Trustees have more limited powers of appropriation.

- *Businesses*: it is common to permit personal representatives to run businesses for as long as they wish, to use other assets, to appoint a manager, and to include an indemnity for the personal representatives.

- *Charging clause*: this should still be included as trustees or executors can only charge if the other trustees and executors all agree.

- *Delegation*: trustees can delegate collectively and individually.

- *Insurance*: in the light of the Trustee Act 2000 it is no longer necessary to modify the statutory power.

- *Investment*: it is common to confer wide investment powers on trustees.

- However wide the investment clause, trustees must have regard to the 'standard investment criteria' and the requirement to obtain advice.

- *Maintenance*: it is common to give the trustees a complete discretion as to whether the income is applied for the maintenance, education or benefit of a beneficiary, and to postpone the entitlement to income to an age greater than 18.

- *Infants*: an infant cannot give a valid receipt, although there are some exceptions.

- *Receipt*: a sole trustee can give a valid receipt, except for the proceeds of sale or other capital money arising under a trust for sale, or capital money arising under the Settled Land Act.

- *Sale*: trustees have wide powers of sale and a wide discretion as to the method of sale.

- Trustees can convey land to beneficiaries or partition the land.

Chapter 3

Duties of trustees

BEFORE ACCEPTANCE OF THE TRUST

3.1   Before accepting a trust, a trustee should consider whether the acceptance of the trust will mean that there is a conflict of interest between the beneficiaries and the trustee; for example it would be wrong for a person in dispute with a beneficiary to be appointed a trustee. At the very least, the trustee should disclose the existence of a conflict or potential conflict of interest.

Another situation where there is a possibility for conflict is trusts of shares in the family company. The family members may be trustees of shares in the family company, owners of shares in the family company in a personal capacity, directors of the company and also full-time employees of the company. There is clearly the potential for conflict in relation to the various positions held by the family members.

DUTIES ON ACCEPTANCE OF THE TRUST

3.2   Once a trustee has accepted the appointment as a trustee, his first task is to read the trust document and ensure that he understands it. If necessary, legal opinion must be sought. The trustee should also find out about the beneficiaries, and the trust property (*Hallows v Lloyd (1888) 39 Ch D 686*). He should also ensure that the trust property is vested in the trustees immediately; s 40 of the Trustee Act 1925 provides that a deed appointing a new trustee will vest in the new trustees any estate or interest in land, any chattel, or the right to recover or receive any debt or other thing in action subject to the trust.

If a new trustee has been appointed to an existing trust, additional duties are imposed. The new trustee should check to ensure that the existing trustees have not committed any breach of trust (*Harvey v Olliver (1887) 57 LT 239*). The new trustee is not liable for the breaches of trust committed by the previous trustees, but he is liable if he fails to take all reasonable efforts to recover losses incurred by the previous trustees.

Trustees are also under a duty to check to see if the beneficial interests have been charged or assigned in any manner, so that they can give effect to the assignment. If they fail to do so, they will then become liable to the third party if money is paid or property handed over to the beneficiary (*Hallows v Lloyd (1888) 39 Ch D 686*). If there has been more than one assignment of the same beneficial interest, the trustees must have regard to the rules concerning priority of interests.

DUTY TO ENSURE FAIRNESS BETWEEN BENEFICIARIES

3.3   There is a general duty imposed on trustees to ensure fairness between beneficiaries. Although this duty applies throughout the existence of the trust, it particularly applies when the trust is first established and where there is a life interest followed by a remainder. It would be unfair to the life tenant to permit the trustees to retain investments which had little or no income, but at the same time showed considerable capital growth. Equally, it would be unfair to the remainderman to permit trustees to retain investments with a large income, but little or no capital growth. As a result, equity has developed some rules which are designed to hold the balance fairly between the life tenant and the remainderman. The relevant rules are as follows:

(a)   *Shares – purchase or sale ex div or cum div*. Shares are sold cum div or ex div. Cum div means that the share price reflects the fact that a dividend is due in the near future, whereas ex div means that the prospect of a dividend has been ignored in fixing the price. No apportionment between income and capital is required, unless it would cause a glaring injustice (see *Re MacClaren's Settlement Trustees [1951] 2 All ER 414* at page 420).

(b)   *Bonus shares*. Companies sometimes issue bonus shares. Are these capital or income? In *Bouch v Sproule (1887) 12 App Cas 385* it was said at page 397:

> 'When a testator or settlor directs or permits the subject of his disposition to remain as shares or stock in a company which has the power either of distributing its profits as dividends, or of converting them into capital, and the company validly exercises this power, such exercise of its power is binding on all persons interested under him, the testator or settlor, in the shares, and consequently what is paid by the company as dividend goes to the tenant for life, and what is paid by the company to the shareholder as capital, or appropriated as an increase of the capital stock in the concern, enures to the benefit of all who are interested in the capital.'

Thus they are regarded as capital. The trustees will either hold the shares, or sell them and reinvest the proceeds. Whichever alternative applies, the life tenant will receive the income from the shares.

(c) *Scrip dividends.* The trustees have an option to take dividends or an allotment of shares, and in deciding whether to take the dividends or the shares, the trustees must act in the best interests of the trust. Are scrip dividends income or capital? In *In re Malam [1894] 3 Ch 578*, Stirling J at page 585 stated that he was bound by the passage in *Bouch v Sproule* quoted above, and in the case before him he held that the tenant for life was entitled only to that part of the value of the new shares attributable to the dividend, the remainder being capital.

In an article in *The Law Society's Gazette* (1992) number 29 at page 19 Beatrice Toll states that 'the only safe course of action is for trustees to treat scrip dividends and demerged shares as capital until there is any judgment that they are income'. The Society of Trust and Estate Practitioners has suggested that the *Malam* approach is correct, and representations have been made to the Inland Revenue with regard to the tax treatment of scrip dividends (see memorandum dated March 1994).

(d) Thomas Tilling Ltd operated a bus and coach business which was nationalised. As compensation the company was issued with a block of 3 per cent British Transport Guaranteed Stock, which was distributed to shareholders. It was held that the stock was to be regarded as income, although in special circumstances the payment could be apportioned between income and capital (*In Re Kleinwort [1951] Ch 860*).

(e) *ICI and Zeneca.* In *Re Lee (deceased) [1993] 3 WLR 498* it was held that the shares in Zeneca which were issued to the shareholders of ICI in satisfaction of a dividend to be declared by ICI were to be treated as capital and not as income. Sir Donald Nicholls V-C said at page 508:

> 'In 1930 the Judicial Committee of the Privy Council considered this area of the law in *Hill v Permanent Trustee Co of New South Wales Ltd [1930] AC 720*. There, a company with an Australian sheep and cattle rearing business sold substantially the whole of its land, livestock and other assets, and ceased to carry on its business. It distributed the proceeds as a dividend described as a distribution of capital assets in advance of the winding up of the company. The Board held the dividend was income, as between tenant for life and remainderman. Of the five well-known propositions stated by Lord Russel of Killowen, at page 731, I should mention two:
>
> "(2) A limited company not in liquidation can make no payment by way of return of capital to its shareholders except

as a step in an authorised reduction of capital. Any other payment made by it by means of which it parts with moneys to its shareholders must and can only be made by way of dividing profits ... (3) Moneys so paid to a shareholder will (if he be a trustee) prima facie belong to the person beneficially entitled to the income of the trust estate. If such moneys or any part thereof are to be treated as part of the corpus of the trust estate there must be some provision in the trust deed which bring about that result ...".'

At page 510 he said:

'Having regard to these considerations, in my view to regard the ICI transaction as a distribution of profits, akin to payment of dividend in specie and hence income, would be to exalt company form over commercial substance to an unacceptable extent. In the last analysis, the rationale underlying the general principles enunciated in *Hill's* case [1930] AC 720 is an endeavour by the law to give effect to the assumed intention of the testator or settlor in respect of a particular distribution to shareholders. When the inflexible application of these principles would produce a result manifestly inconsistent with the presumed intention of the testator or settlor, the court should not be required to apply them slavishly. In origin they were guidelines. They should not be applied in circumstances, or in a manner, which would defeat the very purpose they are designed to achieve. Unless constrained by binding authority to the contrary, I consider the ICI transaction is to be characterised as a company reconstruction, with two capital assets (shares in ICI and Zeneca Group) in the trustees' hands replacing one existing capital asset (shares in ICI).'

(In respect of the tax treatment, see SP 4/94.)

(f) *Payment of expenses.* Should expenses be paid out of capital or income? The rules are as follows:

   (i) Capital must usually bear the cost of administering the estate. It is desirable that all settlements and wills which create trusts should specify whether capital or income is to bear the expenses, or whether the trustees are to have a discretion as to whether they are paid out of income or capital.

   (ii) If trustees carry on a business, losses must normally be paid from income. However, if the business is not carried on under a power in the settlement, but so that it can be sold, any losses must be apportioned between income and capital. Similarly, any income must be apportioned (*Re Hengler [1893] 1 Ch 586*).

(iii) If the power of insurance conferred by s 19 of the Trustee Act 1925 is exercised, the premiums can be paid out of the income or capital funds of the trust.

(iv) Section 57 of the Trustee Act 1925 and s 64 of the Settled Land Act 1925 as extended by s 1 of the Settled Land and Trustee Acts (Courts' General Powers) Act 1943 empower a court to order that repairs should be treated as a capital expense.

(v) If trust property is mortgaged, the principal will normally be payable out of capital, but interest will normally be paid out of income (*Marshall v Crowther (1874) 2 Ch D 199*).

(g) The rule in *Howe v Dartmouth (1802) 7 Ves Jr 137* provides that if there is a residuary gift of personalty for persons in succession, the trustees are under a duty to sell any trust assets which are wasting, hazardous or unauthorised, and any reversionary interests. The proceeds must be invested in authorised investments.

It should be noted that this rule is of limited application. First, it applies only to gifts in wills; it does not apply to *inter vivos* settlements. Secondly, it does not apply to specific gifts. Thirdly, it has no application to land or leaseholds.

(h) A duty to convert may arise in other circumstances, for example if there is an express trust for sale.

(i) If there is a duty to convert, it may be necessary to apportion the income. Assets of a wasting, hazardous or unauthorised nature may yield a large income, but at the same time the capital value may be decreasing rapidly. Unless there is an intention that the life tenant should enjoy the whole of the income, the trustees must apportion the proceeds of sale of these investments so that the life tenant receives interest at 4 per cent per annum. Any income in excess of the 4 per cent is regarded as capital to which the remainderman is entitled. If the income is insufficient to provide the 4 per cent, it must be made up out of income from later years, or the proceeds of sale of the assets.

As the assets may increase or decrease in value, it is clearly essential to determine the date at which the assets must be valued for the purpose of calculating the 4 per cent. The answer to this question depends on whether there is a power to postpone sale. If there is a power to postpone sale, the date for determining the value is one year after death, but if the assets are sold within that year, the value is the actual sale price. If there is no power to postpone sale, the date for determining the value is the date of death (*Re Fawcett [1946] Ch 402*).

Note that the duty to apportion applies to all settled property, whether the settlement is created *inter vivos* or by will, where there is a duty to convert immediately. However, the duty to apportion does not apply on intestacy. Section 33(5) of the Administration of Estates Act 1925 provides that the income (including net rents and profits of real estate and chattels real [i.e. leasehold interests] after payment of rates, taxes, rent, costs of insurance, repairs and other outgoings properly attributable to income) of so much of the real and personal estate of the deceased as may not be disposed of by his will, if any, or may not be required for administration purposes, may, however such estate is invested, as from the death of the deceased, be treated and applied as income, and for that purpose any necessary apportionment may be made between the tenant for life and remainderman.

Note also that the rule does not apply if trustees invest the trust assets in unauthorised investments and no loss results.

(j) The rule in *Re Earl of Chesterfield's Trusts (1883) 24 Ch D 643* deals with reversionary interests. These do not yield any income, which is unfair to the life tenant, and the rule requires that part of the value of the reversionary interest when it falls in or the proceeds of sale if it is sold should be applied as income.

What property is included in the rule? The case refers to a mortgage debt with arrears of interest, or arrears of an annuity with interest, or moneys payable on a life policy which falls in some years after the death of the testator. It also applies to settlements where the remainderman dies before the life tenant.

Note that the rule applies only if there is a duty to convert. Furthermore, it applies only to personalty; it does not apply to freehold land.

How do you calculate the income? It is necessary to ascertain the sum which, put out at interest at 4 per cent per annum on the day of the testator's death, and accumulating at compound interest calculated at that rate with yearly rests and deducting income tax, would, with the accumulations of interest, have produced, at the day of receipt, the amount actually received; and the sum so ascertained should be treated as capital, and the residue as income. 'Yearly rests' means that the interest is calculated at yearly intervals.

(k) The rule in *Allhusen v Whittell (1867) LR 4 EQ 295* deals with liability for debts. It would clearly be unfair to the life tenant if they were paid totally out of income; equally it would be unfair to the remainderman if they were paid out of capital. The rule requires that the debts should be paid partly out of income and partly out of capital. It is necessary to calculate the average income of the estate after income tax, and the debts will then be split proportionately between the income and the capital.

(l)   *Apportionment Act 1870.* Income may be paid periodically, for example rent, and on the death of a testator or a life tenant it may be that a payment of rent will relate to a period before death as well as after death. The Apportionment Act 1870 applies in this situation, and requires that 'all rents, annuities, dividends, and other periodical payments in the nature of income ... shall ... be considered as accruing from day to day, and shall be apportionable in respect of time accordingly'. Thus if rent is paid on a yearly basis in arrear, and the testator or life tenant dies during the year, the rent will have to be apportioned on a daily basis. The part of the rent attributable to the period before death will be deemed to belong to the testator or life tenant, and the part attributable to the period after death will belong to the personal representatives, or the remainderman. If the income is paid in advance, it does not have to be apportioned. If it is paid after death but relates wholly to a period before death, again no apportionment is necessary.

(m) *Income tax.* The rules discussed above do not affect liability for income tax. The crucial date for determining liability for income tax is the date when it is due, so that if a dividend is paid after death, it will not be regarded as part of the income of the deceased for income tax purposes, although for succession purposes it will have to be apportioned.

Finally, it should be remembered that in addition to the specialised rules mentioned above, there is a general duty to act fairly to all beneficiaries. In *Lloyds Bank plc v Duker [1987] 1 WLR 1324* Duker was entitled to 46/80 of the residue of an estate which was held on trust for sale and included shares in a private company. Duker requested that 46/80 of the shares should be transferred to him. It was held that this would benefit Duker at the expense of the other beneficiaries as a majority holding is worth more than a minority holding, and that the shares should be sold on the open market. John Mowbray QC said at pages 1330 and 1331 that he could 'get some help from another general principle. I mean the principle that trustees are bound to hold an even hand among their beneficiaries, and not favour one as against another ...'.

DUTY TO COMPLY WITH THE TERMS OF THE TRUST

3.4   It almost goes without saying that trustees must comply strictly with the terms of the trust and the law relating to trusts. If all the beneficiaries are of full age and capacity, they can of course agree that the terms of the trust should be modified or even that the trust should be terminated. However, if there is one beneficiary or one potential beneficiary who is not of full age, the trust cannot be varied or terminated without an application to the court for approval.

If a payment is due to a beneficiary, the trustees should make it without waiting for the beneficiary to request it (*Hawksley v May [1956] QB 304*).

Trustees holding property on discretionary trusts must comply with the terms of the trust, and if they fail to exercise discretionary powers within a reasonable time, the default trusts will apply. If the trustees must exercise the power, it can still be exercised, but if it is a discretionary power, it will lapse (*Re Locker's Settlement [1978] 1 All ER 216*).

DUTY TO PROVIDE INFORMATION AND ACCOUNTS

3.5   The question of whether trustees are under a duty to disclose documents relating to the trust, and whether there is a difference between the rights of beneficiaries under a fixed interest trust or discretionary trust has been litigated in several cases recently. It is clear that trustees are under a duty to provide beneficiaries on request with information about the trust and investments and a copy of the accounts. Trustees must also produce the title deeds and other documents applying to the trust. A beneficiary is also entitled to inspect the minutes or other record of any meetings held by the directors, although trustees are not under any duty to give reasons for their decisions (*Re Marquess of Londonderry's Settlement [1964] Ch 594*).

There are some limitations on this duty. The beneficiary can be asked to pay the cost of producing the documents, and the trustees can employ agents to help them produce the information required. In addition, a beneficiary is not entitled to see all the documents held by the trustees. In *Foreman v Kingstone [2005] WTLR 823*, a decision of the High Court of New Zealand, the trustees of several family trusts sought directions as to what documents they should disclose to the plaintiffs.

It was directed that the trustees should disclose the following:

(a)   Financial statements.

(b)   Accounts and details of beneficiaries to whom assets had been provided.

(c)   Copies of all deeds appointing trustees.

(d)   Details of all distributions of income and capital.

(e)   Information as to the amount and state of the property in trust funds.

(f)   Information about the management of trust property.

(g)   Details of changes in the structure of the trusts.

(h)   Memoranda of wishes or like communications from the settlor.

The following did not have to be disclosed:

(i)   Information as to their change of policy with regard to the application of provisions in the trust document regarding distributions made to one beneficiary.

(ii)   Legal opinions obtained by the trustees, but not necessarily all communications between the trustees and their legal advisers.

(iii)   Information as to the basis on which they had made their decision.

There is no duty on trustees to have the accounts audited, but if they want to do so, s 22(4) of the Trustee Act 1925 permits this to be done not more than once in every three years.

Section 137(8) of the Law of Property Act 1925 deals with notices of assignment of equitable interests which may have been given to trustees. Any person interested in the equitable interest may require production of the notice on payment of the costs.

If trustees fail to keep accounts, and a beneficiary begins an administration action to compel them to do so, the trustees will be liable in costs.

Solicitors who are trustees are of course subject to the Solicitors Trust Account Rules.

Section 13 of the Public Trustee Act 1906 provides that the condition and accounts of any trust shall, on an application being made and notice given in the prescribed manner by any trustee or beneficiary, be investigated and audited by such solicitor or public accountant as may be agreed on by the applicant and the trustees, or in default of agreement, by the public trustee or some person appointed by him.

DUTY TO TAKE REASONABLE CARE

Under the Trustee Act 2000

3.6   The Trustee Act 2000 describes the duty of care which is applicable to trustees. Section 1(1) provides that whenever the duty under the subsection applies to a trustee, he must exercise such care and skill as is reasonable in the circumstances, having regard in particular:

(a)   to any special knowledge or experience that he has or holds himself out as having; and

(b)   if he acts as trustee in the course of a business or profession, to any special knowledge or experience that it is reasonable to expect of a person acting in the course of that kind of business or profession.

Thus a solicitor who is a trustee will have to exercise a higher duty of care and skill than a lay trustee.

Schedule 1 deals with when the duty of care applies to a trustee. It provides that a duty of care applies to a trustee in connection with investment, acquisition of land, agents, nominees and custodians and insurance. Paragraph 1 provides that the duty of care applies to a trustee when exercising the general power of investment or a power of investment conferred on him by the trust instrument. It also applies when the trustee is carrying out the duty to which he is subject under ss 4 or 5 (duties relating to the exercise of a power of investment or to the review of investments) (Sch 1 para 1).

The duty of care also applies to a trustee when exercising the power under s 8 to acquire land, or when exercising any power to acquire land conferred on him by the trust instrument. It also applies when the trustee is exercising any power in relation to land acquired under these powers (para 2).

With regard to agents, nominees and custodians, para 3(1) provides that the duty of care applies to a trustee:

(a)   when entering into arrangements under which a person is authorised under s 11 to exercise functions as an agent;

(b)   when entering into arrangements under which a person is appointed under s 16 to act as a nominee;

(c)   when entering into arrangements under which a person is appointed under s 17 or 18 to act as a custodian;

(d)   when entering into arrangements under which, under any power conferred by the trust instrument, a person is authorised to exercise functions as an agent or is appointed to act as a nominee or custodian;

(e)   when carrying out his duties under s 22 (review of agent, nominee or custodian, etc).

Paragraph 3(2) provides that, for the purposes of subpara (1), entering into arrangements under which a person is authorised to exercise functions or is appointed to act as a nominee or custodian includes, in particular:

(a)   selecting the person who is to act;

(b)   determining any terms on which he is to act; and

(c)   if the person is being authorised to exercise assets management functions, the preparation of a policy statement under s 15.

Paragraph 4 provides that the duty of care applies to a trustee when exercising the power under s 19 of the Trustee Act 1925 to insure property. It also applies when the trustee is exercising any corresponding power conferred on him by the trust instrument.

The duty of care also applies to other powers conferred by the trust instrument. Paragraph 5 provides that the duty of care does not apply to powers conferred by a trust instrument if or in so far as it appears from the trust instrument that the duty is not meant to apply.

In areas not covered by the Trustee Act 2000, the rules are long established.

Existing duty

3.7   The extent of this duty varies according to whether the trustee is paid or unpaid. In *Speight v Gaunt (1883) 22 Ch D 727* Jessel MR stated that an unpaid trustee 'ought to conduct the business of the trust in the same manner that an ordinary prudent man of business would conduct his own ...'. However, a paid trustee is under a much higher duty. In *Bartlett v Barclays Bank Trust Co Ltd [1980] Ch 515* at page 534 Brightman J said:

> 'A trust corporation holds itself out in its advertising literature as being above ordinary mortals. With a specialist staff with ready access to financial information and professional advice, dealing with and solving trust problems day after day, the trust corporation holds itself out as capable of providing an expertise which it would be unrealistic to expect and unjust to demand from the ordinary prudent man or woman who accepts, probably unpaid and sometimes reluctantly from a sense of family duty, the burdens of trusteeship ... I think that a professional corporate trustee is liable for breach of trust if loss is caused to the trust fund because it neglects to use the special care and skill which it professes to have.'

Whilst the duties imposed on trustees are onerous, there is no liability for an error of judgement. In *Re Chapman [1896] 2 Ch 763* Lopes LJ said at page 778:

> 'A trustee who is honest and reasonably competent is not to be held responsible for a mere error in judgement when the question he has to consider is whether a security of a class authorised, but depreciated in value should be retained or realised, provided he acts with reasonable care, prudence and circumspection.'

Section 61 of the Trustee Act 1925 may also apply to relieve a trustee from liability. It applies where a trustee has acted honestly and reasonably, and ought fairly to be excused for the breach of trust and for omitting to obtain the directions of the court in the matter in which he committed such breach; in these circumstances the court may relieve him either wholly or partly from personal liability.

Trustees are under a duty to take steps to recover all monies owing to them. However, this is not an absolute duty, and there may be circumstances where forbearance is justified. In *Ward v Ward (1843) 2 HL Cas 777n* it was held that trustees were justified in not suing a beneficiary who owed money to the trust as such action would have ruined the beneficiary and the children of the beneficiary who were also beneficiaries. Trustees faced with such a situation should consider obtaining the directions of the court as to the proper course of action. Section 15 of the Trustee Act 1925 gives trustees wide powers with regard to debts, but such powers can only be exercised if it is in the best interests of the trust. The trustees must also discharge the duty of care set out in s 1(1) of the Trustee Act 2000.

If chattels are comprised in the trust assets, the trustees should make a list of all the chattels comprised in the trust. Unless the chattels are valuable, it is usually not a good idea to include them in the settled property as the trustees would be under a duty to ensure that reasonable care was taken of them.

If trustees decide to sell the trust property, or to purchase additional property for the trust, they would be well advised to obtain a professional valuation of the property so that there can be no argument about whether they obtained the best possible price, or paid too much for the property. If trustees receive a better offer for property they are selling, they must at the very least investigate the subsequent offer to see if it is genuine. If there is some doubt as to whether the person who made the higher offer is genuine, for example has another property to sell, or is unlikely to obtain the finance, the trustees would be justified in accepting a lower offer.

If trust property is stolen, trustees will not be liable provided that they have taken reasonable care of the property. However, a trustee is liable if property is delivered to the wrong person as a result of fraud or forgery (see *Law Relating to Trustees*, 16th edition, by Underhill and Hayton (Butterworths)).

DUTY TO ACT JOINTLY

3.8 Trustees must be unanimous in the action they take. In practice, it may be that one trustee is dominant, but nevertheless all the trustees must agree on a particular course of action.

A trust for sale usually includes a power to postpone sale, and in the case of land, s 4(1) of the Trusts of Land and Appointment of Trustees Act 1996 imposes a power to postpone sale in every trust for sale. This power to postpone sale cannot be excluded. The trustees are not liable in any way for postponing the sale of land for an indefinite period. If the trustees wish to exercise the power to postpone sale, they must all agree. On the other hand, if one trustee wants the property sold, then the property should be sold because the trustees are under a duty to sell.

All the trustees must give a receipt for capital, although one trustee can be permitted to give a receipt for income. In the case of land, any capital money must be paid to at least two trustees or a trust corporation in order to protect the purchaser (s 27 of the Law of Property Act 1925).

There are various exceptions to the rule that trustees must act jointly. The trust instrument may of course empower trustees to act by majority decision, and trustees also have the powers of delegation discussed above.

DUTY TO ACT WITHOUT REWARD

3.9   Most solicitors are aware of the rule that trustees are not entitled to be paid for work carried out in their capacity as trustees.

The Trustee Act 2000 confers on trustees an entitlement to remuneration (for a discussion of the provisions, see 2.19 above).

It is usual to include a charging clause in a will or settlement so as to permit a trustee who is a solicitor or other professional person to make his usual charges. Such a clause should be inserted even if the persons initially appointed trustees are not professionally qualified as such persons may be appointed at a later date.

In drafting such a clause, the following points should be borne in mind:

(a)   Trustees may have to do work which is not of a professional nature; it used to be the case that any charging clause had to be wide enough to permit trustees to charge for this work (*Re Ames (1883) 25 Ch D 72*). This is not now necessary as a result of s 29(4) of the Trustee Act 2000.

(b)   Trustees holding shares may be able to appoint themselves directors of companies, and in these circumstances they will be liable to account for all directors' fees paid by the company. However, the trustee will not be liable if he is made a trustee independently of any use of the trust holding (*Re Gee [1948] Ch 284*). In these circumstances, the clause should make it clear what is to happen to the fees.

(c)   A trustee may also receive commissions, for example for arranging insurance. Again the basic rule is that trustees must account for all commissions earned in respect of the trust property, and it is desirable to include a provision in the charging clause as to whether the trustee is entitled to them, or whether the trustee must account to the trust for them.

DUTY NOT TO MAKE PROFITS FROM THE TRUST

3.10   This duty will be familiar to practitioners. It is sometimes known as the rule in *Keech v Sandford (1726) 2 Eq Cas Abr 741*. The facts of that case were that a trustee held a lease on trust for an infant. The landlord refused to renew the lease for the benefit of the infant, but did renew it in favour of the trustee personally. It was held that the trustee held the renewed lease on trust for the infant beneficiary. Lord King LC said he must consider this as a trust for an infant, for if a trustee, on refusal to renew, might have a lease to himself, few trust estates would be renewed to the cestui que trust.

The duty is of very wide application; it clearly applies to any property added to the trust. For example, if trustees own shares, a bonus issue must be held by the trustees on the original trusts. The trustees are not of course entitled to keep the bonus shares for themselves. Trustees who use trust shares to obtain appointment of themselves as directors of a company must account for all benefits received from the company (*Re Macadam [1946] Ch 73*), but if the appointment had nothing whatsoever to do with the trust, then there is no liability to account. For example, if the trustees also owned shares in their personal capacity in a company as well as shares in their capacity as trustees, but used their personal holding to appoint themselves directors, they will not be liable to account (*Re Gee [1948] Ch 284*).

The duty may also apply to the purchase of the freehold reversion. In *Protheroe v Protheroe [1968] 1 WLR 519* a spouse had purchased the matrimonial home. Both contributed to the purchase price, but the property was vested in the sole name of the husband. The effect of this was to make the husband a trustee for both of them. The husband purchased the freehold reversion. There was a divorce, and it was held that the husband must account to his former wife for part of the proceeds when the house was sold. Lord Denning said at page 521:

> 'There is a long established rule of equity from *Keech v Sandford* downwards that if a trustee who owns the leasehold, gets in the freehold, that freehold belongs to the trust and he cannot take the property for himself.'

This decision conflicts with *Phipps v Boardman [1964] 2 All ER 187* where Wilberforce J at first instance said at pages 201–202:

> 'By contrast, with the familiar case of the renewal of a lease, typified by *Keech v Sandford*, which, if made by a person in a fiduciary

position, becomes the property of the trust, the purchase of a reversion does not have this effect, unless the lease is renewable by contract or custom; ... The reason for this is that whereas in the case of a renewal the trustee is in effect buying a part of the trust property, in the case of a reversion, this is not so ...'.

The law on this aspect is thus in doubt.

DUTY NOT TO PURCHASE TRUST PROPERTY

3.11   Most professional trustees will be aware of the duty not to purchase the trust property. Such a purchase is voidable at the instance of a beneficiary, even if the market price was paid for the property. However, the duty is not absolute. In *Holder v Holder [1968] Ch 353* the deceased had appointed his wife, daughter and son to be his executors. The son initially did a few acts in the administration of the estate which were admitted to constitute intermeddling, so that a renunciation by the son was ineffective. Then at an auction the son purchased from the estate some farmland of which he had been tenant. He had not taken any part in organising the auction. It was held that the sale should not be set aside. Harman LJ said at page 392:

'In this case the third defendant was not so acting: his interference with the administration of the estate was of a minimal character, and the last cheque he signed was in August before he executed the deed of renunciation. He took no part in the instructions for probate, nor in the valuations or fixing of the reserves. Everyone concerned knew of the renunciation and of the reason for it, namely that he wished to be a purchaser. Equally, everyone including the three firms of solicitors engaged assumed that the renunciation was effective and entitled the third defendant to bid. I feel great doubt whether the admission made at the Bar was correct, as did the judge, but assuming that it was right, the acts were only technically acts of intermeddling and I find no case where the circumstances are parallel. Of course, I feel the force of the judge's reasoning that if the third defendant remained an executor he is within the rule, but in a case where the reasons behind the rule do not exist I do not feel bound to apply it. My reasons are that the beneficiaries never looked to the third defendant to protect their interests. They all knew that he was in the market as a purchaser; that the price paid was a good one and probably higher than anyone not a sitting tenant would give. Further, the first two defendants alone acted as executors and sellers: they alone could convey: they were not influenced by the third defendant in connection with the sales.'

The rule is not limited in its application to purchases by trustees. It can also extend to purchases by the spouses of trustees, and to purchases by companies in which the trustee has an interest. Such a transaction is not always voidable; it will be if the purchase is in reality a purchase by the trustee. The rule will also apply to a sale to a third party if there is an understanding that the trustee will then purchase the property. However, the rule does not apply if there is no such understanding (*Re Postlethwaite (1888) 37 WR 200, CA*).

If the court decides that the sale is to be avoided, the beneficiaries can insist on the reconveyance of the property if it is still owned by the trustee. However, this can only be done if all the beneficiaries agree. A sale can also be ordered; the trustee will be entitled to be repaid the purchase price, any money spent on the property, and interest on both.

There are various exceptions to this rule. First, the settlement or will may expressly permit a trustee to purchase the trust property. Secondly, if all the beneficiaries are of full capacity, they can agree that a trustee should be permitted to purchase the trust property. In these circumstances, the beneficiaries may need separate legal advice. Thirdly, in the case of a settlement subject to the Settled Land Act 1925, s 68 of this Act permits wide dealings with the tenant for life; he is allowed *inter alia* to purchase the property which is the subject of the settlement. Fourthly, the court has power to permit a sale to a trustee.

It should be noted that there is no prohibition on the purchase by a trustee of the equitable interest of a beneficiary. In *Tito v Waddell (No 2) [1977] 3 All ER 129* at page 241 Megarry V-C said:

'... if a trustee purchases the beneficial interest of any of his beneficiaries, the transaction is not voidable ex debito justitiae, but can be set aside by the beneficiary unless the trustee can show that he has taken no advantage of his position and has made full disclosure to the beneficiary, and that the transaction is fair and honest'.

DUTY TO ENSURE THAT THE ASSETS ARE DISTRIBUTED TO THE CORRECT BENEFICIARIES

3.12   Trustees are under a duty to ensure that the assets of the trust are distributed or the income paid to the correct beneficiaries. This duty is very onerous as it is no defence to prove that payment was made as a result of a mistake as to the construction of a settlement or will (*Hilliard v Fulford (1876) 4 Ch D 389*). Similarly, it is no defence to prove that payment was made relying upon a forged document (*Eaves v Hickson (1861) 30 Beav 136*).

It should also be remembered that beneficiaries can assign their interests; if an assignee claims to be entitled, the trustees should check to ensure that this is the case. A new trustee should familiarise himself with the trust documents – if there was a notice of assignment lodged with them, and the trustee paid the money to the original beneficiary, the trustee would probably be liable to the assignee, but not if new trustees are appointed and there is nothing in the trust papers to indicate that there has been an assignment (*Hallows v Lloyd (1898) 39 Ch D 686*).

If trustees overpay a beneficiary, they can reclaim the overpayment from subsequent payments.

When a trust has come to an end, the trustees are entitled to present accounts to the beneficiaries, and request a formal discharge.

Although the duty imposed on trustees is high, the following are ways to reduce the risk of action by disgruntled beneficiaries:

(a) Section 61 of the Trustee Act 1925 enables a court to relieve a trustee from liability for breach of trust if the trustee has acted honestly and reasonably and ought fairly to be excused.

(b) Trustees and personal representatives can make use of protection by means of advertisements under s 27 of the Trustee Act 1925. Advertisements must be inserted in the *London Gazette*, and in a newspaper circulating in the district in which any land vested in the trustees or owned by the deceased is situated. The trustees must also give such other notices as would have been directed by a court of competent jurisdiction in an action for administration. The notice must require any person interested to send notice of claims to the trustees or personal representatives within the time specified in the notice, not being less than two months. The trustees must also make all the searches which an intending purchaser would make or be advised to make. At the expiration of the specified period, the trustees can distribute the trust assets only having regard to claims of which they had notice. Any disappointed claimant – i.e. a claimant within the time limit but whose claim is ignored – may follow the property, or any property representing the same, into the hands of a beneficiary. It should be noted that s 27 only protects personal representatives and trustees from liability for claims of which they are unaware.

(c) Section 48(1) of the Administration of Justice Act 1985 provides that where:

(i) any question of construction has arisen out of the terms of a will or a trust, and

(ii) an opinion in writing given by a person who has a ten-year High Court qualification, within the meaning of s 71 of the Courts and Legal Services Act 1990, has been obtained on that question by the personal representatives or trustees under the will or trust, the High

Court may, on the application of the personal representatives or trustees and without hearing argument, make an order authorising those persons to take such steps in reliance on the said opinion as are specified in the order.

Subsection (2) provides that the High Court shall not make an order if it appears that a dispute exists which would make it inappropriate for the court to make the order without hearing argument.

(d) Section 26 of the Trustee Act 1925 deals with the situation where trustees are liable for any rent or on any other covenant contained in a lease. If the trustees satisfy all liabilities under the lease or grant up to the date of the conveyance, and where necessary set apart a sufficient fund to answer any future claim that may be made in respect of any fixed and ascertained sum which the lessee agreed to lay out on the demised property, the trustees may then safely distribute the assets. Section 26(1A) provides that where a personal representative or trustee has entered or may be required to enter into an authorised guarantee agreement within the Landlord and Tenant (Covenants) Act 1995 with respect to any lease comprised in the estate of a deceased testator or intestate or a trust estate–

'(a) he may distribute the residuary real and personal estate of the deceased testator or intestate, or the trust estate, to or amongst the persons entitled thereto:

(i) without appropriating any part of the estate of the deceased, or the trust estate, to meet any future liability (or, as the case may be, any liability) under any such agreement, and

(ii) notwithstanding any potential liability of his to enter into any such agreement; and

(b) notwithstanding any such distribution, he shall not be personally liable in respect of any subsequent claim (or, as the case may be, any claim) under any such agreement.'

If a personal representative or trustee has entered into such an agreement, he must have satisfied all liabilities under it which may have accrued and been claimed up to the date of distribution. The lessor has the right to follow the assets into the hands of the persons amongst whom the assets may have been distributed.

(e) If the trustees have been unable to ascertain who is entitled, application can be made to the court for directions.

(f) If the trustees have made all reasonable enquiries, but have not been able to identify all possible beneficiaries, application can be made to the court for a 'Benjamin' order authorising the distribution of the assets in a certain manner. This procedure could be used if, for example, a possible beneficiary is almost certainly dead, for example a member of the RAF who was certified by the Air Ministry to have died in January 1943 having failed to return from a bombing raid over Germany (*Re Green's Will Trusts [1985] 3 All ER 455*).

(g) Illegitimate, legitimated, and adopted children are entitled to share in a gift to children just as if they are legitimate children, subject to any contrary intention. Section 45 of the Adoption Act 1976 provides:

  (i) A trustee or personal representative is not under a duty, by virtue of the law relating to trusts or the administration of estates, to enquire, before conveying or distributing any property, whether any adoption has been effected or revoked if that fact could affect entitlement to the property.

  (ii) A trustee or personal representative shall not be liable to any person by reason of a conveyance or distribution of the property made without regard to any such fact if he has not received notice of the fact before the conveyance or distribution.

  (iii) This section does not prejudice the right of a person to follow the property, or any property representing it, into the hands of another person, other than a purchaser, who has received it.

No such protection is available for illegitimate children, and so in order to obtain protection from claims by illegitimate children of whom they are unaware personal representatives or trustees should advertise under s 27 of the Trustee Act 1925.

(h) As a last resort the trust money can be paid into court.

DUTY TO CONSULT

3.13 So far as practicable, trustees are also under a duty to consult the beneficiaries of full age and beneficially entitled to an interest in possession in the land (s 11(1)(a) of the Trusts of Land and Appointment of Trustees Act 1996). Section 11(1)(b) provides that they must give effect to the wishes of such beneficiaries so far as is consistent with the general interest of the trust; if there is a dispute amongst the beneficiaries, the views of the majority by value prevail. The duty to consult can be excluded, and will not normally apply to a trust created before the Trusts of Land and Appointment of Trustees Act 1996 came into force (1 January 1997), or to a trust created or arising under a will made before 1 January 1997 (s 11(2)).

SUMMARY

3.14
*   Before accepting appointment as a trustee, the trustee should ensure that there is no conflict between the trustee and the beneficiary.

- A new trustee should ensure that he understands the trust document.

- A new trustee should ensure that the trust property is vested in the trustees.

- A person appointed to an existing trust should check to ensure that there has not been any breach of trust.

- Trustees should check to ensure that the beneficial interests have not been charged or assigned.

- Trustees must ensure that all the beneficiaries are fairly treated.

- Trustees must comply with the terms of the trust.

- Trustees must provide information and accounts.

- Trustees must take reasonable care.

- Trustees must act jointly.

- Lay trustees are not entitled to any reward. Professional trustees can charge under the Trustee Act 2000 as long as the other trustees agree.

- Trustees must not make any profit from the trust.

- Trustees are not entitled to purchase the trust property.

- Trustees must ensure that the assets are distributed to the correct beneficiaries.

- Trustees of land may have to consult the beneficiaries.

Chapter 4

Appointment, retirement and removal of trustees

WHO CAN BE A TRUSTEE?

Individuals

4.1   It is of course very common to appoint friends or relatives as trustees. It is possible to appoint bankrupts or persons who have committed serious criminal offences, but the court may remove them. It is clearly undesirable to appoint an infant as a trustee, and s 20 of the Law of Property Act 1925 specifically provides that the appointment of an infant to be a trustee in relation to any settlement or trust shall be void. However, it is clear that an infant does have the capacity to act as a trustee, and in *Re Vinogradoff [1935] WN 68* it was held that an infant could be a trustee of War Stock on a resulting trust.

Although it may not be desirable, there is no legal bar on the appointment of a beneficiary as a trustee.

Trust corporations

4.2   Section 68(18) of the Trustee Act 1925 defines a trust corporation. Many banks and insurance companies are trust corporations in their own right, or have subsidiary companies which operate as trust corporations. As a result of s 3 of the Law of Property (Amendment) Act 1926 the definition also includes the Treasury Solicitor, the Official Solicitor, and the trustee in bankruptcy.

Trust corporations can be appointed as executors or trustees, and whereas two individuals are required to give a valid receipt for capital money arising from land, a sole trust corporation can give a valid receipt (s 14 of the Trustee Act, s 27(2) of the Law of Property Act 1925, ss 18(1), 94 and 95 of the Settled Land Act 1925).

Trust corporations usually have a standard charging clause which should be incorporated in the will or settlement; it normally authorises the trust corporation to charge in accordance with a scale of fees published by the corporation, which may be amended from time to time.

The Public Trustee

4.3   The Public Trustee Act 1906 created the office of Public Trustee. It is a corporation sole, which means that it is never necessary to appoint another trustee. The Public Trustee can be appointed as trustee or executor, and may act jointly or alone. Whilst the Public Trustee can decline to act, he cannot do so solely on the ground that the estate is small. In addition, he cannot be appointed the trustee of a trust for religious or charitable purposes. If the trust assets include a business, the Public Trustee can only run it in order to wind the business up (Public Trustee Rules 1912 r 7(1) and (2)).

The Public Trustee is entitled to charge fees.

Custodian trustees

4.4   As the name implies, the function of a custodian trustee is to hold the property and documents of a trust. There will also be managing trustees who deal with the day-to-day administration of the trust.

A custodian trustee will be a trust corporation or the Public Trustee. It should be noted that the Public Trustee cannot be both a custodian trustee and a managing trustee (Public Trustee Act 1906, s 4(2)(b)).

Judicial trustees

4.5   The Judicial Trustees Act 1896 authorises the court to appoint a fit and proper person to be a judicial trustee. Any person so appointed may be remunerated.

In *Re Ridsdel [1947] Ch 597* at page 605 it was stated that the 'object of the Judicial Trustees Act 1896 ... was to provide a middle course in cases where the administration of the estate by the ordinary trustees had broken down, and it was not desired to put the estate to the expense of full administration ... a solution was found in the appointment of a judicial trustee, who acts in close concert with the court and under conditions enabling the court to supervise his transactions'.

NUMBER OF TRUSTEES

4.6   Section 34 of the Trustee Act 1925 provides that in the cases of settlements or dispositions on trust for sale of land, the number of trustees must not exceed four. Where more than four trustees are named, the four first named who are able and willing to act are the trustees alone. It is permissible to have a sole trustee of land, but a sole trustee, except where the trustee is a trust corporation, cannot give a valid receipt for the proceeds of sale or other capital money arising under a trust of land or capital money arising under the Settled Land Act 1925 (s 14(2) of the Trustee Act 1925).

If the settlement is of personalty, there are no limitations on the number of trustees, but it is unusual to appoint more than four.

DISCLAIMER

4.7   A settlor cannot force someone to be a trustee. It is always open to a person appointed as trustee to disclaim, as long as he has not intermeddled with the estate. Any person appointed as a trustee who wishes to disclaim should do so by deed, although a deed is not essential. Mere inactivity may amount to an implied disclaimer.

NEW TRUSTS

4.8   If a trust is created *inter vivos*, the settlor will normally appoint the trustees, who can include the settlor himself and the beneficiaries. If a trust is created in a will, or arises on intestacy, the personal representatives of the deceased will often be the trustees. It is possible to appoint separate persons as executors and trustees; if the deceased was in business on his own, it may be desirable to appoint as executors persons who know how to run the business. However, if it is intended that the business should be sold and the proceeds held on trust, then it may be that family members should be appointed as trustees. If the same persons are appointed executors and trustees, on the death of the testator they will be personal representatives. At a later date they will become trustees.

If there are no trustees when a trust comes into existence, for example because the settlor failed to appoint any trustees or those appointed did not want to act, there may be a power in the settlement authorising the settlor or a third party to appoint trustees. If there is no such power, the court has an inherent jurisdiction to appoint trustees. However, in *Pappadakis v Pappadakis [2000] WTLR 719* P took out a whole life policy and executed a document headed 'Declaration of Trust'. This was in a standard form, but was not properly completed.

It was held:

1.   The document was an assignment of the policy, but could not operate as such as no trustees were appointed.

2.   As it was not intended to operate as a declaration of trust, equity would not treat it as such.

3.   The document was not as a matter of construction a declaration of trust.

4.   An invalid document cannot be saved by having its terms rectified.

WHAT HAPPENS IF A TRUSTEE DIES?

4.9   If there is more than one trustee, the right of survivorship will apply, and the trust property will automatically vest in the survivor. If a sole trustee dies, the personal representatives of the sole trustee are capable of exercising or performing any power or trust which was given to, or capable of being exercised by, the trustee (s 18 of the Trustee Act 1925).

NEW TRUSTEES

4.10   As has been mentioned, there may be an express power to appoint new trustees in the will or settlement. There is also a statutory power in s 36 of the Trustee Act 1925, which applies if a trustee is dead, or remains out of the United Kingdom for more than 12 months, or desires to be discharged from all or any of the trusts or powers reposed in or conferred on him, or refuses or is unfit to act therein, or is incapable of acting therein, or is an infant. It should be noted that 12 months' absence means continuous absence for 12 months so that the requirement is not satisfied if the trustee remains abroad for more than 112 months, but returns for one week (*Re Walker [1901] 1 Ch 259*). 'Unfit to act' is not referring to mental incapacity, but to other factors like bankruptcy or conviction for a crime of dishonesty. It should also be noted that a personal representative may have completed the administration of an estate, and become a trustee. If the person does not want to be a trustee, he could be discharged under this section.

Section 36(9) provides that where a trustee is incapable, by reason of mental disorder within the meaning of the Mental Health Act 1983, of exercising his functions as trustee and is also entitled in possession to some beneficial interest in the trust property, no appointment of a new trustee in his place can be made under s 36(1)(b) unless leave to make the appointment has been given by the authority having jurisdiction under Part VII of the Mental Health Act 1983.

Section 36(1) provides that if the section applies:

(a)   the person or persons nominated for the purpose of appointing new trustees by the instrument, if any, creating the trust; or

(b)   if there is no such person, or no such person able and willing to act, then the surviving or continuing trustees or trustee for the time being, or the personal representative of the last surviving or continuing trustee,

may, by writing, appoint one or more other persons (whether or not being the persons exercising the power) to be a trustee or trustees in the place of the trustees so deceased, remaining out of the United Kingdom, desiring to be discharged, refusing, or being unfit or being incapable, or being an infant.

If two or more persons are nominated to appoint new trustees, they must all concur in the appointment (*Re Sheppard's Settlement Trusts [1888] WN 234*). If one dies, the survivors cannot exercise it (*Re Harding [1923] 1 Ch 182*). If the trust instrument does not nominate any person to appoint new trustees, the surviving or continuing trustees have the power to do so. It should be noted that if all the trustees appointed in a will predecease the testator, the provision does not apply (*Nicholson v Field (1893) 2 Ch 511*).

The personal representatives of a last surviving or continuing trustee can also exercise this power. Personal representatives need not prove the will before exercising this power, but any trustee appointed will need a grant to prove that he is entitled to exercise the power (*Re Crowhurst Park, Sims-Hilditch v Simmons [1974] 1 All ER 991*).

Care should be taken if the power is hedged with restrictions. In *Re Wheeler [1896] 1 Ch 315* a settlement contained a power to appoint trustees in specified circumstances. It was desired to appoint a trustee in circumstances not covered by the express provision. It was held that the appointment had to be made under the statutory power to appoint new trustees.

If beneficiaries have the power to appoint new trustees, they will generally retain the power even if they cease to be beneficiaries (*Hardaker v Moorhouse (1884) 26 Ch D 417*).

Can a retiring trustee act under the provisions of this section? Section 36(8) specifically provides that the provisions of s 36 relative to a continuing trustee include a refusing or retiring trustee if willing to act in the execution of the provisions of this section. So a retiring trustee can participate in the appointment of a new trustee.

It should be noted that the power is not exercisable by will, and that the personal representatives cannot be compelled to exercise the power. If a beneficiary does not like the proposed appointee, there is nothing the beneficiary can do to prevent the appointment.

Where:

(a)   no person has been nominated for the purposes of appointing new trustees by the instrument, if any, creating the trust; and

(b)   the beneficiaries under the trust are of full age and capacity who together are absolutely entitled to the property subject to the trust,

section 19(2) of the Trusts of Land and Appointment of Trustees Act 1996 provides that the beneficiaries may give a written direction (i) to a trustee or trustees to retire from the trust, and/or (ii) to the trustee(s) for the time being (or, if there are none, to the personal representative of the last person who was a trustee) to appoint by writing as trustee(s) the person(s) specified in the direction.

A trustee who has received such a written direction to retire should make a deed declaring his retirement (s 19(3)). He will then be deemed to have retired from the trust, and to be discharged from the trust, if:

—   reasonable arrangements have been made for the protection of any rights of his in connection with the trust;

—   after he has retired, there will be a trust corporation or at least two persons to act as trustees to perform the trust; and

—   either another person is to be appointed to be a new trustee on his retirement or the continuing trustees by deed consent to his retirement.

When a trustee retires in these circumstances, both he and the continuing trustees must vest the trust property in the continuing trustees, subject to any arrangements for the protection of the retiring trustee (s 19(4)).

Section 20(1) of the Trusts of Land and Appointment of Trustees Act 1996 provides that if a trustee is incapable of exercising his functions as a trustee because of mental disorder, the beneficiaries may give a written direction requiring the person(s) specified in the direction to be trustee(s) in place of the incapable trustee provided that the following conditions are satisfied:

—   there is no person who is both entitled and willing and able to appoint a trustee in place of the incapable trustee under s 36(1) of the Trustee Act 1925; and

— the beneficiaries under the trust are of full age and capacity and (taken together) are absolutely entitled to the property subject to the trust.

Section 20(2) provides that the written direction must be given to:

(a)   a receiver of the trustee;

(b)   an attorney acting for him under the authority of a power of attorney created by an instrument which is registered under s 6 of the Enduring Powers of Attorney Act 1985; or

(c)   a person authorised for the purpose by the authority having jurisdiction under Part VII of the Mental Health Act 1983.

Section 21 provides that, for the purposes of ss 19 or 20, the beneficiaries can give one direction or separate directions. Where separate directions are given, they must each specify for appointment or retirement the same person(s).

Section 21 goes on to provide that a direction under ss 19 or 20 must not specify a person or persons for appointment if the appointment of such person(s) would contravene s 35(1) of the Trustee Act 1925 or s 24(1) of the Law of Property Act 1925 (requirements as to identity of trustees).

Section 8 of the Trustee Delegation Act 1999 confers on the donee of an enduring power a limited power to appoint a new trustee. The section applies to a person who is either:

(a)   both a trustee and attorney for the other trustee (if one other), or for both of the other trustees (if two others), under a registered power; or

(b)   an attorney under a registered power for the trustee (if one) or for both or each of the trustees (if two or three).

(s 36(6A))

(a) applies where one of the trustees is appointed attorney by all the other trustees; (b) applies where a non-trustee is appointed as attorney by all the trustees.

Section 36(6B) provides that the attorney must as attorney under the power intend:

(a)   to exercise any function of the trustee(s) by virtue of s 1(1) of the Trustee Delegation Act 1999; or

(b)   to exercise any function of the trustee(s) in relation to any land, capital proceeds of a conveyance of land or income from land by virtue of its delegation to him under s 25 of the Trustee Delegation Act 1999 or the instrument (if any) creating the trust.

Section 36(6D) states that s 36(6A) is subject to any contrary intention expressed in the instrument creating the power of attorney (or, where more than one, any of them) or the instrument (if any) creating the trust, and has effect subject to the terms of those instruments.

These provisions will assist spouses or cohabitees who are the trustees of the legal estate of the home holding it on trust for themselves as joint tenants or tenants in common in equity. If both spouses grant enduring powers of attorney to each other or lasting powers of attorney, and one becomes mentally incapable, then the other can make use of these provisions to appoint another trustee, thereby satisfying the requirements of s 7 of the Trustee Delegation Act 1999. (These issues are more fully discussed in the author's book *A Practitioners' Guide to Powers of Attorney* published by Tottel Publishing.)

RETIREMENT OF TRUSTEES

4.11   As we have seen, the duties of trustees are onerous, and it may be that a trustee will want to retire because of ill health, or because he is old, or has retired from practice. Retirement is possible in the following circumstances:

(a)   *Express power.* The trust instrument may contain an express power permitting a trustee to retire. This is not very common.

(b)   Section 36 of the Trustee Act 1925 permits a trustee to retire if another is appointed in his place; this section is discussed above.

(c)   Section 39 of the Trustee Act 1925 permits a trustee to retire if after his discharge there will be at least two individuals or a trust corporation to act as trustees. The co-trustees and any person empowered to appoint new trustees must consent by deed, and to the vesting in the co-trustees alone of the trust property. No new trustee need be appointed in the place of the retiring trustee, and the effect of the retirement is to discharge the trustee from the trust.

　　It should be noted that under s 36 it is possible to retire from part of a trust, but under s 39 the trustee retires from the whole trust.

(d)   *Consent of beneficiaries.* A trustee can retire if all the beneficiaries are of full age and capacity and agree. It is possible that the co-trustees must agree to the retirement.

(e)   *Order of the court.* As a last resort, the court can be asked to permit the retirement of a trustee.

(f)   *At the instance of the beneficiaries.* Section 19 of the Trusts of Land and Appointment of Trustees Act 1996 applies where the trust instrument does not nominate any person for the purpose of appointing new trustees (see above).

It should be noted that retirement is not possible if the beneficiaries are quarrelling amongst themselves.

A trustee who retires is not normally liable for breaches of trust committed after he has retired, unless a breach was clearly contemplated when the trustee retired (*Head v Gould [1898] 2 Ch 25*).

REMOVAL OF TRUSTEES

4.12   Beneficiaries who are dissatisfied with the administration of a trust may wish to remove one or all of the trustees. Very rarely, the trust instrument may contain an express power to remove a trustee; if not it may be that a trustee can be removed under s 36 of the Trustee Act or ss 19 or 20 of the Trusts of Land and Appointment of Trustees Act 1996. The court also has an inherent power to remove a trustee, and it will do so if there is 'something which induces the court to think either the trust property will not be safe or that the trust will not be properly executed in the interests of the beneficiaries' (Warrington J in *Re Wrightson [1908] 1 Ch 789* at page 803). Thus if a trustee has become bankrupt, or has been convicted of an offence of dishonesty, the court will remove such a trustee, but the court may not be prepared to do so if the problem is that the trustees cannot agree, unless of course there is complete deadlock, and the trust will not be properly executed.

APPOINTMENT OF ADDITIONAL TRUSTEES

4.13   Section 36(6) of the Trustee Act 1925 confers on:

(a)   the person or persons nominated for the purpose of appointing new trustees by the instrument, if any, creating the trust; or

(b)   if there is no such person, or no such person able and willing to act, then the trustee or trustees for the time being:

the power to appoint an additional trustee or trustees.

Any appointment must be in writing, and the number of trustees must not exceed four.

Because of a difference in wording between s 36(1) and (6), the person making the appointment of a trustee under s 36(1) can appoint himself, but if the appointment is made under s 36(6), the person making the appointment cannot appoint himself.

APPOINTMENT OF NEW TRUSTEES BY THE COURT

4.14   Section 41(1) of the Trustee Act authorises the court to appoint new trustees whenever it is expedient to do so, and it is found inexpedient, difficult or impracticable so to do without the assistance of the court. The subsection then lists some situations when the court may make such an order – if a trustee is incapable by reason of mental disorder within the meaning of the Mental Health Act 1983 of exercising his functions as a trustee, or is bankrupt, or is a corporation which is in liquidation, or has been dissolved. Although the subsection gives the court a wide discretion as to the circumstances in which an appointment will be made, it should be noted that the court will not make an appointment if the trust instrument contains an express power to appoint new trustees, or the power under s 36(1) could be exercised (*Re Gibbon (1882) 45 LT 756*).

There is no objection to the appointment of a beneficiary as a trustee, and the court may still appoint a person as trustee even though the existing trustees object (*Re Tempest (1886) 1 Ch App 485*).

Section 41(4) provides that nothing in the section gives power to appoint an executor or administrator.

Section 42 provides that where the court appoints a corporation, other than the Public Trustee, to be a trustee, the court may authorise the corporation to charge such remuneration for its services as the court may think fit.

Section 43 provides that every trustee appointed by the court has the same powers, authorities, and discretions, and may in all respects act as if he had been originally appointed a trustee by the instrument creating the trust.

HOW MANY TRUSTEES SHOULD BE APPOINTED?

4.15   Section 37(1)(c) of the Trustee Act 1925 provides that it shall not be obligatory to appoint more than one new trustee where only one trustee was originally appointed, or to maintain the original number of trustees where more than two trustees were originally appointed. However, unless only one trustee was originally appointed, and a sole trustee when appointed will be able to give valid receipts for all capital money, a trustee is not to be discharged from his trust unless there will be either a trust corporation or at least two individuals to act as trustees to perform the trust.

Thus a retiring trustee will be discharged if a trust corporation is appointed, or there are two trustees – or, if only one trustee was originally appointed, where a sole trustee can give valid receipts for capital money.

Section 37(2) provides that nothing in the Act is to authorise the appointment of a sole trustee, not being a trust corporation, where the trustee, when appointed, would not be able to give valid receipts for all capital money arising under the trust.

In *Adam & Co International Trustees Ltd v Theodore Goddard (A Firm) [2000] WTLR 349* E and S were trustees. TG prepared a deed of retirement. A was appointed as a single trustee. It was held that the appointment of A as a single trustee was ineffective to discharge E and S because of the provisions of section 37(1)(c) of the Trustee Act 1925.

(For a fuller discussion of s 37 see the article by Michael Jacobs in *Tolley's Trust Law International* Vol 7 No 3 at pages 73–79.)

VESTING OF PROPERTY

4.16   As we have seen, it is the duty of trustees when first appointed to ensure that the trust property is vested in them. If the trustees are appointed by the trust instrument, they can ensure that all the trust assets are vested in them by the appropriate documents; for example a stock transfer form must be used to transfer shares to trustees, and the transfer registered with the company.

If a new trustee is appointed, s 40(1)(b) of the Trustee Act 1925 provides that if a deed appoints a new trustee, the deed will operate to vest in the trustees as joint tenants all the estates, interest, and rights of the trustee in any land, chattel, or the right to recover or receive any debt or other thing in action subject to the trust. A similar provision operates if a trustee is discharged by deed without a new trustee being appointed. These provisions are all subject to any contrary intention expressed in the deed of appointment or discharge.

Section 40(4) provides that the section does not extend:

(a)   to land conveyed by way of mortgage for securing money subject to the trust, except land conveyed on trust for securing debentures or debenture stock;

(b)   to land held under a lease which contains any covenant, condition or agreement against assignment or disposing of the land without licence or consent, unless, prior to the execution of the deed containing expressly or impliedly the vesting declaration, the requisite licence has been obtained, or unless by virtue of any statute or rule of law, the vesting declaration, express or implied, would not operate as a breach of covenant, or give arise to forfeiture;

(c)   to any share, stock, annuity, or property which is only transferable in books kept by a company or other body, or in a manner directed by or under an Act of Parliament.

Thus a deed appointing a new trustee will vest most assets in the new trustees. The major exception is shares, where a stock transfer will be necessary to transfer the shares to the new trustees.

If the title to freehold land is registered, the registrar will give effect to any vesting order or vesting declaration made on the appointment or discharge of a trustee (s 27(5) of the Land Registration Act 2002). It should be noted that although the vesting order or declaration must be lodged at the Land Registry, it is unnecessary to lodge a transfer, although it is common practice to do so. If a transfer is not lodged, the Land Registry will investigate the right of the persons making the appointment to do so unless the appropriate certificate is given by a conveyancer (see Ruoff and Roper's *Registered Conveyancing* 32–18).

It should be noted that ss 44–56 of the Trustee Act 1925 contain provisions dealing with vesting orders.

Re King's Will Trusts [1964] Ch 542 serves as a warning to practitioners in respect of the pitfalls which can be encountered. In that case the deceased left some freehold land on trust. The will was proved by two executors, and, when one died, the other executor appointed another person to be trustee. No deed vesting the property in the executors was executed. Was the deed of appointment effective to vest the land in the new trustee? It was held that it was not. Section 36 of the Administration of Estates Act 1925 requires a written assent to vest property in the trustees, and this must still be done even though the trustees and the personal representatives are the same people. It was also held that s 40 applied only to land vested in the trustee. Although this case may be wrong, it illustrates the point that care is needed if a personal representative has died before a vesting assent has been executed. The proper procedure in this situation is for the personal representative to vest the property in himself as trustee, and then appoint a new trustee; alternatively, a grant of letters of administration with the will annexed should be obtained.

EVIDENCE OF A VACANCY IN A TRUST

4.17   How is a purchaser from a trustee to be certain that one of the grounds specified in s 36 (power of appointing new or additional trustees) is satisfied? In order to prevent the purchaser having to make enquiries, s 38 of the Trustee Act 1925 provides that a statement contained in any instrument by which a new trustee is appointed for any purpose to the effect that the trustee has remained out of the United Kingdom for more than 12 months or refuses or is unfit to act, or is incapable of acting, or that he is not entitled to a beneficial interest in the trust property in possession, shall, in favour of a purchaser of the legal estate, be conclusive evidence of the matter stated. Thus a purchaser need look no further than the instrument appointing the new trustees. However, the section is somewhat limited in that it applies only to land.

SUMMARY

4.18

- Any person can be appointed a trustee, although some may be undesirable!

- In the case of land, the number of trustees should not exceed four.

- A trustee can disclaim.

- If a trustee dies, normally the trust property automatically vests in the survivor; if a sole trustee dies, his personal representatives can appoint an additional trustee.

- Section 36 authorises the appointment of replacement and additional trustees subject to various conditions.

- Trustees can retire in certain circumstances.

- Trustees can be removed if necessary.

- If a new trustee is appointed in a deed, the deed operates to vest in the new trustees most trust property.

Chapter 5

Resulting and constructive trusts

RESULTING TRUSTS

5.1   In certain circumstances although the donor has transferred property, there will be a resulting trust in favour of the donor. Megarry J in *Re Vandervell's Trusts (No 2) [1974] Ch 269* at page 294 said:

'(3)   Before any doctrine of resulting trust can come into play, there must at least be some effective transaction which transfers or creates some interest in property.

(4)   Where A effectually transfers to B (or creates in his favour) any interest in any property, whether legal or equitable, a resulting trust for A may arise in two distinct classes of case. For simplicity, I shall confine my statement to cases in which the transfer or creation is made without B providing any valuable consideration, and where no presumption of advancement can arise; I shall state the position of transfers without the specific mention of the creation of new interests.

(a)   The first class of case is where the transfer to B is not made on any trust. If, of course, it appears from the transfer that B is intended to hold on certain trusts, that will be decisive, and the case is not within this category; and similarly if it appears that B is intended to take beneficially. But in other cases there is a rebuttable presumption that B holds on resulting trust for A. The question is not one of the automatic consequences of a dispositive failure by A, but one of presumption; the property has been carried to B, and from the absence of consideration and any presumption of advancement B is presumed to have not only to hold the entire interest on trust, but also to hold the beneficial interest for A absolutely. The presumption thus establishes both that B is to take on trust and also what that trust is. Such resulting trusts may be called "presumed resulting trusts".

(b)   The second class of case is where the transfer to B is made on trusts which leave some or all of the beneficial interest undisposed of. Here B automatically holds on a resulting trust for A to the extent that the beneficial interest has not been carried to him or others. The resulting trust here does not depend on any intentions or presumptions, but is the automatic consequence of A's failure to dispose of what is vested in him. Since *ex hypothesi* the transfer is on trust, the resulting trust does not establish the trust but merely carries back to A the beneficial interest that has not been disposed of. Such resulting trusts may be called "automatic resulting trusts".

(5)   Where trustees hold property in trust for A, and it is they who, at A's direction, make the transfer to B, similar principles apply, even though on the face of the transaction the transferor appears to be the trustees and not A. If the transfer to B is on trust, B will hold any beneficial interest that has not been effectively disposed of on an automatic resulting trust for the true transferor, A. If the transfer to B is not on trust, there will be a rebuttable presumption that B holds on resulting trust for A.'

There are many situations when a resulting trust will come into operation. Some of these situations are:

- purchase in the name of another;

- failure of the trust;

- failure to dispose of all the settlor's interest;

- dissolution of unincorporated associations; and

- disaster funds.

It should be noted that there are no formal requirements for a resulting trust (s 53(2) of the Law of Property Act 1925).

Purchase in the name of another

5.2   If property is purchased in the name of another, there is a presumption that there is a resulting trust in favour of the person who provided the money (*Dyer v Dyer (1788) 2 Cox Eq 92*). However, if the person who provided the purchase price is the parent or stands *in loco parentis* to the person in whose name the property is vested, then there is no presumption of resulting trust. In *Shephard v Cartwright [1955] AC 431* at page 445 Viscount Simonds stated:

' ... the law is clear that, on the one hand, where a man purchases shares, and they are registered in the name of a stranger, there is a resulting trust in favour of the purchaser; on the other hand, if they are registered in the name of a child or one to whom the purchaser then stood *in loco parentis* there is no such resulting trust, but a presumption of advancement. Equally it is clear that the presumption may be rebutted but should not give way to slight circumstances.'

It should be noted that there is no presumption of advancement if a mother makes a gift of property to a child.

There is a presumption of advancement in respect of gifts between husband and wife; this is considered in chapter 9.

Failure of the trust

5.3   If a trust fails for any reason, there will be a resulting trust in favour of the settlor. An example of this is provided by the case of *Re Ames' Settlement [1946] Ch 217* where the father of the husband transferred £10,000 to the trustees of a marriage settlement. The husband had a life interest in the property, and in default of issue the persons who would have been the next of kin of the husband had he died were entitled. The marriage was annulled, and when the husband died without issue, it was held that there was a resulting trust in favour of the settlor's executors (the settlor having died some time before).

In *Morice v Bishop of Durham (1804) 9 Ves 399, (1805) 10 Ves 522* there was a bequest for such objects of benevolence and liberality as the trustee in his own discretion shall most approve. It was held that this could not be a charitable legacy, and that the testator's next of kin were entitled.

Failure to dispose of all the settlor's interest

5.4   It may be that the trusts established by the settlement will not exhaust the beneficial interest completely. In *Re Flower's Settlement Trusts [1957] 1 All ER 462, CA* the settlor created a discretionary trust which was to last for his lifetime. This trust was void during the lifetime of the settlor. After the death of the settlor, the income was to be paid to the settlor's wife for life, and then the settlor's children became absolutely entitled. It was held that there was a resulting trust in favour of the settlor during his life.

Practitioners should ensure that a settlement disposes of all the interest of a settlor as otherwise the settlor may be deemed to have retained a benefit, and may be assessable to income tax on the income of the settlement. It is thus clear that great care is required when drafting a settlement to ensure that the beneficial interest is exhausted.

Dissolution of unincorporated associations

5.5   Problems have also arisen with regard to the dissolution of unincorporated non-charitable associations, and the entitlement to surplus funds. The property of such associations may be held on trust for the members, or it may be subject to a contract between the members which is contained in the rules of the association. If there is a resulting trust, there is a possibility that the Crown will be entitled to the property as *bona vacantia*, but there is now a tendency to hold that there is a contractual relationship in these cases. In *Re Recher's Will Trusts [1972] Ch 526* a will contained a gift to an unincorporated association. It was in fact held that the gift was invalid, but Brightman J said at page 539:

> 'In the absence of words which purport to impose a trust, the legacy is a gift to the members beneficially, not as joint tenants or tenants in common so as to entitle each member to an immediate distributive share, but as an accretion to the funds which are the subject-matter of the contract which the members have made *inter se*.'

In *Re Bucks Constabulary Fund (No 2) [1979] 1 WLR 936* Walton J said at page 943:

> 'Before I turn to a consideration of the authorities, it is I think pertinent to observe that all unincorporated societies rest in contract to this extent, but there is an implied contract between all of the members *inter se* governed by the rules of the society. In default of any rule to the contrary – and it will seldom, if ever, be that there is such a rule – when a member ceases to be a member of the association he *ipso facto* ceases to have an interest in its funds.'

Disaster funds

5.6   Although very few practitioners will be asked to deal with funds established to aid the victims of disasters, problems have been encountered with the disposal of surplus assets; for example see *Re Gillingham Bus Disaster Fund [1958] Ch 300*. If such a trust is established, provision should be made for the distribution of any surplus funds.

CONSTRUCTIVE TRUSTS

5.7   In certain situations the courts will impose a trust. For example, a trustee who holds a lease as trustee and renews it for his own benefit will hold the lease as constructive trustee for the beneficiaries (*Keech v Sandford (1726) Sel Cas Ch 61*).

In *Paragon Finance plc v D B Thakerar & Co (a firm) [1999] 1 All ER 400*, Millett LJ summarised the principles applicable to constructive trusts. He said at pages 408–409:

> '... the expressions "constructive trust" and "constructive trustee" have been used by equity lawyers to describe two entirely different situations. The first covers those cases ... where the defendant, though not expressly appointed as trustee, has assumed the duties of a trustee by a lawful transaction which was independent of and preceded the breach of trust and is not impeached by the plaintiff. The second covers those cases where the trust obligation arises as a direct consequence of the unlawful transaction which is impeached by the plaintiff.
>
> A constructive trust arises by operation of law whenever the circumstances are such that it would be unconscionable for the owner of property (usually but not necessarily the legal estate) to assert his own beneficial interest in the property and deny the beneficial interest of another. In the first class of case, however, the constructive trustee really is a trustee. He does not receive the trust property in his own right but by a transaction by which both parties intend to create a trust from the outset and which is not impugned by the plaintiff. His possession of the property is coloured from the first by the trust and confidence by means of which he obtained it, and his subsequent appropriation of the property to his own use is a breach of that trust.'

A trustee is not allowed to take advantage of his position as a trustee so as to enrich himself. This principle is the reason for imposing liability in the following situations.

Renewal of a lease

5.8   The case of *Keech v Sandford* has already been mentioned, where it was held that a trustee must hold the renewed lease for the benefit of the trust.

Similarly, a trustee must hold any additions to the trust property on trust for the beneficiaries. In *Aberdeen Town Council v Aberdeen University (1877) 2 App Cas 544* at page 549 Lord Cairns said:

> ' ... whenever a trustee, being the ostensible owner of property acquires any benefit as the owner of that property, that benefit cannot

be retained by himself, but must be surrendered for the advantage of those who are beneficially interested'.

Duty to account for profits

5.9   A trustee is under a duty to account for profits made from the trust. In *Swain v Law Society [1981] 3 All ER 797* at page 807 Stephenson LJ said:

> 'With certain exceptions, neither directly or indirectly may a trustee make a profit from his trust. This rule is part of the wider principle that in order to protect a trustee against the fallibility of human nature he may not put himself in a position where his duty and his interest may conflict ... It is not only trustees who need this protection against fallibility. Similar principles apply to all other persons who occupy a fiduciary position. They must refund with interest all profits which they have made by means of their position unless they made them with full knowledge and approval of the persons to whom they owe a fiduciary duty.'

Trustee de son tort

5.10   A stranger who behaves as if he were a trustee will *become* a trustee, and be subject to the same duties as properly appointed trustees. In *Mara v Browne [1896] 1 Ch 199* at page 209 AL Smith said:

> ' ... if one, not being a trustee and not having authority from a trustee, takes upon himself to intermeddle with trust matters or to do acts characteristic of the office of trustee he may thereby make himself what is called in law a trustee of his own wrong, or as it is also termed, a constructive trustee.'

Liability of stranger who assists in a breach of trust

5.11   In *Royal Brunei Airlines Sdn Bhd v Tan [1995] 3 All ER 97*, a company acted as agent for an airline. All payments for tickets should have been paid into a separate account, but they were paid into the current account used for the business. The respondent was the managing director of the company, and its major shareholder. The company proved to be insolvent, and the plaintiff airline sued the respondent. On appeal, it was stated that the issue was whether the breach of trust, which is a prerequisite to accessory liability, must itself be a dishonest and fraudulent breach of trust by the trustee. At page 109, Lord Nicholls said:

'A liability in equity to make good resulting loss attaches to a person who dishonestly procures or assists in a breach of trust or fiduciary obligation. It is not necessary that, in addition, the trustee or fiduciary was acting dishonestly, although this will usually be so where the third party who is assisting him is acting dishonestly. "Knowingly" is better avoided as a defining ingredient of the principle, and in the context of this principle the *Baden* scale of knowledge is best forgotten'.

At page 105 dishonesty was defined as not acting as an honest person would in the circumstances.

In *Twinsectra v Yardley [2002] 2 All ER 377* L acted as solicitor for Y. Another firm of solicitors, S, acted for Y in obtaining a loan from T.

T paid £1m to S, who gave an undertaking that the money would only be applied in the acquisition of property on behalf of Y.

Y assured S that the money would be applied in the purchase of a property, and S paid the money to L. L paid the money out on Y's instructions. Y did not apply £358,000 in the acquisition of property, and the money was lost.

The House of Lords stated that solicitors held money in a client account in trust. However, L was held to be not liable.

Lord Hutton said at page 384:

'... there are three possible standards which can be applied to determine if a person has acted dishonestly. There is a purely subjective standard, whereby a person is only regarded as dishonest if he transgresses his own standard of honesty, even if that standard is contrary to that of reasonable and honest people. ... Secondly, there is a purely objective standard whereby a person acts dishonestly if his conduct is dishonest by the ordinary standards of reasonable and honest people, even if he did not realise this. Thirdly, there is a standard which combines an objective test and a subjective test, and which requires that before there can be a finding of dishonesty it must be established that the defendant's conduct was dishonest by the ordinary standards of reasonable and honest people and that he himself realised that by those standards his conduct was dishonest.'

At page 387 he continued:

'... I think that it would be less than just for the law to permit a finding that a defendant had been "dishonest" in assisting in a breach of trust where he knew of facts which created the trust and its breach but had not been aware of what he was doing would be regarded by honest men as being dishonest …

Dishonesty requires knowledge by the defendant that what he was doing would be regarded as dishonest by honest people, although he should not escape a finding of dishonesty because he sets his own standards of honesty and does not regard as dishonest what he knows would offend the normally accepted standards of honest conduct.'

In *Barlow Clowes international Ltd v Eurotrust International Ltd [2005] WTLR 1453* it was alleged that H and S had acted dishonestly in misappropriating assets.

Lord Hoffmann in the Privy Council referred to Lord Hutton's judgment in the *Twinsectra* case, and said at page 1459:

'The reference to "what he knows would offend the normally accepted standards of honest conduct" meant only that his knowledge of the transaction had to be such as to render his participation contrary to normal acceptable standards of honest behaviour. It did not require that he should have had reflections about what those normally acceptable standards were.'

In *Twinsectra*, the solicitor who had paid the money out did not consider that he was bound by the undertaking, and so was not dishonest by normal standards.

On the facts, H and S were held liable.

How can agents like solicitors or accountants or stockbrokers avoid being held liable as constructive trustees? The best advice is to err on the cautious side – if there is the slightest suspicion, beware!

Note that in *Brown v Bennett and Others (1998) The Times, 3 January*, it was held that a person who was merely guilty of a breach of the duties of a director was not liable as a constructive trustee.

In *Satnam Investments Ltd v Dunlop Heywood & Co Ltd [1999] 3 All ER 652*, M Ltd was given confidential information as a result of which it purchased a site with development potential. It was alleged that M Ltd was a constructive trustee of the site. It was held that mere knowledge of a breach of fiduciary duty did not by itself make a person a constructive trustee. Even if the information was property, it could not be traced into the development site. Furthermore, M Ltd could not be liable for knowingly assisting in the breach of trust in the absence of any finding of dishonesty by the judge.

Stranger receiving trust property as constructive trustee

5.12   It is clear that a stranger who receives trust property must account to the trustees for it unless the stranger is a bona fide purchaser without notice.

The stranger may become personally liable, although the mere receipt of trust property is not sufficient to make the stranger so liable. When will a stranger become personally liable? In *Bank of Credit and Commerce International v Akindele [2001] Ch 437* Nourse LJ said at page 455:

> '... just as there is now a single test of dishonesty for knowing assistance, so ought there to be a single test of knowledge for knowing receipt. The recipient's state of knowledge must be such as to make it unconscionable for him to retain the benefit of the receipt'.

Acquisition pursuant to an oral arrangement

5.13   In *Yaxley v Gotts [2000] 1 All ER 711,* Y, a builder, was interested in purchasing the freehold of a property he wanted to refurbish and let as flats. He asked BG to provide a loan to enable him to purchase the freehold, but BG decided to acquire the property himself. In fact, BG's son, AG, purchased the property. It was agreed that Y would acquire the ground floor flats in return for working on the flats, and acting as the managing agent for the landlord. AG was aware of these arrangements when he purchased the property. Y spent £9,000 refurbishing the property, and also acted as the landlord's managing agent. The Court of Appeal held that Y was entitled to a rent-free long lease of the ground floor of the property as there was a constructive trust in his favour.

In *Banner Homes Group plc v Luff Developments Ltd and another [2000] 2 All ER 117,* L Ltd and B plc agreed in principle (a) to acquire a development site, and (b) that it should be acquired through a new company which they would own in equal shares. As a result of the agreement, L Ltd acquired an off-the-shelf company, S Ltd. S Ltd acquired the development site with funds provided by L Ltd. L Ltd then informed B plc that it was withdrawing from the proposed joint venture. The Court of Appeal held that L Ltd held one half of the shares in S Ltd on constructive trust for B plc.

Acquisition by tenant of freehold on behalf of tenants

5.14   In *Hooper v Gorvin [2001] WTLR 575* the Waterside Estate was let under various leases. There was a dispute about the payment of a service charge, and G was appointed to act on behalf of the tenants with a view to acquiring the freehold. G purchased the freehold himself.

It was held that G held the freehold on trust.

Lottery tickets

5.15   In *Abrahams v Trustee of the property of Anthony Emmanuel Abrahams [2000] WTLR 593* Mrs A paid for a lottery ticket for herself and her husband in a lottery syndicate. She continued paying, despite having separated from her husband, and beginning divorce proceedings. On the list recording who had paid, Mr Abrahams was still shown as having paid, although Mrs A considered that she would be entitled to two shares in any winnings. Mr A became bankrupt.

The syndicate won in excess of £3.6m.

It was held that Mrs A was entitled to two shares.

The share payable to Mr A was held in trust for Mrs A, and his trustee in bankruptcy was not entitled to it.

Promissory estoppel

5.16   If a person A makes a promise to another, B, and B acts to his detriment relying on the promise, then A will not be allowed to go back on his promise.

In *Campbell v Griffin [2001] WTLR 981,* C, who had spent part of his childhood in a childrens' home, became Mr and Mrs A's lodger. Initially, this had been a commercial arrangement, but gradually Mr and Mrs A came to regard C as their son. He helped with domestic chores, and towards the end of Mr and Mrs A's life, became a carer. Both Mr and Mrs A made promises to him that he would have a home for life.

It was held that the doctrine of proprietary estoppel applied, and C was awarded £35,000 from the proceeds of the sale of the house (about £160,000).

The court held that once it was proved that promises had been made, and that there has been conduct by the applicant of such a nature that inducement may be inferred, then there is a presumption of reliance.

In *Hyett v Stanley and others [2003] WTLR 1269,* F was the sole legal owner of a farm. He separated from his wife in 1988, and in subsequent divorce proceedings she did not pursue a claim in respect of the farm because she understood that it would be given to the two sons of the marriage.

F commenced a relationship with H, and in 1992 at the instance of H, F restructured his finances. F and H executed a legal charge to Barclays Bank which contained a joint and several covenant by F and H to repay the money outstanding. The reason why H had to give the covenant was that her income was required to support the charge. H was concerned about what would happen if the relationship broke down, and F told her that as her name was on the charge she had a right to the farm. H admitted that she was not concerned with what would happen if F died.

An insurance policy on the joint lives of both parties was also taken out.

On appeal, it was held that H was entitled to one half of the farm.

It was also held that the policy had been taken out with the clear intention of repaying the mortgage, and H's claim to be reimbursed for the amount paid to redeem the mortgage was rejected. She was also ordered to pay to the executors an amount they had expended in part redemption of the mortgage.

In *Evans v HSBC [2005] WTLR 1289* Doreen was a wartime evacuee from Liverpool. She lived with M and her husband in West Wales. She did return to Liverpool, but decided to return to West Wales. M and her husband had no children, but regarded Doreen as their daughter.

Doreen married in 1955, and had two sons. M regarded the two sons as her grandchildren and led them to believe that they would inherit her assets. As a result, one of the sons, K, gave up a career in Cardiff to return to West Wales. The other son, C, also moved back to West Wales.

M died partially intestate, and her sisters were entitled to part of her estate.

HHJ Williams QC said at page 1306:

> 'The detriment need not consist of the expenditure of money; nor need it be a quantifiable financial detriment, so long as it is substantial. Whether the alleged detriment is sufficiently substantial is to be tested by whether it would be unjust or inequitable to allow the assurance to be disregarded.'

It was held that both K and C had acted to their detriment relying upon M's promise.

K had given up his career in Cardiff, and not proceeded with the purchase of an investment property. However, the purchase of the house in which he lived was not a detriment.

C had acted to his detriment by borrowing money from his brother to purchase a house in West Wales. He had obtained a Local Authority grant to refurbish the house, and as he was not living in it, he might have to repay the grant.

However, the judge did not award the whole estate to K and C.

This doctrine has been applied in a commercial context in recent years.

In *Kinane v Mackie Conteh [2005] WTLR 345* MC was the managing director of AMS Ltd. He was introduced to K who was prepared to lend the company £50,000, which was to be repaid within 120 days with a return of 100%. K wanted security, and MC offered his house as security. The loan was made, but was not repaid.

The court of appeal held there was an agreement to create a new interest in land, and that this was unenforceable because it was not in writing or evidenced in writing, and did not come within s 53(1)(c) of the Law of Property Act 1925.

However, the doctrine of proprietary estoppel applied as K had acted to his detriment relying on the promise of an equitable charge. K had an equitable charge which could be enforced.

In *Cobbe v Yeomans Property Management [2005] WTLR* C was a property developer. Y owned a site with potential for redevelopment. L was the secretary of the company.

C and Y entered into negotiations with a view to C obtaining planning consent. C employed various professionals at a cost to himself of at least £69,000, and was successful in obtaining planning permission. There was no written agreement, and both parties contemplated that there would be a formal written agreement once planning permission had been obtained.

Y refused to implement the oral agreement; there was some dispute about its exact terms.

It was held that the doctrine of estoppel applied, and C was awarded one half of the increase in value attributable to obtaining planning permission.

In *Munt v Beasley [2006] EWCA Civ 370* Mr Beasley owned a house divided into two flats and occupied the ground floor flat. Mr Munt purchased the first floor flat, and believed that the lease included the loft of the house. He converted the loft into living space, and Mr Beasley was aware of what was happening and acquiesced in it.

It was held that Mr Beasley was estopped from challenging the conversion. Rectification of the lease to include the lost slack was also ordered.

Availability of remedy at common law

5.17   A constructive trust will not be imposed if there is a remedy available at common law (*Box and Others v Barclays Bank plc [1998] The Times 30 April*).

SUMMARY

5.18

(1) A resulting trust in favour of the settlor may arise in the following circumstances:

- purchase in the name of another;
- failure of the trust;
- failure to dispose of all the settlor's interest;
- dissolution of an unincorporated association;
- disaster funds.

(2) A constructive trust may arise in the following circumstances:

- renewal of a lease by the trustees;
- profits made by the trustee from trust property;
- a person intermeddling with the trust property;
- a stranger receiving trust property;
- an acquisition pursuant to an oral agreement.

Chapter 6

Breach of trust and protection of trustees

BREACH OF TRUST

6.1 A trustee who commits a breach of trust is liable to make good any loss which results. It is, however, necessary for there to be a causal connection between the breach and the loss before a trustee will be liable (*Re Miller's Trust Deed (1978) 75 LS Gaz 454*). On the other hand, the rules regarding remoteness of damage in contract and tort have no application.

In *Target Holdings Ltd v Redferns [1996] 1 AC 421*, solicitors were acting for the purchaser and the mortgagor of a property. In breach of trust and before the property had been purchased and charged to the finance company, which was in fact done a month later, the solicitors paid money received from the finance company. The mortgagee sued for breach of trust. It was held that the solicitors were not necessarily liable for all losses suffered by the mortgagee. At page 439 Lord Browne-Wilkinson said:

> 'Equitable compensation for breach of trust is designed to achieve exactly what the word compensation suggests: to make good a loss in fact suffered by the beneficiaries and which, using hindsight and common sense, can be seen to have been caused by the breach'.

In *Swindle v Harrison [1997] 4 All ER 705,* H mortgaged her house to secure a loan to assist with the purchase of a restaurant. Part of the purchase price was to come from a loan by a brewery. This loan was not forthcoming. The plaintiff solicitors loaned the money secured by a first charge on the hotel. The business failed, and H lost her house.

The solicitors sued to enforce the charge. H counterclaimed alleging that the plaintiffs had failed to disclose that they were making a profit on the loan, and that they knew that the loan from the brewery would not be forthcoming.

It was held that even if there had been a breach of duty, there had to be a causal link between the breach and the loss. There was no such link here; H's loss was caused by her decision to mortgage her house to provide a loan for the business.

The breach of trust can take various forms. It may be that trust assets are applied for the benefit of the wrong beneficiaries, or it may be that there is a breach of some other duty of the trustees, for example the duties associated with investment. Whilst most settlements will contain an express investment clause authorising the trustees to invest in a wide range of investments, this does not permit trustees to invest in any investments regardless of their desirability, or to fail to periodically review the investments. Section 4(3) of the Trustee Act 2000 directs trustees to have regard:

(a)   to the suitability to the trust of the investments of the same kind as any particular investment proposed to be made or retained and of that particular investment as an investment of that fund; and

(b)   to the need for diversification of investments of the trust, in so far as is appropriate to the circumstances of the trust (the standard investment criteria).

Section 5 requires trustees to obtain advice as to whether an investment is satisfactory and to obtain periodic advice as to whether an investment is satisfactory having regard to the standard investment criteria.

The duty imposed on trustees not to profit from the trust has already been discussed. A beneficiary can seek an account of the profits made by the trustee, or alternatively the beneficiary can claim compensation for the losses suffered. It should be stressed that these remedies are alternatives and not cumulative.

A trustee who is liable for breach of duty is also liable for interest on the compensation which has to be paid.

LIABILITY FOR ACTS OF CO-TRUSTEES

6.2   A trustee is not liable for the acts of his co-trustees. However, whilst this is the general principle, it may be that a trustee will be guilty of a breach of his own personal duties as a trustee, and as a result liable. When will a trustee be liable in this situation? In *Cases and Commentary on the Law of Trusts*, 10th edition, by Hayton (Sweet and Maxwell) at pages 770 and 771 it is stated that a trustee will be liable in the following circumstances:

'1.   If he leaves a matter in the hands of his co-trustee without inquiry.

2.   If he stands by while a breach of trust, of the facts of which he is cognisant, is being committed by his co-trustee … .

3.   If he allows trust funds to remain in the sole control of his co-trustee … .

> 4.   Apparently also if, becoming aware of a breach of trust committed or contemplated by his co-trustee, he takes no steps to obtain redress.'

In Underhill and Hayton: Law of Trusts and Trustees 16th edition it is stated at page 938:

> '1.   A trustee is not vicariously answerable for the receipts, acts, or defaults of his co-trustee, but only for his own acts or defaults such as:
>
>   (a)   where he hands the trust property to his co-trustee without seeing to its proper application;
>
>   (b)   where he allows his co-trustee to receive the trust property without making due inquiry as to his dealing with it;
>
>   (c)   where he becomes aware of a breach of trust, either committed or mediated, and abstains from taking the needful steps to obtain restitution and redress, or to prevent the meditated wrong.'

However, the liability of trustees is joint and several so that if one trustee who is innocent of any wrongdoing, is sued, then that innocent trustee can seek an indemnity from the guilty trustee or trustees.

INDEMNITY

6.3   If there are two or more trustees, and they are liable for breach of trust, the liability is joint and several. A beneficiary can therefore pursue his remedy against one trustee to the exclusion of the other trustees, but in this situation the trustee sued will have a right to a contribution from the other trustees, although the amount which can be recovered is limited to 'such as may be found by the court to be just and equitable having regard to the extent of that person's responsibility for the damages in question' (Civil Liability (Contribution) Act 1978, s 2(1)).

A trustee who is liable for a breach of trust and is also a beneficiary is liable to contribute to the loss to the extent of his beneficial interest. Thereafter the loss is shared equally between the trustees liable for the breach (*Chillingworth v Chambers [1896] 1 Ch 685*).

In some circumstances there is no right to an indemnity. A trustee guilty of fraud will not be entitled to an indemnity, and a trustee who is a solicitor or is otherwise professionally qualified may not be entitled to an indemnity. However, the mere fact that one trustee is professionally qualified does not mean that

that trustee must indemnify lay trustees. In *Head v Gould [1898] 2 Ch 250* Kekewich J said at page 265:

> ' ... but I do not myself think that Byrne J or any other judge intended to hold a man is bound to indemnify his co-trustee against loss merely because he was a solicitor, when that co-trustee was an active participator in the breach of trust complained of, and is not proved to have participated merely in consequence of the advice and control of the solicitor'.

LOSS AND GAIN

6.4   It may be that one unauthorised transaction has resulted in a loss, and another in a profit. The basic rule is that trustees cannot offset the profit against the loss, but this may be possible if the transactions are in reality one. In *Bartlett v Barclays Bank Trust Co Ltd (No 1) [1980] Ch 515*, Brightman J said at page 538:

> 'The general rule as stated in all the textbooks, with some reservations, is that where a trustee is liable in respect of distinct breaches of trust, one of which has resulted in a loss and the other in a gain, he is not entitled to set off the gain against the loss, unless they arise in the same transaction: ... The relevant cases are, however, not altogether easy to reconcile ... The Guildford development stemmed from exactly the same policy and (to a lesser degree because it proceeded less far) exemplified the same folly as the Old Bailey project. Part of the profit was in fact used to finance the Old Bailey disaster. By sheer luck the gamble paid off handsomely, on capital account. I think it would be unjust to deprive the bank of this element of salvage in the course of assessing the cost of the shipwreck.'

What is the position if the trustees are clearly guilty of breach of trust, but there is no loss to the trust estate? In *Hulbert v Avens [2001] WTLR 387* the defendants were the trustees of three separate trusts, and the plaintiffs were the beneficiaries under these trusts.

The defendants incurred a liability for CGT, which was not paid when it should have been. However, the interest earned on moneys retained was in excess of the interest and penalties due to the Revenue.

It was held that the date for assessing any losses incurred by the beneficiaries was the date of the trial, and the measure of damages was the loss actually suffered by the beneficiaries. As the beneficiaries received more than they would have done had there been no breach of trust, they had not suffered any loss.

Even though there had been a breach of trust, the trustees were entitled to be paid, provided they would otherwise be entitled to remuneration.

The trustees had also made a loan to one of the beneficiaries when she was absolutely entitled, which had been repaid with interest. It was held that this was in order as the trustees needed to retain assets so as to satisfy the CGT liability.

DATE FOR CALCULATING THE LOSS

6.5   In *Jaffray v Marshall [1993] 1 WLR 1285* it was held that if there is a continuing breach of trust the measure of damages is the highest intermediate value between the date of the breach and the date of the judgment.

FOLLOWING AND TRACING

In equity

6.6   If trust assets have been misapplied, the beneficiaries may be able to trace them and recover them from the person in whom they are vested. If the trust assets are still in the possession of a person, they can be followed. Tracing is where the trust assets have been converted into another asset. Usually a fiduciary relationship is required. In *Re Diplock [1948] Ch 465* at page 530 it was said that:

> ' ... equity may operate on the conscience not merely of those who acquire a legal title in breach of some trust, express or constructive, or of some other fiduciary obligation, but of volunteers provided as a result of what has gone before some equitable proprietary interest has been created and attaches to the property in the hands of the volunteer'.

It would clearly be unjust to permit tracing into the hands of a bona fide purchaser of the legal estate without notice of the right to trace. Knox J in *Cowan de Groot Properties Ltd v Eagle Trust plc [1992] 4 All ER 700* said at page 767:

> ' ... there can ... be no independent right to trace against a purchaser for value under a contract for sale where the contract is not liable to be set aside and there is no valid claim to impose a constructive trust'.

In *Bishopsgate Investment Management Ltd v Homan [1994] 3 WLR 1270*, it was held that the remedy of tracing was not available if trust money was paid into an overdrawn bank account. It made no difference whether the account was overdrawn at the time of the payment, or subsequently became overdrawn.

The right is also lost if it would be inequitable to enforce the remedy of tracing. In *Re Diplock [1948] Ch 465* money was distributed to a charity in breach of trust. The charity used the money to improve some buildings. The remedy of tracing was refused. Also in that case it was refused against a beneficiary that had used the money to settle debts. In addition, the remedy is lost if the property cannot be identified. It is also lost if it would be inequitable to order restitution (*Lipkin Gorman v Karpnale Ltd [1991] 2 AC 548*).

In *Re Hallett's Estate (1880) 13 Ch D 696* money held by one Hallett, which was subject to a trust, was paid into his bank account. It was held that Hallett must be taken to have withdrawn his own money first. In *Re Oatway [1903] 2 Ch 356* a trustee mixed trust funds and his own money in a bank account, and then used the money to purchase an investment in his own name. It was held that the trustee could not maintain that the investment represented his own money alone.

If the trustee has mixed trust funds with his own private funds, the 'beneficiary will be entitled to every portion of the blended property which the trustee cannot prove to be his own, according to *Lewin on Trusts*, 16th edition at page 223, which statement was approved by Ungoed-Thomas J in *Re Tilley's Will Trusts [1967] Ch 1179* at page 1193. He said:

'If, of course, a trustee deliberately uses trust money to contribute with his own money to buy property in his own name, then I would see no difficulty in enabling a beneficiary to adopt the purchase and claim a share of the resulting profits ...

It seems to me that if, having regard to all the circumstances of the case objectively considered, it appears that the trustee has in fact, whatever his intention, laid out trust moneys in or towards a purchase then the beneficiaries are entitled to the property purchased and any profits which it produces to the extent to which it has been paid for out of the trust moneys.'

In *Space Investments Ltd v Canadian Imperial Bank of Commerce Trust Co (Bahamas) Ltd [1986] 1 WLR 1072* a bank was a trustee. Under the settlements the bank was authorised to deposit trust money with itself. It did so, and then became insolvent. It was held that the remedy of tracing was not available to the trustees of settlements where the money had been deposited with the bank because the trust money could be lawfully deposited with the bank, and then became the property of the bank.

In *In re Goldcorp Exchange Ltd (in receivership) [1995] 1 AC 74*, a company dealt in gold and other precious metals. Some bullion was allocated to specific customers, whilst other bullion was not. The customers who had not had bullion allocated to them were refused tracing, but those who had were allowed some remedy.

In *Foskett v McKeown and others [1997] 3 All ER 392* a number of people, including the plaintiff, had agreed to purchase from M plots of land on a site to be developed in the Algarve. The site was never developed, and M used the money belonging to the plaintiff and other purchasers to pay several annual premiums of £10,220 payable under a life assurance policy. M committed suicide, and a sum in excess of £1 million was paid under the policy. The plaintiff claimed that the purchasers were entitled to the proceeds of the policies, and the judge at first instance held that they were entitled to 53.46 per cent of the proceeds. On appeal, it was held that the purchasers were entitled to a charge over the proceeds of the policy in order to recover such of their money as could be traced into the premiums together with interest thereon. The House of Lords has now reversed the decision of the Court of Appeal, and has held that the purchasers were entitled to a proportionate share of the policy proceeds ([2000] 3 All ER 97).

At common law

6.7   A similar remedy is available at common law, but it is more limited than the equitable remedy, although it may apply where there is no remedy in equity, for example where there is no fiduciary relationship. In *Agip (Africa) Ltd v Jackson [1991] Ch 547*, Fox LJ said at page 563:

> ' ... tracing at common law does not depend upon the establishment of an initial fiduciary relationship. Liability depends upon receipt by the defendant of the plaintiff's money and the extent of the liability depends on the amount received. Since liability depends upon receipt the fact that a recipient has not retained the asset is irrelevant. For the same reason dishonesty or lack of inquiry on the part of the recipient are irrelevant. Identification in the defendant's hands of the plaintiff's asset is, however, necessary. It must be shown that the money received by the defendant was the money of the plaintiff. Further, the very limited common law remedies make it difficult to follow at law into mixed funds'.

In *Lipkin Gorman v Karpnale Ltd [1991] 2 AC 548*, where a partner in a firm of solicitors withdrew money from the client account in order to gamble, Lord Templeman said at page 559:

' … the law imposes an obligation on the recipient of stolen money to pay an equivalent sum to the victim if the recipient has been unjustly enriched at the expense of the true owner'.

In *Trustees of the property of FC Jones & Sons v Jones [1996] 4 All ER 721*, the partners of a firm committed an act of bankruptcy, but before they were made bankrupt, a cheque for £11,700 was paid to the wife of one of the partners. The wife used the money to invest in potato futures, and made a handsome profit. It was held that she must account not only for the original sum, but also the profit. Nourse LJ said at page 732:

> 'In my view, Mrs Jones cannot in conscience retain the profit any more than the original £11,700. She had no title to the original. She could not have made the profit without her use of it. She cannot, by making a profit through the use of money to which she had no title, acquire some better title to the profit'.

SUBROGATION

6.8   Subrogation is a remedy similar to tracing. The idea is that a person stands in the shoes of another person, and can take over the rights of action of that person.

In *Boscawen v Bajwa [1996] 1 WLR 328*, a building society sent an advance to the purchaser's solicitors, who transferred the money to the vendor's solicitors to hold to their order. The vendor's solicitors used the money to redeem the existing mortgage. The sale then fell through. It was held that the building society could trace the money, and was entitled by way of subrogation to a charge on the proceeds of sale of the property.

CRIMINAL LIABILITY

6.9   It may be that a breach of trust will involve criminal liability. Section 1 of the Theft Act 1968 provides that a person is guilty of theft if he dishonestly appropriates property belonging to another with the intention of permanently depriving the other of it. Section 5(2) provides that, where property is subject to a trust, the persons to whom it belongs shall be regarded as including any person having a right to enforce the trust, and an intention to defeat the trust shall be regarded accordingly as an intention to deprive of the property any person having that right.

A trustee guilty of breach of trust may also be guilty of other offences, for example false accounting.

IDENTIFYING THE TRUSTEES OF A DISCRETIONARY TRUST

6.10   In *Re Murphy's Settlements [1998] 3 All ER 1* the plaintiff's father was the defendant. The defendant and the plaintiff's mother both created settlements under which the plaintiff was within the class of potential beneficiaries. The plaintiff also alleged that other settlements had been created, and that he was probably within the class of beneficiaries. The plaintiff sought disclosure by his father of the names and addresses of the trustees of the settlement. Disclosure was ordered. A defendant who is not otherwise an appropriate party to the proceedings can be ordered to identify the name and address of a third party if the defendant has, albeit quite innocently, become mixed up in wrongdoing. Disclosure can also be ordered in equity even though there is no suggestion of wrongdoing.

LIABILITY OF TRUSTEES OF CLUBS

6.11   Many lay persons act as trustees of sports and social clubs. The case of *Marston Thompson & Evershed v Benn [1998] CL 4871* should be in the mind of all such trustees and professional advisers of such trustees. B and the other trustees of a club executed legal charges over property of the club, but three years later the club ceased to trade. It was held that the trustees were personally liable. They could limit their liability by agreement, but this had not been done. In addition, in the circumstances, B was not entitled to an indemnity.

PROTECTION OF TRUSTEES

6.12   Trustees may commit a breach of trust innocently. In such circumstances it would be unfair to make them responsible for the breach of trust, and there are various defences available to them.

SECTION 61 OF THE TRUSTEE ACT 1925

6.13   The section provides that 'if it appears to the court that a trustee ... is or may be personally liable for any breach of trust, whether the transaction alleged to be a breach of trust occurred before or after the commencement of this Act, but has acted honestly and reasonably, and ought fairly to be excused for the breach of trust and for omitting to obtain the directions of the court in the matter in which he committed such breach, then the court may relieve him either wholly or partly for the same'.

What is reasonable conduct in this context? It seems that the duty is to act in a business-like manner, or to act as if the trust property had been his own (*Re Turner [1897] 1 Ch 536* at page 542, and *Re Stuart, Smith v Stuart [1897] 2 Ch 583*).

INDEMNITY BY BENEFICIARY

6.14   Section 62(1) of the Trustee Act 1925 provides that where a trustee commits a breach of trust at the instigation or request or with the consent in writing of a beneficiary, the court may, if it thinks fit, make such order as to the court seems just, for impounding all or any part of the interest of the beneficiary in the trust estate by way of indemnity to the trustee or persons claiming through him. Thus a trustee can claim the interest of a beneficiary if the trustee has committed a breach of trust at the behest of a beneficiary, or with the written consent of the beneficiary.

CONCURRENCE OF BENEFICIARY

6.15   A trustee may be able to escape liability for breach of trust if a beneficiary has concurred in the breach of trust. The extent of this protection was outlined in the case of *Re Pauling's Settlement Trusts, Younghusband v Coutts & Co [1961] 3 All ER 713* where Wilberforce J said at page 730:

> 'The result of these authorities appears to me to be that the court has to consider all the circumstances in which the concurrence of the cestui que trust was given with a view to seeing whether it is fair and equitable that, having given his concurrence, he should afterwards turn round and sue the trustees: that, subject to this, it is not necessary that he should know that what he is concurring in is a breach of trust, provided that he fully understands what he is concurring in, and that it is not necessary that he should himself have directly benefited by the breach of trust.'

LIMITATION OF ACTIONS

6.16   Section 21(3) of the Limitation Act 1980 provides that an action by a beneficiary to recover trust property or in respect of any breach of trust, not being an action for which a period of limitation is prescribed by any other provision of this Act, shall not be brought after the expiration of six years from the date on which the right of action accrued.

Thus the normal limitation period for actions for breach of trust is six years; if the beneficiary is entitled to a future interest in property, time does not begin to run until the interest falls into possession. So if a remainderman is complaining about a breach of trust, time will not begin to run until the life tenant has died.

Section 38(1) of the Act provides that 'trust' and 'trustee' have the same meanings respectively as in the Trustee Act 1925; s 68(17) of the Trustee Act provides that 'trust' and 'trustee' extend to implied and constructive trusts, and to cases where the trustee has a beneficial interest in the trust property, and to the duties incident to the office of a personal representative.

Section 21(1) of the Limitation Act 1980 provides that no period of limitation prescribed by the Act shall apply to an action by a beneficiary under a trust, being an action:

(a)   in respect of any fraud or fraudulent breach of trust to which the trustee was a party or privy; or

(b)   to recover from the trustee trust property or the proceeds of trust property in the possession of the trustee, or previously received by the trustee and converted to his use.

Section 22 provides that subject to s 21(1) and (2) of the Act:

(a)   no action in respect of any claim to the personal estate of a deceased person or to any share or interest in any such estate (whether under a will or on intestacy) shall be brought after the expiration of twelve years from the date on which the right to receive the share or interest accrued; and

(b)   no action to recover arrears of interest in respect of any legacy, or damages in respect of such arrears, shall be brought after the expiration of six years from the date on which the interest became due.

Paragraph 9 of Sch 1 to the Limitation Act 1980 provides that where land is subject to a trust, and is in possession of the person entitled to a beneficial interest in land, no right of action to recover the land shall be treated as accruing during that possession to any person in whom the land is vested as tenant for life, statutory owner or trustee, or to any other person entitled to a beneficial interest in the land.

If no period of limitation is specified in the Act, then the doctrine of laches will apply. The idea behind this doctrine is that a potential plaintiff must not delay in bringing an action; the court will take into account various factors like hardship and the balance of justice before deciding if an action is barred by laches. In *Weld v Petre [1929] 1 Ch 33* Lawrence LJ at pages 51–52 cited with approval the following passage in *Lindsay Petroleum Co v Hurd (1874) LR 5 PC 221*:

'Now the doctrine of laches in Courts of equity is not an arbitrary or a technical doctrine. Where it would be practically unjust to give a remedy, either because the party has, by his conduct, done that which might fairly be regarded as equivalent to a waiver of it, or where by his conduct and neglect he has, though perhaps not waiving that remedy, yet put the other party in a situation in which it would not be reasonable to place him if the remedy were afterwards to be asserted, in either of these cases, lapse of time and delay are most material. But in every case, if an argument against relief, which otherwise would be just, is founded upon mere delay, that delay of course not amounting to a bar by any statute of limitations, the validity of the defence must be tried upon principles substantially equitable. Two circumstances, always important in such cases, are, the length of the delay and the nature of the acts done during the interval, which might affect either party and cause a balance of justice or injustice in taking the one course or the other, so far as relates to the remedy.'

In *Coulthard v Disco Mix Club Ltd and others [1999] 2 All ER 457* the plaintiff made various claims. Most of the claims based on common law were clearly statute barred, but the question arose as to whether a simple duty to account could be a fiduciary duty. It was held that it was not a fiduciary duty even when it was owed by a person in a fiduciary position. The question of whether s 5 of the 1980 Act, which provides a limitation period of six years for actions founded on simple contract, applied to a breach of fiduciary duty and constructive trust claims was also argued. It was held that it did. Jules Sher QC said at page 477:

'Two things emerge from these passages. First, where the court of equity was simply exercising a concurrent jurisdiction giving the same relief as was available in a court of law the statute of limitation would be applied. But, secondly, even if the relief afforded by the court of equity was wider than that available at law the court of equity would apply the statute by analogy where there was correspondence between the remedies available at law or in equity.'

In *Kershaw v Whelan (No 2) The Times 10 February 1997*, K, who was disabled, sought to sue the solicitor representing his stepmother in relation to his father's estate. The claim was statute barred in law, but the claim was allowed to proceed as the solicitor had concealed a letter.

Earnshaw v Hartley [1999] 3 WLR 709 is a case where paragraph 9 of Sch 1 was applied. There were four children – three daughters and a son. The parents died intestate leaving a farm. The son remained in occupation of the farm for many years. On his death, the daughters sued to recover their ¾ share. It was argued that the daughters' claim was barred because the son had been in adverse possession for more than 12 years, but this argument was rejected. It was held that the adverse possession claim was defeated by Sch 1, paragraph 9 to the

Limitation Act 1980. The son was entitled to possession of the farm as a beneficiary. Therefore, time did not begin to run until the son had ceased to be in possession. So the 12 years limitation period did not start to run against the daughters until the son died.

In *James v Williams [1999] 3 All ER 309* three children were entitled to a house on the death intestate of their mother. Two of the children continued to reside in the house. No grant of letters of administration was taken out. Many years later the third child claimed a third of the property. The claim was successful.

The defendant relied on s 15(1) of the Limitation Act 1980 which provides that the limitation period for an action to recover any land expires after 12 years. The plaintiff argued that there was a constructive trust, and that accordingly there was no limitation period.

It was held that the plaintiff was entitled to a one-third share, although credit had to be given for the money properly spent on repairs.

The Court of Appeal said that William (one of the children who had remained in occupation) was an executor *de son tort*, and that normally an executor *de son tort* could not be a constructive trustee. However, there were cases when that would be appropriate. Lord Justice Aldis stated that, as a general rule, a constructive trust attaches by law to property which is held by a person in circumstances where it would be inequitable to allow him to assert full beneficial ownership of the property. It was held that this was such a case as the son, William, knew very well that he was not solely entitled to the property.

LITIGATION AND TRUSTEES' COSTS AND EXEMPTION CLAUSES

6.17   In *Alsop Wilkinson v Neary [1995] 1 All ER 431* the first defendant was a partner in a firm of solicitors, and misappropriated in excess of £1 million from the firm. He established two settlements, in which the major beneficiaries were the first defendant, his wife and their issue. In an action to set aside the two settlements, the trustees applied by summonses in the actions for directions on two issues – whether or not to defend the actions, and for a pre-emptive cost order. It was held (at page 435) that in a case where the dispute is between rival claimants to a beneficial interest in the subject matter of a trust, the duty of the trustees is to remain neutral and offer to submit to the court's directions, leaving it to the rivals to fight their battles.

It was also held that whilst the court has jurisdiction to make an order at an early stage in the proceedings regarding the ultimate incidence of costs, it would not be right to do so in the circumstances. The correct procedure was for the trustees to plead that they would comply with any order made in the proceedings, and leave it to the rivals to fight out their battles. At page 437, it was stated that the following factors are relevant:

'(1)   the strength of the party's case;

(2)   the likely order as to costs at the trial;

(3)   the justice of the application;

(4)   any special circumstances.'

Exemption clauses

6.18   In *Armitage v Nurse, The Times, 31 March 1997*, each trustee was exempted from liability by a clause in the settlement 'unless such loss or damage shall be caused by his own actual fraud'. It was held that the clause could exclude liability for gross negligence.

In *Wight v Olswang, The Times, 18 May 1999*, a settlement contained a general exemption clause for the trustees, and also a clause which only applied if the trustees were unpaid. There was clearly a conflict between the two clauses, and it was held that in this situation any doubt should be resolved against the trustees.

In *Walker and others v Stones and another [2000] 4 All ER 412*, S and O were partners in a firm of solicitors. They were also the trustees of a discretionary trust, whose main beneficiaries were the children of the chairman of Brent Walker Group plc. The main asset of the trust was a shareholding in a company, which owned shareholdings in another company, which owned certain French vineyards.

In 1990 S guaranteed a bank loan, and charged the shares owned by the trust as security. The guarantee was called in.

The beneficiaries sued S and O. S and O relied on an exemption clause in the trust deed exempting them from liability arising in the execution of the trust and the powers thereof for any loss caused to the trust by any matter save wilful fraud or dishonesty on the part of S and O. The beneficiaries argued that this clause only covered things done in the actual execution of the trust.

There was no allegation of wilful fraud, and so the only question was whether the trustees had acted dishonestly.

It was held:

(a)   That the clause extended to anything done by the trustees in the purported execution of the trust, and was not limited to things done in the actual execution of the trust.

(b)   As there was no evidence that O had been dishonest, the action against him was dismissed.

(c)   As far as S was concerned, the test was not whether the solicitor genuinely believed he was acting honestly. It was also necessary to consider whether the honest belief was so unreasonable that by any objective standard no reasonable solicitor trustee could have thought what he did or agreed to do was for the benefit of the beneficiaries. On this basis, S had been dishonest, and was liable.

(d)   The breaches of trust committed by S fell outside the ordinary business of the partnership of solicitors. Accordingly, the other partners were not liable for the breach of trust.

Thus, there is an objective element in deciding if a trustee has acted honestly or dishonestly.

LIEN

6.19   In *X v A [2000] 1 All ER 490* the trust assets included land. The sole trustee was concerned about the potential liability for remediation costs of contaminated land. It was held that the trustee had a lien on the trust assets in respect of this potential liability.

SUMMARY

6.20
- A trustee who commits a breach of trust which results in a loss to the trust estate is liable for the loss.
- Normally a loss on one transaction cannot be offset against a profit on another transaction.
- A trustee is not normally liable for the acts of a co-trustee, but this may be a breach of his own personal duties as trustee.
- Beneficiaries may be able to trace trust assets into the hands of the recipients.
- Breach of trust may involve criminal liability.
- The court may relieve the trustee from liability if he has acted honestly and reasonably.

- The interest of a beneficiary who instigates a breach of trust may be impounded to indemnify the trustees.

- A beneficiary who has concurred in a breach of trust may not be able to sue the trustees.

- Lapse of time may bar an action against beneficiaries.

- An exemption clause may protect trustees.

- Trustees may be entitled to a lien.

Chapter 7

Variation of trusts

7.1 Beneficiaries may wish to vary a trust, or possibly to terminate it. If all the beneficiaries are of full capacity, there is no reason why they should not agree to break up a trust. However, if there is a possibility that there may be an infant entitled, the beneficiaries will not be able to enter into an agreement terminating the trust. This will be the case even if it is highly unlikely that such a beneficiary will become entitled. In many trusts, the beneficiaries frequently include both adult and infant beneficiaries when first set up. However, it may be that as the years go by all the beneficiaries will come of age, and so whilst it may not be possible to break up the trust when it is first established, it will be possible to do so once all the beneficiaries are of full age and capacity.

The court has a limited inherent jurisdiction to vary the terms of a trust. As trustees and beneficiaries may have legitimate reasons for varying a trust, Parliament has intervened to extend this jurisdiction.

The Matrimonial Causes Act 1973, the Mental Health Act 1983 and the Mental Capacity Act 2005 all empower the court to vary settlements and to make settlements in the situations where they apply.

Section 53 of the Trustee Act 1925 provides that where an infant is beneficially entitled to any property the court may, with a view to the application of the capital or income thereof for the maintenance, education, or benefit of the infant, make an order:

(a)   appointing a person to convey such property; or

(b)   in the case of stock, or a thing in action, vesting in any person the right to transfer or call for a transfer of such stock, or to receive the dividends or incomes thereof, or to sue for and recover such thing in action, upon such terms as the court may think fit.

Section 57(1) of the Trustee Act 1925 provides that if trustees do not have power to enter into various transactions concerning any property vested in trustees, the court can confer the necessary powers on the trustees if the transaction is expedient. However, the court can only exercise the power if the transaction arises in the administration or management of the trust, and so it cannot be used to vary beneficial interests.

Section 64 of the Settled Land Act 1925 empowers the court to make an order permitting the tenant for life to carry out some transaction which would not otherwise have been authorised. The transaction must in the opinion of the court be for the benefit of the settled land. This section was applied in *Hambro v Duke of Marlborough [1994] 3 All ER 332* where it was held that the court had power to approve the variation of a settlement so as to give a tenant in tail in remainder an interest under a protective trust, even though the tenant in tail did not agree.

VARIATION OF TRUSTS ACT 1958

7.2   The powers described above are all limited, and the Variation of Trusts Act 1958 substantially extended the power to vary. Section 1(1) permits the court to approve a variation on behalf of the following:

(a)   any person having, directly or indirectly, an interest, whether vested or contingent, under the trusts who by reason of infancy or other incapacity is incapable of assenting; or

(b)   any person (whether ascertained or not) who may become entitled, directly or indirectly, to an interest under the trusts as being at a future date or on the happening of a future event a person of any specified description or a member of any specified class of persons, so however that this paragraph shall not include any person who would be of that description, or a member of that class, as the case may be, if the said date had fallen or the said event had happened at the date of the application to the court; or

(c)   any person unborn; or

(d)   any person in respect of any discretionary interest of his under protective trusts where the interest of the principal beneficiary has not failed or determined.

It should be noted that the court has no power to approve a variation on behalf of a known beneficiary of full capacity.

Paragraph (b) was applied in *Re Suffert [1961] Ch 1* where the applicant was the beneficiary under a protective trust. In the events which happened, the applicant had a power of appointment, and if she did not exercise the power, her statutory next of kin were entitled to the settled funds. At the date of the application to the court, the applicant's next of kin were three people who were all of full age and capacity, but only one agreed to the arrangement proposed by the applicant. Buckley J held that he could not approve the arrangement on behalf of the two next of kin who did not agree. They were members of the class on the date of death of the applicant, and would have been if the date of death had been the date of the application. These people therefore came within the exception to s 1(1)(b), and the court had no power to approve the proposed arrangement on behalf of the next of kin who did not agree.

The arrangement must vary or revoke all or any of the trusts, or enlarge the powers of the trustees of managing and administering any of the property the subject of the trusts. The courts have refused to sanction any arrangement which is in effect the creation of a new settlement. In *Re Ball's Settlement [1968] 2 All ER 438* at page 442 Megarry J said:

'If an arrangement changes the whole substratum of a trust, then it may well be that it cannot be regarded merely as varying that trust. But if an arrangement, while leaving the substratum, effectuates the purpose of the original trust by other means, it may still be possible to regard that arrangement as merely varying the original trusts, even though the means employed are wholly different and even though the form is completely changed.'

The variation must also be for the benefit of the persons listed above, apart from those within (d). Usually the benefit will be financial, and frequently will be designed to save tax. However, the courts may take other benefits into account. In *Re Weston's Settlements [1969] 1 Ch 223* at page 245 Lord Denning MR said:

'The court should not consider merely the financial benefit to the infants or unborn children but also their educational and social benefit. There are many things in life more worthwhile than money. One of these things is to be brought up in this our England, which is still "the envy of less happier lands". I do not believe it is for the benefit of children to be uprooted from England and transported to another country simply to avoid tax.'

In *Goulding and another v James and another [1997] 2 All ER 239* June and Marcus Goulding – the beneficiaries under the will trusts – applied to the court for a variation under s 1(1)(c) of the Variation of Trusts Act 1958. The proposed variation was partly in favour of a grandchildren's trust fund, and would benefit unborn great grandchildren of the testatrix, Mrs Froud. However, the variation was contrary to the wishes of the testatrix. The variation was sanctioned. Mummery LJ said at pages 249–251:

'In my judgment the legal position is as follows. (1) The court has a discretion whether or not to approve a proposed arrangement. (2) That discretion is fettered by only one express restriction. The proviso to s 1 [of the Variation of Trusts Act 1958] prohibits the court from approving an arrangement which is not for the benefit of the classes referred to in (a), (b) or (c) [of s 1(1) of the 1958 Act] ... (3) It does not follow from the fact of benefit to unborns that the arrangement must be approved ... (4) That overall discretion ... is to be exercised with regard to all relevant factors properly considered in the statutory context ... (5) Viewed in that context, an important factor in this case is that Mrs June Goulding and Mr Marcus Goulding [the only grandchild of Mrs Froud] are *sui juris* and Mrs Froud's intentions and wishes related to their beneficial interests under the testamentary trusts rather than to the contingent interests of her unborn great grandchildren whom the court is concerned to protect ... (8) The fact that the rules of court require a living settlor to be joined as a party to proceedings under the 1958 Act does not mean that the court attaches any overbearing or special significance to the wishes of a settlor.'

Ralph Gibson said at page 252:

'Where there is an application under the Variation of Trusts Act 1958 for approval of an arrangement agreed by the beneficiaries, capable of giving assent, it is not clear to me why evidence of the intention of the testator can be of any relevance whatever if it does no more than explain why the testator gave the interests set out in the will and the nature and degree of feeling with which such provisions were selected. If the arrangement agreed by the beneficiaries is to do no more with their interests than the beneficiaries are able in law to do in accordance with the provisions of the will, I can see no relevance in evidence which shows no more than the original intention or motivation of the testator.'

SUMMARY

7.3

- The court has a limited inherent power to authorise a variation of a trust.
- Various statutes have conferred limited powers on the court to vary a trust.
- The Variation of Trusts Act 1958 confers a wide power of variation, but the court cannot approve a variation on behalf of a person of full age and capacity.

Part II

Particular Trusts

Chapter 8

Lifetime gifts of money to children

8.1   If money is given to parents for the benefit of children, it is unlikely that the donor will expressly impose a trust. However, if there is a clear intention to create a trust, one will be created, even though the word 'trust' was not used. Words like 'Here's £50 for Junior' might very well be sufficient to create a trust in favour of the child.

When a baby is born, delighted relatives and friends will more often than not give the proud parents rattles and furry toys to amuse the new arrival. Some will give money, and as the child grows up, increasingly he or she will be given money at Christmas or on his or her birthday. What should the parents do with this money? Can it be invested in the child's name? Can they spend it freely for the benefit of the child, or are there restrictions on what they can do with it? The aim of this chapter is to answer these questions.

CAN MONEY BE INVESTED IN A BANK OR BUILDING SOCIETY IN THE CHILD'S NAME?

8.2   A minor can open a current account, but it must not be overdrawn (*Nottingham Permanent Benefit Building Society v Thurstan [1903] AC 6 HL*). Further, paragraph 5(3) of Sch 2 to the Building Societies Act 1986 provides that a person who is a minor may, if the rules do not otherwise provide, be admitted as a member of a building society and give all necessary receipts. In addition, paragraph 2 of Sch 7 to the 1986 Act provides that:

> 'Any receipt or acknowledgement given to a building society by a person who is a minor in respect of the payment to him of any sum due in respect of a deposit made by him with the society shall not be invalid on the ground of his minority.'

However, minors cannot vote, hold office in the society, nominate or join in nominating a person for election as a director of the society.

Thus it is in order for a child to operate a bank or building society account, and in fact most banks and building societies permit minors to operate current and deposit accounts, and frequently encourage them to do so with gifts. However, if the child is not old enough to operate an account, the parents may decide to invest the money in their own names. What rights and duties do the parents then have?

Has a trust been created?

8.3   It may be that a trust is created when money is given to parents for the benefit of children. It would seem that with most gifts to parents for the benefit of their own children, it will be clear who is to benefit, and there will be no difficulty with regard to certainty of objects. However, if there are both stepchildren and children of both parents in the family, a gift to 'children' is ambiguous, and it would be for the court to decide whether the expression included the children of both parents and the stepchildren. If the court is unable to do so, the trust is void.

Are any formalities necessary for the creation of a trust?

8.4   The answer to this question is provided by s 53(1) of the Law of Property Act 1925. Paragraph (b) of that subsection provides that a declaration of trust respecting any land or any interest therein must be manifested and proved by some writing signed by some person who is able to declare such trust or by his will. Section 53(1)(c) requires that a disposition of an equitable interest or trust subsisting at the time of disposition must be in writing signed by the person disposing of the same, or by his agent lawfully authorised in writing or by will. It is clear that if the declaration of trust relates to any property other than land or an interest in land or an equitable interest or trust, an oral declaration is sufficient.

Thus a donor who gives money to parents can create a trust in favour of the children without any written document.

Are parents subject to any duties as trustees?

8.5   Assuming that a trust is created, the parents will of course be subject to all the duties and obligations imposed on trustees. Amongst these duties and obligations are the duties imposed with regard to investment.

Frequently, a will or other document creating a trust instrument will include an express power of investment, which will give the trustees an absolute discretion as to how the trust funds should be invested. With a gift to parents to hold on trust for children, it is highly unlikely that the donor will have given any express

125

power, although it might be implied, for example if the donor says 'Use it as you think fit'. If there is no such express or implied power, then the investments must be made in accordance with the Trustee Act 2000. This Act and the duties imposed by it have been discussed in CHAPTER 2.

Parents may be very surprised to learn that they are subject to these duties with regard to the investment of money given to them for the benefit of their children, assuming that a trust has been created. However, if only a small sum of money is involved, the trustees could probably discharge their obligations under the Trustee Act 2000 by investing all the money in National Savings Certificates. Although advice should be obtained before making any investment, few parents will do this, and it would seem to be a very onerous requirement if there is only a small sum to be invested.

Can the parents spend the money for the benefit of the children?

8.6   The answer to this question depends in part on any powers which may have been given to the parents by the donor. When handing the money over, the donor might have said 'Here's £20; spend it on the children for me'; clearly this is an express authority to apply all the money for the benefit of the children. However, if there is no such express or implied authority, then the answer to the question depends on ss 31 and 32 of the Trustee Act 1925.

It will be recalled that s 31(1) provides that if an infant is entitled to trust property, the trustees may at their sole discretion pay to the parent or guardian or apply for or towards his or her maintenance, education, or benefit the whole or such part of the income of that property as may in all the circumstances be reasonable. Under s 31(2) the trustees must have regard to the following factors in deciding whether or not to exercise their discretion:

- the age of the infant;
- his requirements and generally the circumstances of the case; and
- what other income is applicable for the same purposes.

In so far as the income is not applied for the benefit of the children, under s 31(2) it must be accumulated until the child attains the age of 18 years, or marries under that age. If the child is then entitled to the property absolutely, the trustees must hold the accumulated income in trust for such person absolutely. It is thus clear that the parents have power to apply the whole of the income for the benefit of the children.

A power to advance capital is contained in s 32 of the Trustee Act. Section 32(1) enables trustees to advance up to one-half of the capital to which a beneficiary is or might be entitled. They have an absolute discretion as to whether or not to make the advancement, and if they do so, the beneficiary must bring any money so received into account when he becomes absolutely entitled. Once one-half has been advanced, there is no power to advance any more capital (*Re Marquess of Abergavenny's Trusts [1981] 2 All ER 643*). So if the parents of two children are given £500 to be held on trust for the children in equal shares, they can advance up to £125 to each child. But when the child attains 18, or marries under that age, and becomes absolutely entitled, the £125 will have to be brought into account.

The personal representatives of a deceased person, where under that person's will or intestacy a minor is entitled, will have the powers and duties set out above. Provided they have not been appointed trustees under s 42 of the Administration of Estates Act 1925, they can appoint a trust corporation or two or more individuals including the personal representatives to be the trustees for the minor. On such appointment, the personal representatives are discharged from all further liability in respect of such gift.

Taxation

8.7   Minors are subject to income tax, capital gains tax and inheritance tax in the same way as adults. There are anti-avoidance provisions which will deem income to be that of a parent. All these matters are discussed in more detail in chapter 13.

TRUSTS FOR BEREAVED MINORS

8.8   It may be that a donor will wish to settle property or money for the benefit of children. Trusts for bereaved minors have considerable advantages as far as IHT is concerned; they are considered in more detail in chapter 13.

SUMMARY

8.9

- A minor can hold a bank or building society account, but it must not become overdrawn.

- Gifts of money for the benefit of children may create a trust in their favour.

- Parents are subject to the same duties as other trustees, and have the same powers.

8.9 Lifetime gifts of money to children

This chapter is based on an article which was published in *Trust Law and Practice* (now *Tolley's Trust Law International*) in October 1988.

Chapter 9

The family home

TRUST OF LAND

9.1   For most people the largest purchase which they will make is that of a house to live in. Frequently it will be transferred into the joint names of husband and wife or cohabitees, and will be held by them in trust for themselves (ss 34 or 36(1) of the Law of Property Act 1925). They will either be joint tenants or tenants in common; the difference between joint tenants and tenants in common is discussed later in this chapter.

At first sight, these provisions look rather strange, but they are a convenient way of dealing with jointly owned property. The maximum number of trustees is four, and as a purchaser is not affected by the trusts provided he pays the purchase money to two trustees or a trust corporation, it facilitates conveyancing. Otherwise, a purchaser might have to deal with countless joint owners – an impossible task!

TRANSFER INTO THE NAME OF ONE PARTY

9.2   It may be that the home has been transferred into the name of one party, whilst the other party has contributed towards the purchase price. If it is the wife who has contributed, then the effect is that the husband will hold the property on trust for both of them in equity. If it is the husband who has contributed to the purchase price, there is a presumption that he intended to advance the money to the wife and, unless this presumption is rebutted, the husband will not have any equitable interest in the property. It is doubtful if this is still good law.

The effect of indirect contributions was considered in *Lloyds Bank v Rosset [1991] 1 AC 107*. This case was concerned with s 70(1)g of the Land Registration Act 1925 which conferred an overriding interest on a person in occupation of land if they also had an equitable interest in the land. In the *Rosset* case a house was purchased in the sole name of the husband. The wife did not contribute financially, but she did contribute to the renovation of the property. It was held that she did not have an equitable interest in the property, and therefore

129

did not have an overriding interest within s 70(1)(g) of the Land Registration Act 1925. Lord Bridge of Harwich said at page 132:

'The first and fundamental question which must always be resolved is whether, independently of any inference to be drawn from the conduct of the parties in the course of sharing the house as their home and managing their joint affairs, there has at any time prior to acquisition, or exceptionally at some later date, been an agreement, arrangement or understanding reached between them that the property is to be shared beneficially. The finding of an agreement or arrangement to share in this sense can only, I think, be based on evidence of express discussions between the partners, however imperfectly remembered and however imprecise their terms may have been. Once a finding to this effect is made, it will only be necessary for the partner asserting a claim to a beneficial interest against the partner entitled to the legal estate to show that he or she has acted to his or her detriment or significantly altered his or her position in reliance on the agreement in order to give rise to a constructive trust or proprietary estoppel.

In sharp contrast with this situation is the very different one where there is no evidence to support a finding of an agreement or arrangement to share, however reasonable it might have been for the parties to reach such an arrangement if they had applied their minds to the question, and where the court must rely entirely on the conduct of the parties both as the basis from which to infer a common intention to share the property beneficially and as the conduct relied on to give rise to a constructive trust. In this situation direct contributions to the purchase price by the partner who is not the legal owner, whether initially or by payment of mortgage instalments, will readily justify the inference necessary to the creation of a constructive trust. But, as I read the authorities, it is at least extremely doubtful whether anything less will do.'

In *Re Rogers' Question [1948] 1 All ER 328* a husband purchased a house in his own name. The wife contributed £100, and the husband borrowed £900. It was held that the parties were entitled in the proportions one-tenth for the wife and nine-tenths for the husband. If nine-tenths of the proceeds of sale were insufficient to discharge what was due under the mortgage, the husband would have to make up the difference. Evershed LJ said at pages 328–329:

'What the judge must try to do in all cases is, after seeing and hearing the witnesses, to try to conclude what at the time was in the parties' minds and then to make an order which, in the changed conditions, now fairly gives effect to what the parties, in the judge's finding, must be taken to have intended at the time of the transaction itself.'

In *Drake v Whipp (1996) 28 HLR 531*, the plaintiff and the defendant purchased a barn with the intention of converting it into a residence. It was conveyed into the sole name of the defendant. Both parties contributed to the purchase price and to the cost of the conversion work. They also worked on the conversion. It was held that there was a constructive trust as there was a common intention between the parties that they were to share beneficially. The plaintiff had also acted to her detriment. It was held that the defendant held the barn on trust for the plaintiff as to one-third and for himself as to two-thirds.

In *Savill v Goodall (1993) 25 HLR 588*, the defendant was the secure tenant of a council house. She cohabited with the plaintiff, and exercised her right to buy. It was agreed that the house would be purchased jointly, and that the plaintiff would pay the mortgage. It was held that as the parties had intended to own the home jointly, they owned it jointly. It was also held that the plaintiff was to bear the mortgage if the house was sold.

In *Mollo v Mollo [2000] WTLR 227,* AM and CM married in 1966, and had two children. They divorced in 1987 and met for the first time after the divorce in 1992. CM then visited her sons and was horrified by their living conditions. They were both out of work actors. She decided to purchase a house to be divided into three flats, one for each son, and one for the use of AM and CM when they came to this country. The house was purchased in her name, and she made it clear that she expected AM to contribute one half of the price. AM could not afford to do so, but he did contribute towards the cost, and paid the cost of improvements, most of which he carried out himself.

CM then locked AM and the sons out of the property. It was agreed that it should be sold.

AM and the sons claimed an equitable interest in the property.

It was held that the sons did not have any equitable interest in the property as there was no evidence that there was any intention that they should have an equitable interest in the property, and they had not contributed to the purchase price.

AM had contributed money and worked on the property. On a broad brush approach, he was entitled to 25% of the proceeds.

In *Carlton v Goodman [2002]* C agreed to help G to obtain a mortgage to enable him to purchase a house. She did not contribute to the purchase price or the mortgage instalments. There was no agreement with regard to the ownership of the house. On G's death, it was held that there was not a resulting trust in favour of C.

In *Ali v Khan [2002] EWCA Civ 974,* K transferred the family home to two of his six children, S and H, who became the registered proprietors. They borrowed the consideration of £25,000. K continued to pay all the household bills.

H assigned her share to S, and S claimed possession of the property.

The claim failed. It was held that there had been no intention to transfer the beneficial interest.

In *Firth v Mallender [2001] WTLR 1109,* G cohabited with M in his house. She paid for improvements to the property. On her death her executor argued that M should refund the cost of the improvements on various grounds. However, it was held that the claim failed as the evidence was that G was happy to spend her own money on improvements to a house in which she hoped to live for many years. Presumably the decision would have been different if the evidence was to the effect that she had made it clear she expected to be reimbursed.

Tenants of council houses can sometimes buy them at a considerable discount. Frequently the tenants are elderly, and cannot afford to fund the purchase. In that situation a child may fund the purchase price. Does this mean that there is a trust in favour of the child? In *Buggs v Buggs [2004] WTLR 799,* DB was married to JB. They took out a further advance to enable them to assist DB's mother to purchase a council house at a considerable discount. DB and JB divorced, and DB's mother then made a will giving the house as to 20% to DB and 80% to his brother. JB alleged that there was a trust in her favour.

It was held that there was no evidence of any common intention that the house should be owned by DB and JB. In addition, there was no evidence that DB's mother entered into the transaction with the intention that the property should become the property of DB and JB.

The evidence did not support a trust in favour of DB and JB.

Quantification of equitable interests

9.3   A house is vested in the name of one party to a relationship. The other party has contributed to the purchase price or the mortgage. The parties fall out. How do you quantify the interests of the parties?

The parties may have agreed their respective shares at the outset. If not, as will often be the case, does the court do a mathematical calculation to determine the value of each party's share, or does the court decide having regard to all relevant facts?

In *Oxley v Hiscock [2004] WTLR 709,* O and H cohabited. In 1991 a property was purchased which was vested in the sole name of H. O and H contributed unequal amounts to the purchase price.

The relationship broke down, and litigation ensued as to who was entitled to the proceeds of sale, and the proportions.

Chadwick LJ said at pages 747–748:

'... the first question is whether there is evidence from which to infer a common intention, communicated by each to the other, that each shall have a beneficial share in the property. In many cases ... there will have been some discussion between the parties which provides the answer to that question. ... In other cases – where the evidence is that the matter was not discussed at all – an affirmative answer will readily be inferred from the fact that each has made a financial contribution. ...

In those circumstances, the second question to be answered in cases of this nature is "what is the extent of the parties' respective beneficial interests in the property?" Again, in many such cases, the answer will be provided by evidence of what they said and did at the time of acquisition. But, in a case where there is no evidence of what they said and did at the time of acquisition ... It must now be accepted that ... the answer is that each is entitled to that share which the court considers fair having regard to the whole course of dealing between them in relation to the property. And, in that context, "the whole course of dealing between them in relation to property" includes the arrangements which they make from time to time in order to meet the outgoings (for example, mortgage contributions, council tax and utilities, repairs, insurance and housekeeping) which have to be met if they are to live in the property as their home'.

The judge also expressed the view that there is no difference in outcome in cases of this nature whether the true analysis lies in constructive trust or proprietary estoppel.

In *Pinfield v Eagles [2005] EWHC 577 (Ch) Oxley v Hiscock* was applied to a dispute between business partners with regard to the ownership of shares.

What is the position if the house is in the name of both parties to a relationship, and they have been registered as joint tenants in equity? It could be argued that the registration as joint tenants was conclusive, and that evidence that one party contributed more was irrelevant. However, in *Stack v Dowden [2005] EWCA 887* S and D cohabited and had four children. They purchased the family home as joint tenants both at law and in equity, but they were not advised about the difference between joint tenants and tenants in common. The relationship broke down and there was litigation as to their respective shares in the family home. The evidence was that S had contributed more than D. S limited her claim to 65% of the home, and was awarded this.

It was held that the mere fact that the parties had been registered as if they were joint tenants in equity did not stop a court holding that their beneficial interests were different. In the absence of any agreement, the court had a discretion to decide what the shares should be applying *Oxley v Hiscock*.

However, in *Clarke v Harlow [2005] WTLR 1473* C and H met in 1977, and cohabited until 2003. H was a successful solicitor, but C had various jobs, some full time, some part time.

In 2001 a property, Bank House, was purchased, and it was declared in the transfer that the parties were joint tenants. It was understood that H would pay the mortgage instalments, and the cost of refurbishing the property.

When the relationship broke down, H argued that C was not entitled to one half of the proceeds on the principle of equitable accounting.

It was held that in the absence of fraud or mistake, the declaration of trust in the transfer was conclusive. It was open to the court to infer an agreement to vary this, but such an inference would only be made in exceptional circumstances. There was no duty to account unless there had been a breach of some duty or obligation owed by one party to the other.

Once the parties separate, then equitable accounting can apply. In this case, all the improvements were carried out before the separation. There was no suggestion that C would contribute to the cost. In addition, it had always been understood that H would pay the mortgage instalments, so there was no room for the doctrine of equitable accounting.

The Children Act 1989

9.4   Usually in disputes between co-owners there is no statutory power to order one cohabitee to transfer the house to the other. However, under the Children Act 1989 there is power to order the transfer of houses or the settlement of houses for the benefit of the children.

The Children Act 1989, Schedule 1 provides as follows:

> '1(1)   On an application made by a parent or guardian of a child, or by any person in whose favour a residence order is in force with respect to a child, the court may:
>
> (a)   in the case of an application to the High Court or a county court make one or more of the orders mentioned in subparagraph (2).
>
> 1(2)   The orders referred to in sub-paragraph (1) are:

(d)   an order requiring a settlement to be made for the benefit of the child, and to the satisfaction of the court, of property:

  (i)   to which either parent is entitled (either in possession or in reversion); and

  (ii)   which is specified in the order.

(e)   an order requiring either or both parents of a child:

  (i)   to transfer to the applicant, for the benefit of the child; or

  (ii)   to transfer to the child himself,

such property to which the parent is, or the parents are, entitled (either in possession or reversion) as may be specified in the order.

In *W v W [2004] WTLR 321* the mother and father of two girls purchased a house in their joint names before the children were born. The relationship broke down, and the father obtained a residence order. The mother applied under the Trusts of Land and Appointment of Trustees Act 1996 for an order for the sale of the house, the father applied for an order under Sch 1 of the Children Act 1989 seeking a transfer of the mother's interest in the family home during the minority of the children. The father requested that both applications should be heard together, but the judge at first instance dealt with the application under the 1996 Act and adjourned the father's application. He made an order for the sale of the house.

On appeal, it was held that both applications should have been heard together. The court also expressed the view that the judge who dealt with the application for the residence order under s 8 of the Children Act should also deal with the Sch 1 application.

The order of the judge at first instance was confirmed. The reason for this was that both parties were legally aided, and the court was very conscious of the costs implications. In addition, the court was of the view that if the house was sold, the father would be able to buy another house in the same neighbourhood with his share of the proceeds.

PROPRIETARY ESTOPPEL

9.5   It may be that a third party acquires a proprietary right in land if A encourages B to take certain action, and B does so to his detriment. In *Pascoe v Turner [1979] 1 WLR 431*, the plaintiff, who was a businessman, and the defendant, who was a widow, cohabited in a house owned by the plaintiff. The relationship broke down, but the plaintiff assured the defendant that the house and its contents were hers. She spent money on repairs and improvements. It was held that she was entitled to a conveyance of the house.

In *Re Basham (deceased) [1987] 1 All ER 405* the plaintiff had looked after the deceased for a number of years. The deceased had led her to believe that she would inherit his property on his death. When the deceased died intestate, his two nieces were entitled to his estate. The plaintiff brought an action against the nieces, and it was held that she was entitled to the estate. Edward Nugee QC, sitting as a Deputy Judge of the High Court, said at page 410:

> 'Where one person (A) has acted to his detriment on the faith of a belief, which was known to and encouraged by another person (B), that he either has or is going to be given a right in or over B's property, B cannot insist on his strict legal rights if to do so would be inconsistent with A's belief.'

He continued:

> 'The principle is commonly known as proprietary estoppel, and since the effect of it is that B is prevented from asserting his strict legal rights it has something in common with estoppel. But in my judgment, at all events where the belief is that A is going to be given a right in the future, it is properly to be regarded as giving rise to a species of constructive trust, which is the concept employed by a court of equity to prevent a person from relying on his legal rights where it would be unconscionable for him to do so. The rights to which proprietary estoppel gives rise, and the machinery by which effect is given to them, are similar in many respects to those involved in cases of secret trusts, mutual wills and other comparable cases in which property is vested in B on the faith of an understanding that it will be dealt with in a particular manner ...'

In *Gillett v Holt and another [2000] 2 All ER 289,* G had worked for H for almost 40 years. H indicated that he would leave the bulk of his estate to G, and made wills to that effect. The relationship between G and H broke down, and H made a new will in favour of the second defendant, excluding G entirely. G sued H and the second defendant alleging that H had become subject to an obligation founded on proprietary estoppel to give the bulk of his estate to him. The Court of Appeal decided in G's favour. At page 301, Robert Walker LJ stated:

> 'This judgment considers the relevant principles of law, and the judge's application of them to the facts which he found, in much the same order as the appellant's notice of appeal and skeleton argument. But although the judgment is, for convenience, divided into several sections with headings which give a rough indication of the subject matter, it is important to note at the outset that the doctrine of

proprietary estoppel cannot be treated as subdivided into three or four watertight compartments. Both sides are agreed on that, and in the course of the oral argument in this court it repeatedly became apparent that the quality of the relevant assurances may influence the issue of reliance, that reliance and detriment are often intertwined, and that whether there is a distinct need for a 'mutual understanding' may depend on how the other elements are formulated and understood. Moreover, the fundamental principle that equity is concerned to prevent unconscionable conduct permeates all the elements of the doctrine. In the end the court must look at the matter in the round.'

(For a fuller discussion of promissory estoppel, see Chapter 5.)

DISPUTE AS TO WHETHER THE PROPERTY SHOULD BE SOLD

9.6   It may be that there will be a dispute between the co-owners as to whether the house should be sold, for example if the relationship between the parties breaks down. If the parties are married, then the dispute will probably be resolved in the divorce proceedings. If the parties are not married, then any dispute is now regulated by s 14 of the Trusts of Land and Appointment of Trustees Act 1996.

Section 14(1) of the 1996 Act provides that any trustee or beneficiary may apply to the court. Section 14(2) provides that the court may make any such order:

'(a)   relating to the exercise by the trustees of any of their functions (including an order relieving them of any obligation to obtain the consent of, or to consult, any person in connection with the exercise of any of their functions), or

(b)   declaring the nature or extent of a person's interest in property subject to the trust,

as the court thinks fit.'

Section 14(3) provides that the court may not use s 14 to make any order as to the appointment or removal of trustees. Section 18(1) provides that s 14 does not apply to personal representatives.

Section 17 makes it clear that s 14 applies even if the trustees have disposed of all the land which was the subject of the trust.

Section 15(1) provides that the matters to which the court is to have regard in determining an application for an order under s 14 include:

'(a) the intentions of the person or persons (if any) who created the trust,

(b) the purposes for which the property subject to the trust is held,

(c) the welfare of any minor who occupies or might reasonably be expected to occupy any land subject to the trust as his home, and

(d) the interests of any secured creditor of any beneficiary.'

If the application is concerned with the exercise of any of the powers conferred on the trustees by s 13, the court must also have regard to the circumstances and wishes of each of the beneficiaries who is (or, apart from any previous exercise by the trustees of those powers, would be) entitled to occupy the land under s 12 (s 15(2)). For a discussion of ss 12 and 13, see 9.8 below.

In respect of any other application, s 15(3) provides that the court must also have regard to the circumstances and wishes of any beneficiaries who are of full age and entitled to an interest in possession in property subject to the trust or, where the beneficiaries are not in agreement, of the majority of beneficiaries (according to the value of their combined interests). This provision does not apply to the exercise of the power of trustees to transfer land to the beneficiaries, as conferred by s 6(2).

Three cases decided before the Trusts of Land and Appointment of Trustees Act 1996 came into force illustrate how the court might operate such provisions.

In *Bedson v Bedson [1965] 2 QB 666* a draper's business and house were conveyed to husband and wife as joint tenants in equity. The intention was to provide a home for the husband and wife and their three children, and a livelihood. The wife left the matrimonial home, and obtained an order for the maintenance of the children. The court refused to order the sale of the property because the property was still providing a livelihood for the husband, and was enabling him to pay maintenance.

A different conclusion was reached in *Jones v Challenger [1901] 1 QB 176*. The matrimonial home was conveyed to husband and wife as joint tenants. The wife left, and the husband divorced her on the grounds of her adultery. The court ordered the sale of the house.

In *Mortgage Corporation v Silkin [2000] 2 FCR 222*, on an application by a mortgage for an order for sale, Neuberger J said at page 239:

'... it does not seem to me unlikely that the legislature intended to relax the fetters on the way in which the court exercised its discretion ... so as to tip the balance somewhat more in favour of families and against banks and other chargees ... . As a result of section 15, the court has greater flexibility than heretofore, as to how

it exercises its jurisdiction on an application for an order for sale ... .
Once the relevant factors to be taken into account have been
identified, it is a matter for the court as to what weight to give to
each factor in a particular case.'

A different approach may be adopted if one of the co-owners is bankrupt (see
9.12 below).

THE NATURE OF JOINT TENANCY AND TENANCY IN COMMON

9.7   If property is conveyed to spouses on trust for sale for themselves as
joint tenants, they are regarded as owning the whole property rather than a part
of it. There are four 'unities' which have to be satisfied before a joint tenancy
can exist, namely time, title, interest and possession.

Unity of time means that the property must vest in the joint tenants at the same
time. If A is the sole owner of a property, and conveys it to B and himself as
trustees for sale to hold the net proceeds on trust for themselves as tenants in
common, and later conveys his interest to C, B and C will not be joint tenants,
unless of course they agree that this should be the case.

Unity of title means that the joint owners must all have acquired their title from
the same document, although tenants in common can agree that they should be
joint tenants.

Unity of interest means that the estate must be of the same extent, nature and
duration. There can be no joint tenancy between the freeholder and the lease-
holder of the same property, or between a life tenant and the freehold rever-
sioner.

If there is a joint tenancy, the right of survivorship applies. This means that if
one joint tenant dies, the other or others are entitled to his interest in the
property, irrespective of who might be entitled to the property under the will or
intestacy of the deceased. This right does not apply to tenants in common. They
are all entitled to possession, but if one is not in possession, he cannot claim rent
from the others (*Jones (A E) v Jones (F W) [1977] 2 All ER 231*).

The transfer to joint owners may specify whether they are joint tenants or
tenants in common in equity, but if it does not do so, various rules assist the
court to decide on the exact nature of the interest. If the purchase money has
been contributed in unequal shares, or it is a commercial property, the court will
normally hold that the purchasers are tenants in common.

If a joint tenancy is created, it can be converted into a tenancy in common by any act which destroys one or more of the unities, for example:

- assignment by one joint tenant of his interest; or
- partition of the land between the joint tenants.

It can also be severed by mutual agreement, or by notice served under s 36(2) of the Law of Property Act 1925, but not by will. A notice under s 36(2) must be in writing, and must immediately sever the joint tenancy. Under s 196(4) the notice can be served in a registered letter; as long as the section is complied with, it is immaterial whether or not the notice actually reaches the persons to be served.

THE RIGHT OF BENEFICIARIES TO OCCUPY TRUST LAND

9.8   Section 12 of the Trusts of Land and Appointment of Trustees Act 1996 confers the right to occupy land subject to a trust on a beneficiary entitled to an interest in possession in such land if at that time:

> '(a)   the purposes of the trust include making the land available for his occupation (or for the occupation of beneficiaries of a class of which he is a member or of beneficiaries in general), or
>
> (b)   the land is held by the trustees so as to be so available.'

The right in s 12 is subject to s 13. Section 13(1) provides that where two or more beneficiaries are entitled under s 12 to occupy land, the trustees of land may exclude or restrict the entitlement of any one or more (but not all) of them.

Section 13(2) provides that trustees may not:

> '(a)   unreasonably exclude any beneficiary's entitlement to occupy land, or
>
> (b)   restrict any such entitlement to an unreasonable extent.'

Section 13(3) provides that the trustees may impose reasonable conditions on any beneficiary in relation to his occupation of land by reason of his entitlement under s 12. Subsection (5) provides that the conditions which may be imposed on a beneficiary include, in particular, conditions requiring him:

> '(a)   to pay any outgoings or expenses in respect of the land, or
>
> (b)   to assume any other obligation in relation to the land or to any activity which is or is proposed to be conducted there.'

Where a beneficiary has been excluded, s 13(6) provides that any other beneficiary may be required to:

'(a) make payments by way of compensation to the beneficiary whose entitlement has been excluded or restricted, or

(b) forgo any payment or other benefit to which he would otherwise be entitled under the trust so as to benefit that beneficiary.'

Once a beneficiary is in occupation, he cannot be excluded unless he consents or the court has given approval (s 13(7)).

Section 13(4) provides that the matters to which the trustees are to have regard in exercising their s 13 powers include:

(a) the intentions of the person(s) who created the trust;

(b) the purposes for which the land is held; and

(c) the circumstances and wishes of each of the beneficiaries who is (or, apart from any previous exercise by the trustees of those powers, would be) entitled to occupy the land under s 12.

How would the trustees operate these provisions? Assume that a testator creates a trust under which his children have a life interest in the family home. One child does not want to live in the family home. The other children could be ordered to pay him compensation for not being there. If the children cannot get on together, one could be excluded from the house, and those in occupation could be ordered to pay compensation.

PURCHASE OF COUNCIL HOUSES

9.9   It has been very common for the tenants of council houses to purchase them, often at a substantial discount. If the house is sold within three years, the discount may have to be repaid (s 155 of the Housing Act 1985).

Who is entitled to exercise the option?

9.10   Secure tenants have the right to buy the dwelling house of which they are tenants, or if the landlord does not own the freehold, or they are tenants of a flat, to be granted a lease (s 118(1) of the Housing Act 1985). Section 118(2) provides that where a secure tenancy is a joint tenancy then, whether or not each of the joint tenants occupies the dwelling house as his only or principal home, the right to buy belongs jointly to all of them or to such one or more of them as may be agreed between them. Such agreement is not valid unless the person or at least one of the persons to whom the right to buy is to belong occupies the dwelling house as his only or principal home.

The secure tenant may exercise this right by written notice served on the landlord (s 122 of the Housing Act 1985). Under s 123(1) of the Housing Act a secure tenant may in his notice under s 122 require that not more than three members of his family who are not joint tenants but occupy the dwelling house as their only or principal home should share the right to buy with him. Section 123(2) provides that he may validly do so in the case of any such member only if:

(a)   that member is his spouse or has been residing with him throughout the period of 12 months ending with the giving of the notice; or

(b)   the landlord consents.

Section 123(3) provides that where by such a notice any members of the tenant's family are validly required to share the right to buy with the tenant, the right to buy belongs to the tenant and those members jointly and he and they shall be treated for the purposes of that part of the Act as joint tenants.

It may be that the tenants are elderly, and do not have the capital required to exercise the option. In these circumstances, can children provide the purchase price? Can the house be transferred into the names of the children? It would seem that there is no objection to children providing the purchase price. The secure tenant can execute a declaration of trust recording the contribution of the children, and stating the proportions to which the secure tenant and the children are entitled in equity.

EFFECT OF DIVORCE

9.11   The court has wide powers in matrimonial proceedings to make orders with regard to the matrimonial home; this aspect is considered in more detail in chapter 15.

Most solicitors will be aware of the need to warn matrimonial clients about the possibility of severing any joint tenancy of the matrimonial home, which can simply be done by notice under s 36(2) of the Law of Property Act. The client may decide to take no action, perhaps hoping that they will outlive the other spouse, and become absolutely entitled to the whole of the property because of the right of survivorship!

It is debatable whether divorce proceedings have the effect of severing a joint tenancy. In *Re Draper's Conveyance [1969] 1 Ch 486* the matrimonial home was vested in husband and wife as joint tenants. The marriage broke down, and the wife applied for an order for the sale of the matrimonial home under the Married Women's Property Act 1882. It was held that the joint tenancy had been severed. On the other hand, in *Harris v Goddard [1983] 1 WLR 1203* the situation was similar, but there was merely a prayer in the divorce petition that the court might make such order with regard to the matrimonial property as might be just. It was held that the joint tenancy had not been severed.

It may be that the purchaser of a council house will be ordered to transfer the house to his or her spouse or former spouse. In these circumstances, any discount does not have to be repaid, even if the order is made within three years of the purchase.

With regard to improvements, s 37 of the Matrimonial Proceedings and Property Act 1970 provides:

'It is hereby declared that where a husband or wife contributes in money or money's worth to the improvement of real or personal property in which or in the proceeds of sale of which either or both of them has or have a beneficial interest, the husband or wife so contributing shall, if the contribution is of a substantial nature and subject to any agreement between them to the contrary express or implied, be treated as having then acquired by virtue of his or her contribution a share or an enlarged share, as the case may be, in that beneficial interest of such an extent as may have been then agreed or, in default of such agreement, as may seem in all the circumstances just to any court before which the question of its existence or extent of the beneficial interest of the husband or wife arises (whether in proceedings between them or in any other proceedings).'

BANKRUPTCY

9.12   Section 335A of the Insolvency Act 1986 deals with an application by a trustee of a bankrupt's estate under s 14 of the Trusts of Land and Appointment of Trustees Act 1996 (powers of court in relation to trusts of land). Section 335A(2) provides that on an application for the sale of land under s 14 the court shall make such order as it thinks just and reasonable having regard to:

(a)   the interests of the bankrupt's creditors;

(b)   where the application is made in respect of land which includes a dwelling house which is or has been the home of the bankrupt or the bankrupt's spouse or former spouse:

    (i)   the conduct of the spouse or former spouse, so far as contributing to the bankruptcy,

(ii) the needs and financial resources of the spouse or former spouse, and

(iii) the needs of any children; and

(c) all the circumstances of the case other than the needs of the bankrupt.

Section 335A(3) provides that where such an application is made after the end of the period of one year beginning with the first vesting of the bankrupt's estate in a trustee, the court shall assume, unless the circumstances of the case are exceptional, that the interests of the bankrupt's creditors outweigh all other considerations.

Section 336 of the Insolvency Act 1986 provides that where a spouse's rights of occupation under the Family Law Act 1996 are a charge on the estate or interest of the other spouse, that charge binds the trustee in bankruptcy. Any proceedings under s 33 of the 1996 Act must be in the court having jurisdiction in relation to the bankruptcy.

Section 336(4) provides that on an application for sale, the court shall make such order as it thinks just and reasonable having regard to factors almost identical to those discussed above in respect of s 335A(2). Section 336(5) provides that where such an application is made after the end of the period of one year beginning with the first vesting of the bankrupt's estate in a trustee, the court shall assume, unless the circumstances of the case are exceptional, that the interests of the bankrupt's creditors outweigh all other considerations.

Section 337 applies where:

(a) a person who is entitled to occupy a dwelling house by virtue of a beneficial estate or interest is adjudged bankrupt; and

(b) any persons under the age of 18 with whom that person had at some time occupied that dwelling house had their home with that person at the time when the bankruptcy petition was presented and at the commencement of the bankruptcy.

In this situation, s 337(2)(a) provides that the bankrupt has the following rights as against the trustee of his estate:

(i) if in occupation, a right not to be evicted or excluded from the dwelling house or any part of it, except with the leave of the court,

(ii) if not in occupation, a right with the leave of the court to enter into and occupy the dwelling house.

The bankrupt has these rights whether or not the bankrupt's spouse has matrimonial home rights under Part IV of the Family Law Act 1996. The rights of the bankrupt are a charge, having the like priority as an equitable interest created immediately before the commencement of the bankruptcy, on so much of his estate or interest in the dwelling house as vests in the trustee.

Section 337(4) provides that any application for leave such as is mentioned in subs (2)(a) or otherwise by virtue of this section for an order under s 33 of the Family Law Act 1996 shall be made to the court having jurisdiction in relation to the bankruptcy. Section 337(5) provides that on such an application the court shall make such order under s 33 of the Family Law Act 1996 as it thinks just and reasonable having regard to the interests of the creditors, to the bankrupt's financial resources, to the needs of the children and to all the circumstances of the case other than the needs of the bankrupt.

Section 337(6) provides that where such an application is made after the end of the period of one year beginning with the vesting of the bankrupt's estate in a trustee, the court shall assume, unless the circumstances of the case are exceptional, that the interests of the bankrupt's creditors outweigh all other considerations.

How will these provisions be applied by the courts? This matter was discussed in *Re Citro [1990] 3 WLR 880*, where Nourse LJ reviewed the authorities, and said at page 892:

> 'The broad effect of these authorities can be summarised as follows. Where a spouse who has a beneficial interest in the matrimonial home has become bankrupt under debts which cannot be paid without the realisation of that interest, the voice of the creditors will usually prevail over the voice of the other spouse and a sale of the property ordered within a short period. The voice of the other spouse will only prevail in exceptional circumstances. No distinction is to be made between a case where the property is still being enjoyed as the matrimonial home and one where it is not.
>
> What then are exceptional circumstances? As the cases show, it is not uncommon for a wife with young children to be faced with eviction in circumstances where the realisation of her beneficial interest will not produce enough to buy a comparable home in the same neighbourhood, or indeed elsewhere. And, if she has to move elsewhere, there may be problems over schooling and so forth. Such circumstances, while engendering a natural sympathy in all who hear of them, cannot be described as exceptional.'

The courts may adopt a different attitude if there is no question of bankruptcy (see *Mortgage Corporation v Silkin [2000] 2 FCR 222* at page 238 and 9.6 above).

TAXATION

Capital gains tax

9.13   It is well known that there is an exemption from CGT in respect of private residences.

Section 222(1) of the Taxation of Chargeable Gains Act 1992 provides that the relief applies to a gain accruing to an individual on the disposal of a dwelling house or part of a dwelling house which is, or has at any time in his period of ownership been, his only or main residence, or of land which he has for his own occupation and enjoyment with that residence as its gardens or grounds up to half a hectare. The exemption can apply to a larger area if a larger area is required for the reasonable enjoyment of the dwelling house as a residence having regard to the size and character of the dwelling house.

Second homes

9.14   Where a taxpayer owns two homes, it may be difficult to decide which home is the main residence. Section 222(5) provides that the individual may conclude that question by notice to the inspector given within two years from the beginning of the period when the individual was entitled to two homes. The notice can be varied by giving another notice to the inspector, which can be backdated for two years. If no notice is served, the inspector determines which house is the main residence; there is a right of appeal to the General or Special Commissioners.

Effect of periods of absence

9.15   Section 223(1) provides that the gain on the disposal of a main residence shall not be chargeable to tax if the dwelling house has been the individual's only or main residence throughout the period of ownership except for all or any part of the last 36 months of that period. If these conditions are not satisfied, s 223(2) provides that the following fraction of the gain shall not be chargeable:

> 'the length of the periods of ownership during which the dwelling-house was the only or main residence inclusive of the last 36 months divided by the length of the period of ownership.'

Disregard of certain periods

9.16   Section 223(3) provides for the disregard of some periods of absence if both before and after the period there was a time when the dwelling house was the individual's only or main residence. The periods which can be disregarded are:

(a)   a period of absence not exceeding three years (or periods of absence which together did not exceed three years);

(b)   any period of absence throughout which the individual worked in an employment or office all the duties of which were performed outside the United Kingdom; or

(c)   any period of absence not exceeding four years (or periods of absence which together did not exceed four years) throughout which the individual was prevented from residing in the dwelling house or part of the dwelling house in consequence of the situation of his place of work or in consequence of any condition imposed by his employer requiring him to reside elsewhere, being a condition reasonably imposed to secure the effective performance of his duties.

ESC D3 provides that if spouses are living together, and one spouse is required to live elsewhere because of his employment, the other spouse is similarly treated. ESC D4 exempts individuals from the requirement that after the period of absence the dwelling house should be the only or main residence of the individual if the employee is obliged to work in another place.

ESC D49 provides for the disregard of no more than a year if the individual has a house built, or an existing house is altered or redecorated.

Occupation by beneficiary under a settlement

9.17   Section 225 exempts from any charge to CGT the gain made on the disposal of a dwelling house where during the period of ownership of the trustee, the dwelling house has been the only or main residence of a person entitled to occupy it under the terms of the settlement. This relief extends to personal representatives on the disposal of a dwelling house where the persons entitled to at least 75% of the proceeds of sale have occupied the dwelling house as their only or main residence both before and after death.

Business use

9.18   Section 224(1) provides for the apportionment of any gain where part of the dwelling house is used exclusively for the purposes of a trade or business, or of a profession or vocation. Note that no apportionment is required if the use is not exclusive. Section 224(2) deals with the situation where there is a change in the use of the dwelling house, and provides that the relief may be adjusted in such manner as the Commissioners consider to be just and reasonable.

Lettings

9.19   Section 223(4) provides that where a house has been let at any time during the individual's period of ownership, any gain is only chargeable to the extent that it exceeds the lesser of:

- the part of the gain which is not chargeable; and
- £40,000.

This relief can only be claimed if the house has been occupied by the taxpayer.

Thus, if a house has been let, and the gain attributable to the period of occupation is £35,000, and the gain attributable to the period of letting is £45,000, the chargeable gain will be £10,000. If, however, the gain attributable to the period of occupation is £60,000, £5,000 of the gain will be chargeable.

SP 14/80 provides that the taking in of a lodger will not cause the relief to be lost in whole or in part.

Occupation by a dependent relative

9.20   Although it is of decreasing importance, there is also exemption for a dwelling house which was on 5 April 1988 or at any earlier time in the period of ownership the sole residence of a dependent relative of the individual provided rent free and without any other consideration (s 226(1)). Section 226(6) defines dependent relative as:

'(a)   any relative of his, or of his spouse, who is incapacitated by old age or infirmity from maintaining himself; or

(b)   his mother or his spouse's mother, whether or not incapacitated, if she is widowed, or living apart from her husband, or a single woman in consequence of dissolution or annulment of marriage.'

The exemption will be lost if the acquisition or the expenditure was made for the purpose of realising a gain (s 224(3)).

Inheritance tax

9.21   Various schemes – some more risky than others – have been devised to take the home out of charge to IHT, and to avoid the requirement that the donor should continue to live in the house without infringing the reservation of benefit rules. Many of the lifetime schemes will mean that there is now a charge to income tax if the home is not part of the occupier's estate for inheritance tax purposes, which will probably put an end to most of these schemes.

The author has never liked any of the schemes designed to save inheritance tax as he believes that it is important for clients to retain the ability to deal freely with their houses.

SUMMARY

9.22

- In the case of co-ownership, the court will not order a sale of the property if the original purpose remains to be fulfilled.

- The four unities are essential for a joint tenancy.

- The transfer to co-owners should indicate if they are joint tenants or tenants in common.

- A joint tenancy can be converted into a tenancy in common.

- The discount obtainable on the purchase of a council house may have to be repaid if the house is sold within three years of purchase.

- In the case of bankruptcy, the house will normally be sold in order to pay the creditors.

- CGT – private residence exemption. A person who owns two homes can elect which should be treated as the main residence.

- Relief may be restricted if part of the dwelling house is used exclusively for business purposes, or the house is let.

Chapter 10

Life insurance

TYPES OF POLICY

10.1   There are three types of policy:

- whole life policies;
- endowment policies; and
- term policies.

Under a whole life policy, a sum of money is payable on the death of the life assured. Sometimes married couples take out a policy in the joint names of both spouses – the insured amount may be payable on the death of the first to die, or the death of the survivor.

Strictly an endowment policy provides for the payment of a sum of money on the expiry of a specified period if the insured is still alive. Usually the policy also provides that a sum is payable on the death of the insured within that period.

Term policies provide for payment if the assured does not live for a specified period, or dies before a specified age. If the assured is still alive at the end of the specified period, or the specified age, nothing is payable under the policy.

Policies may be without profits, with profits, and unit linked. If the policy is without profits, the amount to be paid under the policy is specified at the outset. If the policy is with profits, the amount to be paid under the policy is specified, but bonuses may be added to the policy whilst it is in force, and a reversionary bonus added when it matures. If the policy is unit linked, the amount payable is linked to the value of the units in which the funds of the policy holder have been invested.

QUALIFYING POLICIES

10.2   Most policies will be qualifying policies, and income tax will not be payable on the proceeds. In order to be classified as a qualifying policy, the policy must be certified by the Inland Revenue, and comply with the conditions contained in Sch 15 to the Income and Corporation Taxes Act 1988. If it is a non-qualifying policy, any gain will be subject to income tax.

Note that an endowment policy which cannot last for more than ten years cannot be a qualifying policy. In addition, a policy for which a single premium is paid cannot be a qualifying policy.

USES OF LIFE POLICIES

10.3   The following are the main uses of life policies:

- protection of dependants;
- payment of school fees;
- home purchase;
- protection against the death of a partner;
- protection against the death of a senior manager; and
- paying or saving IHT.

Taxation

Inheritance tax

10.4   The declaration of trust will constitute a potentially exempt transfer after 22 March 2006 if the transfer is to:

- an individual;
- a gift into a disabled trust; or
- a gift into a bereaved minor' s trust on the coming to an end of an immediate post death interest.

(s 3 of the Inheritance Tax Act 1984 as amended.)

Trusts for disabled persons are discussed in more detail in Chapter 13.

A transfer of a policy to any trust apart from a trust for a disabled person is a chargeable *inter vivos* transfer.

Frequently no IHT will be payable on the transfer of a policy because of exemptions like the annual exemption and the normal expenditure out of income exemption. In addition, the value transferred will be nil if no premiums have been paid; otherwise under s 167(1) of the Inheritance Tax Act 1984 it will be not less than:

> '(a)   the total of the premiums or other consideration which, at any time before the transfer of value, has been paid under the policy ... , less
>
> (b)   any sum which, at any time before the transfer of value, has been paid under, or in consideration of any right conferred by the policy ...'.

In general terms, this means that the value transferred will be the higher of the market value, surrender value or the total premiums paid. If the insured continues to pay the premiums due in respect of such a policy, each premium is a potentially exempt transfer or chargeable disposal. However, if any tax does become payable it may be possible to make use again of the annual exemption, or the exemption for usual expenditure out of income.

A policy the subject of a declaration of trust will not form part of the estate of the insured for inheritance tax purposes; if a spouse or children with a vested interest in the policy predecease the insured, the policy will form part of their estates.

Capital gains tax

10.5   Under s 210(2) of the Taxation of Chargeable Gains Taxes Act 1992 no chargeable gain will accrue on the disposal of, or of an interest in, the rights under any policy of assurance or contract for a deferred annuity on the life of any person, unless the person making the disposal is not the original beneficial owner of the policy or contract and he acquired the rights or interest for a consideration in money or money's worth.

Protection of dependants

10.6   A new policy can be made the subject of an express declaration of trust, and most life offices have their own standard form trust. Existing policies can be assigned, but the assignment must comply with the Policies of Assurance Act 1867:

- the assignment must be made either by endorsement on the policy or by a separate instrument in the words or to the effect set forth in the schedule to the Act, such endorsement or separate instrument being duly stamped;
- written notice of the date and purport of the assignment must be given to the assurance company.

Divorce

10.7   If there is a divorce, it was held in *Gunner v Gunner and Sterling [1949] P 77* that a declaration of trust under the Married Women's Property Act 1882 was a post-nuptial settlement. Presumably a declaration of trust outside the Married Women's Property Act 1882 will also be a post-nuptial settlement. Clearly a court would have power to make a property adjustment order under s 24 of the Matrimonial Causes Act 1973.

Family provision

10.8   Under s 10 of the Inheritance (Provision for Family and Dependants) Act 1975 the court can order a donee to disgorge the whole or part of a gift provided that the court is satisfied:

'(a)   that, less than six years before the date of the death of the deceased, the deceased with the intention of defeating an application for financial provision under this Act made a disposition, and

(b)   that full valuable consideration for that disposition was not given by the person to whom or for the benefit of whom the disposition was made ... or by any other person, and

(c)   that the exercise of the powers conferred by this section would facilitate the making of financial provision for the applicant under this Act'.

Subsection (7) states that disposition includes the payment of a sum of money under a policy of assurance.

Under subsections (3) and (4) the amount that the donee can be ordered to disgorge must not exceed the amount of the payment or the value of the property at the date of death, as the case may be.

If the declaration of trust of the policy was within six years of death, and the other conditions are satisfied, the donee can be ordered to pay the value of the policy to an applicant. On the other hand, if the declaration was more than six years before death, it is only the premiums paid in the six years which may have to be paid to an applicant.

The effect of the settlor's bankruptcy

10.9   A declaration of trust will have the effect of removing the policy from the estate of the settlor, unless the trusts fail, in which event there will be a resulting trust in favour of the settlor.

There are various other provisions rendering transactions void in the case of the bankruptcy of the settlor or donor.

Section 172 of the Law of Property Act 1925 renders voidable conveyances of real or personal property made with intent to defraud creditors. Section 339 of the Insolvency Act deals with transactions at an undervalue, and these are defined in s 339(3) so as to include gifts by an individual to a person or transactions with a person on terms that provide for the individual to receive no consideration. Under s 341 if the gift or transaction was made within two years of the date of presentation of the bankruptcy petition, the court has jurisdiction; if it was made between two and five years it must be proved that the individual was either insolvent at the time of the gift or transaction, or became insolvent as a result of the gift or transaction. Under s 342 the court has wide powers to make orders with regard to such transactions.

Section 423 of the Insolvency Act applies to similar gifts or transactions as s 339, but there is no requirement that the individual making the gift or entering into the transaction should be bankrupt; under s 423(3) the court can only make an order if it:

'is satisfied that it was entered into by him for the purpose–

(a)   of putting assets beyond the reach of a person who is making, or may at some time make, a claim against him, or

(b)   of otherwise prejudicing the interests of such a person in relation to the claim which he is making or may make'.

Payment of school fees

10.10   As regards school fees, if the school fees are required immediately, there is little scope for tax planning. However, if the fees are not required for ten years, it is possible to fund them by means of a series of with profit or unit linked endowment policies. The premiums should be exempt from IHT as they will usually come within one of the exemptions from IHT.

It is sometimes possible to deposit a lump sum with a school in advance payment of school fees, which the school will then use to purchase an annuity. There should be no IHT liability on the initial transfer (disposition for the education of a child).

A parent may also purchase a deferred annuity as a means of funding school fees.

Home purchase

10.11   Life policies were often used to fund the purchase of houses. The borrower pays only the interest due on a mortgage relying upon an endowment policy to repay the capital. Such mortgages lost some of their popularity when it became clear that many endowment policies would not yield enough to pay off the mortgage.

Protection against the death of a partner

10.12   It is common for partners to insure their own lives so that the proceeds can be used to fund any payment due to the estate of a deceased partner.

Paying IHT

10.13   If a potentially exempt transfer has been made, it is common to take out a term policy to cover the IHT should the donor die within seven years of the gift. The policy should be made the subject of a declaration of trust. The donor can make gifts of cash to the trustees to fund future premiums – such gifts will usually come within the annual exemption, or some other exemption. Alternatively, the donee can take out the policy.

Policies can also be used to fund liability to IHT on death. Spouses or civil partners or cohabitees can take out a joint life policy which will pay out on the death of the survivor. This policy can then be made the subject of a declaration of trust in favour of the children of the marriage who will usually be liable for the inheritance tax payable on the death of the survivor. The policy will not then be part of the estate of the surviving parent.

Loan to trustees

10.14   The settlor creates a discretionary trust for the benefit of his children and grandchildren. The settlor then makes a loan to the trustees, and the trustees use the loan to purchase a bond. The trustees surrender 5% each year – this can be done without incurring any tax liability. The trustees give this money to the settlor in repayment of loan. On the death of the settlor only the amount of the outstanding loan is chargeable to IHT.

Even though the settlor is not within the class of beneficiaries, it is arguable that there has been a reservation of benefit if the trustees repay the loan. This can be alleviated by someone other than the settlor creating the original settlement, and

155

transferring a nominal amount to the trust. The real settlor then makes the loan to the trustees.

Discounted gift trust

10.15   Another idea is the discounted gift trust. This again involves invest-ment in a bond. The settlor then creates a trust under which the settlor is entitled to the income, but not the capital. The actuarial value of the right to receive the income is then calculated. Before 22 March 2006, the settlor would be deemed to have made a PET of the balance of the premium. As long as the settlor lived for seven years after the creation of the trust, no IHT was payable on the balance of the fund. If the settlor died within seven years, IHT was payable. If the settlor died after three years, IHT was payable, but taper relief reduced the amount of IHT payable.

As from 22 March 2006, the creation of such a trust will be a chargeable transfer as far as IHT is concerned. However, the value of assets transferred to the trust will often be within the nil rate band.

Reverter to settlor

10.16   This scheme will no longer work as the reverter to settlor exemption has been abolished.

This scheme made use of the reverter to settlor exemption for IHT purposes under which if assets reverted to the original settlor, no IHT was payable.

The settlor took out a series of endowment policies maturing in successive years. These were placed in a flexible interest in possession trust for the benefit of children or grandchildren, but if the settlor was alive when a policy matured, it reverted to the settlor.

The original settlement was a PET for IHT purposes, but no IHT was payable if the policy matured and the proceeds reverted to the settlor. On the death of the settlor other beneficiaries were entitled, but as long as seven years had elapsed from the original settlement, no IHT was payable.

The trustees would have had the power to extend the policy and to distribute capital to the other beneficiaries, so if the settlor did not need any money when a policy was about to mature, the trustees could extend the policy.

Bond funding premiums

10.17   This idea again involves the use of a bond and surrendering 5% each year.

The bond was made the subject of a trust.

Before 22 March 2006 that would have been a PET, but as long as the settlor survived for seven years, it would not have had any IHT consequences. Now it will be a chargeable disposal as far as IHT is concerned.

The trustees surrendered 5% of the bond each year, and used that to invest in a life policy on the life of the settlor for the benefit of children and grandchildren.

On the death of the settlor that policy was free of IHT, and will pass to the beneficiaries under the trust without any IHT liability.

Special bypass trust

10.18   Many clients are in pension schemes.

Often these schemes provide for the payment of a lump sum. This lump sum is frequently payable at the discretion of the trustees of the pension scheme as if the deceased employee's estate had a right to it, it would be part of his estate for IHT purposes.

This scheme will not save any IHT on the death of the employee as none is payable if it is payable at the discretion of the trustees of the pension scheme. However if nothing is done, then the lump sum will be part of the estate of the employee's spouse assuming that the surviving spouse has not spent it!

So the idea is to prevent it being subject to IHT on the death of the surviving spouse. The way to achieve this is for the employee to create a discretionary trust in his or her lifetime. The class of beneficiaries includes the surviving spouse and children. The employee then requests the trustees to pay the lump sum to the trustees of the discretionary trust.

The trustees of the discretionary trust can then apply the lump sum for the benefit of the surviving spouse but if any is left over, it will not be subject to IHT on the death of the surviving spouse.

'Back-to-back' policies

10.19   Most clients would love to increase their income, but at the same time not diminish their capital. The next scheme is a way of doing this. The client takes out an annuity. Part of the annuity is used to fund a life policy which on the death of the annuitant pays out the amount of capital used to purchase the annuity.

This scheme could be abused, and it will only work if the life policy would have been issued even if not linked to the annuity.

10.20 *Life insurance*

SUMMARY

10.20

(1)   Policies may be whole life, endowment or term policies; they may also be with profits, without profits or unit linked.

(2)   Policies can be used for the following purposes:

- protection of dependants;

- school fees;

- home purchase;

- protection against the death of a partner;

- paying IHT; or

- other schemes involving products of the life insurance industry.

(3)   A declaration of trust may be ineffective if the donor becomes bankrupt.

This chapter is in part based on an article which appeared in *Trust Law International* Vol 3 No 4. Readers are also referred to the chapter on insurance in *Tolley's Estate Planning*.

Chapter 11

Pensions

11.1 The rules for the taxation of pension schemes have been revised and simplified, and came into effect for the tax year 2006/2007. There is now one set of rules applying to all pension schemes.

There are two methods of providing pensions:

- the state scheme;
- pension schemes.

STATE SCHEME

11.2 In order to qualify for the state scheme, claimants or the spouse or civil partner of a claimant must have paid National Insurance contributions, although there are some exceptions to this. The state pension is payable as soon as retirement age has been reached. Pension credit ensures that every pensioner has a minimum level of income.

S2P, which replaces SERPS, provides additional income for some pensioners.

PENSION SCHEMES

Contributions

11.3 Members of pension schemes can contribute all of their earnings to a pension scheme subject to an overall annual limit. For 2006/2007 the annual limit is £215,000; this will increase each year. In order to see if the annual limit is exceeded, the contributions of both the employer and employee are aggregated together. If the member has no earnings, then the maximum contribution is £3,600.

Employees receive tax relief on their contributions within the annual limit. Employers can also deduct the contributions made to a pension scheme when calculating the profits of the company.

Lifetime allowance

11.4   There will be a lifetime allowance, and if the value of the member's pension pot exceeds the lifetime allowance, then a tax charge will arise in certain circumstances. The lifetime allowance for 2006/2007 is £1.5m; this will increase each year. Whether the pension fund exceeds the lifetime limit is determined when a benefit crystallisation event occurs; this will normally be when the employee begins to draw the pension, or when the employee attains the age of 75.

If a person's pension pot is in excess of the limit, then the excess will be subject to tax at 25% or 55% depending on whether the excess is taken as income or a cash sum.

Investments

11.5   Pension schemes can invest in a wide range of investments. However, there is no tax advantage with regard to investment in residential property, and there are other restrictions. If the member of a pension scheme or a family member makes a non-commercial use of any of the assets in the scheme, then there will be a 40% charge. Thus if a child of the member occupies premises owned by the scheme for business purposes, and does not pay any rent, there will be a 40% tax charge.

Retirement age

11.6   The retirement age is 55 for those born after 5 April 1960; for those born before it is 50. There are some exceptions to this, for example someone who has to retire due to ill health.

Benefits

11.7   It is left for individual schemes to define what benefits will be paid, provided that they comply with pension rules.

Benefits under such a scheme may be salary related, or alternatively they may be calculated on a money purchase basis. If they are salary related, they may be related to final salary or average salary. If it is final salary, it will be linked to the salary earned in the last year of employment. If it is an average, as its name implies, it will be linked to the average salary over, say, the last three years of employment.

A member of a pension scheme may draw an unsecured pension. If the member is under the age of 75 this could take the form of a tax-free lump sum. The member can then elect to be paid a pension from the rest of the fund, or alternatively the member could purchase some short-term annuities.

Another possibility is for the member to purchase an annuity.

If the member does not claim any pension until they have attained the age of 75, then the only pension the member can receive is a scheme pension, a lifetime annuity or an alternatively secured pension.

Death benefits

11.8   If a member of a pension scheme dies before retirement age, the fund can be paid out as a tax-free lump sum provided that it is still within the lifetime allowance. A dependant's pension can also be paid.

If the member dies after retirement, then the benefit will depend on what benefit the member was receiving.

IHT and lump sum death benefits

11.9   Frequently, pension schemes provide for the payment of a lump sum should the employee die before retirement age. If the payment is at the discretion of the trustees, it will not form part of the employee's estate for IHT purposes. On the other hand, if the employee's estate has a right to the money, it will form part of the employee's estate for IHT purposes.

If the death benefit does form part of the employee's estate, and is only payable to the employee's personal representatives, the benefit should be left to the spouse. The spouse may then be able to pass the money to the children if it is not required, making use of the inter vivos exemptions from IHT, or if they are not available, by making potentially exempt transfers.

It seems that no formalities are required for any such directions or requests to the trustees apart from compliance with the rules of the scheme (*Re Danish Bacon Co Ltd Staff Pension Fund Trusts [1971] 1 WLR 248*).

Chapter 12

Employee trusts, options and incentives

UNAPPROVED SCHEMES

12.1   Companies may wish to give benefits to their employees by means other than salaries, perhaps as a means of ensuring that key employees remain with the company, perhaps as a means of remunerating employees in a tax advantageous manner, or perhaps to reward loyalty and hard work.

There are two possible methods of doing this, by:

(a)   the grant of shares to an employee; or

(b)   the grant of options to employees to purchase shares.

Income tax

12.2   Whichever method is adopted, these will be classed as employment income, and will be taxed under s 9 of the Income Tax (Earnings and Pensions) Act 2003. The effect is as follows:

(i)   fully paid shares given to an employee – the employee will be taxed on the market value of those shares; or

(ii)   partly paid shares made available to an employee – the employee will be taxed on the difference between the cost of the shares and the price paid.

The emolument will be subject to the PAYE system. There may also be a liability for National Insurance ('NI') contributions. This liability is now to a large extent co-extensive with liability for PAYE.

Capital gains tax

12.3   There will be a liability to capital gains tax ('CGT') if the employee disposes of the shares at a profit; the base cost of the employee will be the amount on which he was charged income tax. However, taper relief will frequently mean that CGT is not a problem. As a result of the Finance Act 2000 taper relief applies to all holdings in unquoted companies, but prior to that Act, it only applied if the employee owned 5 % of the shares in the company.

As far as the company is concerned, there will not be any CGT liability with regard to the issue of new shares. If, however, existing shares are transferred, there may be a liability to CGT.

APPROVED SHARE SCHEMES

12.4   There are various statutory provisions providing for approved schemes; if a scheme is approved, the consequences are usually as follows:

Income tax

12.5   Normally there is no charge to income tax, and no duty is imposed on the employer to deduct tax under the PAYE system, but if there is any liability for income tax, the income must be taxed under the PAYE system.

National Insurance contributions

12.6   Usually there will be no liability.

Capital gains tax

12.7   The rules are the same as those which apply to unapproved schemes.

TYPES OF SCHEMES

12.8   Practitioners may encounter various schemes. Each of these will be considered in turn. Readers are warned, however, that it is a very complicated subject, and it is only possible to give an overview. A more detailed treatment is contained in *Revenue Law – Principles and Practice*, (published by Tottel Publishing) chapter 45 and *Tolley's Estate Planning*.

Unapproved employee trusts

12.9   Companies may establish discretionary trusts, usually as a means of providing additional incentives for employees, but also sometimes as a means of providing welfare benefits. The class of beneficiaries would include the employees and their dependants.

Payments of contributions by the company will normally be deductible in computing the profits of the company for corporation tax purposes in accordance with normal principles concerning the deductibility of expenses. This means that they must be of an income nature, and be incurred wholly and exclusively for the purposes of the trade. If that is not the purpose, then the contributions will not be deductible.

As it is a discretionary trust, the trustees are liable to income tax at 32.5% on all dividend income, and 40% on all other income. If the trustees distribute the income, then in the hands of the employee, the market value will be taxable as an emolument. As this could result in double taxation, ESC A68 permits the trustees to recover the tax they have paid subject to various conditions, although it is not possible for them to recover the 10% non-recoverable tax paid on dividends.

A transfer of shares to an employee trust is a deemed disposal at market value of those shares. However, s 239 of the Taxation of Chargeable Gains Act 1992 usually means that no CGT will be payable. When the section applies, the disposal and acquisition are to be treated, for the purposes of the Act, as being made for such consideration as to secure that neither a gain nor a loss accrues on the disposal.

If the trustees distribute shares to the beneficiaries, then the beneficiaries have become absolutely entitled to the shares. This triggers a deemed disposal of those shares at market value by the trustees, and if that is more than the base cost of the trustees, then there is a potential liability for CGT. This could result in a double charge to tax as the employee will be liable to income tax. ESC D35 provides that where in such circumstances as the employee is liable to income tax on the full market value of the assets transferred, the trustees will not be charged CGT on any gain arising on the transfer of those assets. The requirement that the employee should be liable to income tax on the full market value means that the concession will not apply if the employee has been given an option to purchase the shares as they will not be paying full market value. For this reason, these trusts are sometimes established offshore. It is probable that ss 86 and 87 of the Taxation of Chargeable Gains Act 1992 will not apply to these trusts as long as they are bona fide commercial arrangements.

Inheritance tax is payable on the creation of a discretionary trust, on every tenth anniversary, and when a beneficiary becomes absolutely entitled to the assets of the trust. If, however, the trust comes within ss 13, 28 and 86 of the Inheritance Tax Act 1984 no inheritance tax should be payable.

Unapproved schemes

Restricted securities (ss 422 – 434 ITEPA)

12.10 Companies may issue shares to employees which are subject to restrictions on the disposal of such shares, for example performance criteria.

If the shares will cease to be restricted securities within five years after acquisition, then there will be no charge to income tax on the difference between the market value of the shares and the price paid by the employee. However, there will be a charge to income tax if a chargeable event occurs, for example if the shares cease to be restricted. There may also be a charge to capital gains tax on a disposal of the shares.

Convertible securities (ss 435 – 446 ITEPA)

12.11 As the name implies, these are shares which can be converted into another class of shares, for example if certain performance targets are met.

When the shares are first given to the employee, they will be valued ignoring the conversion rights, so if the employee pays the full market value, there will not be any charge to income tax. However, if the employee pays less than the full market value, there will be a charge to income tax on the difference between the market value and the price paid.

If the shares are converted, then the employee will be taxed in accordance with formulae prescribed in ss 440 and 441 ITEPA.

Securities with artificially depressed market value (ss 446A – 446P)

12.12 It may be that the value of shares has been artificially depressed otherwise than for genuine commercial reasons. The employee will be assessed to income tax on the difference between the market value assuming that the value had not been artificially depressed and the actual market value or the price paid.

Securities acquired for less than market value (ss 446Q – 446W)

12.13 Securities may be issued for less then the market value, in which event there will be a charge to income tax on the difference between the market value and the price paid. If the purchase price is left outstanding as a debt due form the employee, it may be taxable as a loan if the employee is a higher paid employee or director. If the shares are issued at market value, but only part of the purchase price is paid, then it will be treated as if the company had made an interest free loan to the employee, and income tax will be payable.

Shares disposed of for more than the market value (ss 446X – 446Z)

12.14   A company may agree to buy back shares from an employee if the price drops. If that happens, there will be a charge to income tax on the difference.

Post-acquisition benefits (ss 447 – 450)

12.15   There will be a charge to income tax if an employee receives some benefit from a security which is not otherwise subject to income tax.

Share options (ss 471 – 484)

12.16   It may be that directors or employees will be given options to purchase shares. There is no charge to income tax on the grant of the option, but there will be a charge whenever shares are acquired pursuant to a right to acquire them.

Approved schemes

Approved share incentive plans (ss 488 – 515)

12.17   A company establishes a trust. The purpose of the trust is to hold shares given to or purchased by an employee. If the employee holds the shares in the trust for certain specified periods, there is no charge to income tax.

Approved savings-related share option schemes (ss 516 – 519)

12.18   These are different from other schemes in that the savings of the employee are used to fund the purchase of the shares. The company grants options to purchase shares, and at the same time the employee takes out a Save As You Earn ('SAYE') contract. The SAYE contract must last for three, five or seven years, and the employee must contribute a regular fixed amount each month, the minimum being £5, and the maximum being £250. At the end of the fixed period, a tax-free bonus is paid. The proceeds are then used to exercise options.

Approved company share option plans (ss 521 – 526)

12.19   There are limits on the value of the shares which can be made subject to options held by the employee.

Compliance with the various rules means that there is no charge to income tax on the grant or exercise of the option, although there will be a charge on any gain made on the sale of the shares.

Enterprise management initiatives (ss 527 et seq)

12.20   Paragraph 4 of Schedule 5 provides that an option is a qualifying option if it is granted for commercial reasons in order to recruit or retain key employees in a company, and not as part of a scheme or arrangement the main purpose, or one of the main purposes, of which is the avoidance of tax.

Paragraph 5(1) provides that an employee may not hold unexercised qualifying options which:

(a)   are in respect of shares with a total value of more than £100,000; and

(b)   were granted by reason of his employment;

    (i)   with one company; or

    (ii)   with two or more companies which are members of the same group.

An employee is an eligible employee in relation to the relevant company only if his committed time amounts to:

(a)   at least 25 hours per week; or

(b)   if less, 75 % of his working time.

If the conditions are complied with, there is no charge to income tax on the grant of the option or the exercise of the option, but there may be a liability for CGT.

SUMMARY

12.21
- Schemes for rewarding employees may be approved or unapproved.

12.21 *Employee trusts, options and incentives*

- If a scheme is approved, generally no income tax is payable, but capital gains tax may be payable on any gain.

- If the scheme is unapproved, income tax and capital gains tax may be payable.

Chapter 13

Settlements and Trusts

PURPOSE

13.1   A client with assets to spare may be prepared to make absolute gifts of those assets to relatives, and in many cases this will be satisfactory. It has the great merit of simplicity in that the gift will be a potentially exempt transfer, and IHT will not be payable if the donor survives for seven years. In addition, the expense of administering a trust will be avoided, and the beneficiary can do what he likes with the assets.

For a variety of reasons, some clients will not wish to make absolute gifts, and instead will wish to create settlements. A donor may not consider that children or grandchildren are mature enough to deal with large sums of money, or it is possible that more children or grandchildren will be born, or the donor may wish to retain some control over the property. This last aspect is particularly relevant with small companies where the donor may wish to divest himself of shares, but may still want to retain control of the company; he can achieve this object by appointing himself a trustee.

The Finance Act 2006 has substantially changed the rules with regard to the taxation of trusts; the rules are discussed later in this chapter.

WHICH TYPE OF TRUST?

13.2   A donor can choose between the following types of trust:

- precatory trusts;
- fixed trusts;
- discretionary trusts;
- secret trusts;
- trusts for bereaved minors;
- powers of appointment;

- protective trusts; and

- trusts for disabled persons.

Precatory trusts

13.3   This is where the donor gives money or property to an individual expressing the wish that the individual should use the property in a certain manner, but without imposing any binding obligation. An example of such a gift is:

> 'I give £500,000 to A and it is my wish but without imposing any trust on A that he should distribute this money in a manner I shall indicate to him'.

The disadvantage of a precatory trust is that the beneficiary may keep all the money for himself.

Precatory trusts are often used in connection with jewellery. A testatrix may leave a will giving jewellery to executors or a daughter, but expressing the wish without imposing any binding obligation on the executors or daughter, that the executors or daughter will distribute the jewellery in accordance with a note the testatrix will leave. If the executors and daughter decide to keep the jewellery, there is little anyone named in the note could do about it, but most executors and daughters will feel a considerable moral obligation to comply with the wishes of the testatrix.

Fixed trusts

13.4   These are trusts where the interests of the beneficiaries are clearly defined. They can be inflexible, but there are ways of avoiding this inflexibility; for example a life tenant could be given power to appoint, with a gift in default of appointment, or the trustees could be given power to advance all the capital.

If there is a gift in remainder to the children, the settlor should decide whether they should have contingent or vested interests, and whether the class closing rules should be modified.

Discretionary trusts

13.5   These are trusts where the trustees have a discretion as to which member of a class of beneficiaries is to benefit. They have the merit of flexibility, but the settlor or testator loses control over the ultimate destination of the property. This loss of control can be alleviated to a certain extent by appointing the settlor a trustee in the case of an inter vivos settlement. The settlor can also indicate to the trustees how he would like the trust and discretions exercised, and although the trustees are in no way bound by these suggestions, they will often give effect to them.

In exercising their discretion, the trustees must consider all possible beneficiaries. If the trustees refuse to exercise their discretion, potential beneficiaries can apply to the court. The court can remove the trustees, or exercise the discretion itself.

Secret trusts

13.6   These are useful if the testator does not want to disclose the identity of a beneficiary. If it is a fully secret trust, it must be communicated during the testator's lifetime, either before or after the will. If it is a half secret trust, there is some doubt about whether the trust can be communicated after the will. In *Re Keen, Evershed v Griffiths [1937] Ch 236 CA*, T gave his trustees £10,000 to be held upon trust and disposed of by them among such persons 'as may be notified by me to them or either of them during my lifetime ...'. Shortly before he executed the will, T gave the trustees a sealed envelope containing the name of a beneficiary. It was held that the trust was ineffective, and Lord Wright expressed the view in effect that communication of the half secret trust after the will was executed would be ineffective.

Trusts for bereaved minors (formerly accumulation and maintenance settlements)

13.7   Prior to the Finance Act 2006 settlors or testators could create trusts for the benefit of young persons and provided various conditions were satisfied, these enjoyed privileged status as far as IHT is concerned, but not as far as CGT or income tax was concerned. They were known as accumulation and maintenance settlements. It is not now possible to create accumulation and maintenance settlements, but instead parents can create trusts for bereaved minors in their wills. The taxation consequences of these trusts are considered below.

Powers of appointment

13.8   When there is no restriction on who can be the beneficiaries, the power is a general power. It is a special power where the class of beneficiaries is limited. If it is a special power, care should be taken in drafting the power. The class of beneficiaries should not be too restricted, but on the other hand it should not include persons whom the client would not have wanted to benefit. For example, a power to appoint for the benefit of my son A might permit appointments in favour of A's wife and children. It should also be remembered that the person empowered to make the appointment cannot delegate the exercise of the discretion – appointment in favour of a discretionary trust is not permissible.

In *Re Hay's Settlement Trusts [1981] 3 All ER 786* Megarry V-C said at page 79:

> '... the duties of a trustee which are specific to a mere power seem to be threefold ... the trustee must, first, consider periodically whether or not he should exercise the power; second, consider the range of objects of the power; and third consider the appropriateness of individual appointments'.

Protective trusts

13.9   A further possibility is the creation of protective trusts within s 33 of the Trustee Act 1925. The idea behind protective trusts is that some beneficiaries need protection from themselves – they may be spendthrifts, or likely to go bankrupt.

Section 33(1) provides that if property is directed to be held on protective trusts for the benefit of any person (the principal beneficiary) for his life or for any less period, the income is to be paid to the principal beneficiary until an event happens which could result in the principal beneficiary losing the right to receive the income or any part of the income. This event can be the act of the principal beneficiary – for example, assigning his interest – or the operation of law – for example, if the principal beneficiary becomes bankrupt.

Section 33(1)(ii) provides that if the principal beneficiary is deprived of his right to receive the income or part of it, the income is to be applied for the maintenance or support or otherwise for the benefit of:

> '(a)   the principal beneficiary, and his or her wife or husband, if any, and his or her children or more remote issue, if any; or
>
> (b)   if there is no wife or husband or issue of the principal beneficiary in existence, the principal beneficiary and the persons who would, if he were actually dead, be entitled to the trust property ...;
>
> as the trustees in their absolute discretion, without being liable to account for the exercise of such discretion, think fit.'

Trusts for vulnerable or disabled persons

13.10   Trusts for vulnerable or disabled persons may qualify for special treatment as far as tax is concerned; this is considered later.

COMPLETELY AND INCOMPLETELY CONSTITUTED TRUSTS

13.11   There are two equitable maxims which apply:

- 'Equity will not perfect an imperfect gift.'
- 'Equity will not assist a volunteer.'

Usually this aspect will not cause any problems in the case of wills. However, if a settlor is creating an inter vivos trust, it is essential that the trust property is properly vested in the trustees, or that there has been a declaration of trust.

Land

13.12   The settlor must execute a transfer of the legal estate.

Shares

13.13   In *Milroy v Lord (1862) 4 De GF & J 264* the settlor executed a voluntary deed purporting to transfer 50 shares in a bank to Samuel Lord, and at a later date gave him the share certificates. The shares were to be held on trust for the plaintiffs. The settlor had granted Lord a general power of attorney which empowered him to transfer the shares. Registration in the books of the bank was necessary in order to effect the transfer, but this was never done. It was held that no trust existed. Turner LJ said:

> '... in order to render a voluntary settlement valid and effectual, the settlor must have done everything which, according to the nature of the property comprised in the settlement, was necessary to be done in order to transfer the property and render the settlement binding upon him'.

In *Re Fry [1946] Ch 312* Ambrose Fry was domiciled and lived in America. He executed a transfer of shares in an English company. Under regulations then in force, the consent of the Treasury to the transfer was necessary. Fry signed the necessary forms to obtain the consent, but died before the consent was obtained. It was held that the gift was ineffective.

In *Re Rose [1952] Ch 499* the settlor owned shares in a company, and under the articles of association of the company the directors could refuse to register a transfer. On 30 March the settlor executed two transfers of shares in the company, and they were registered on 30 June. For tax purposes it was necessary to decide if the transfer was effective on 30 March or 30 June. It was held that the transfer was effective on 30 March.

In *Pennington v Waine [2002] WTLR 387* the articles of a association of a company incorporated Part II of Table A to the Companies Act 1948 subject to certain amendments. This meant that there were conflicting articles. Article 8(A) permitted shares to be transferred to a privileged class, which included the executors of a shareholder; article 8(B) prohibited the transfer of any shares unless they had first been offered to the existing members at a fair value. However, regulation 30 of Table A provided that any person becoming entitled to a share in consequence of the death or bankruptcy of a member could elect to be registered as a member or have some person nominated by him registered as a member.

AC signed a share transfer transferring 400 shares in C Ltd to her nephew, HC. The transfer was sent to the auditors of the company, who took no further action. HC was appointed a director of the company. It was held that the transfer was effective to transfer the shares despite Article 8(B).

There was a sequel to this case. Whilst it was held in Pennington that the transfer was effective, it had not been registered with the company. Has there been a breach of the articles of the company? In *Hurst v Crampton Bros (Coopers) Ltd [2003] WTLR 659* it was held that the transfer of shares was a breach of this article. It was held that 'transfer' meant parting with the share, and that its meaning was not restricted by the reference to 'sale' later on, and so there had been a breach of the articles of association of the company.

There was a further sequel to this case in *Pennington v Waine [2003] WTLR 1011.* In her will AC made specific gifts of some of the shares in C Ltd to HC and PW. Her residuary estate was to be divided between sixteen beneficiaries. On her death, it was argued that the rights of pre-emption adeemed the specific gifts, so that they fell into the residuary estate.

This argument was rejected. C had made a specific gift of the rights to the shares, and this gift of the rights was not adeemed by the pre-emption rights.

There has been yet another sequel, *Pennington v Waine [2005] WTLR 559.* In her will, AC appointed JP and JR as executors; JR was removed as an executor and replaced by SB.

It was held:

- Articles 8(A) and (B) and Regulations 30 and 31 did not fit together very well. If there was a conflict, articles 8(A) and (B) were to prevail.

- JP and JR were within the privileged class under Article 8(A). JR could remain a member even though she had been removed as an executor.

- JP and JR could transfer the shares to persons who would hold it on the same trusts as themselves without triggering the pre-emption provisions in Article 8(B).

- With regard to the 400 shares, the subject of the lifetime gift, the court should not dictate to the valuers how a fair value should be fixed. It should be a current valuation.

- The only litigation to be considered was that between the company and third parties.

- Article 8(B) permitted the purchase of part of a shareholding. The auditors needed to determine a value for each share by valuing the company as a whole and then dividing that by the number of issued shares.

As far as practitioners are concerned, the message is clear – if you are dealing with a transfer of shares in a private company, make sure that there is compliance with the restrictions in the articles.

Chattels

13.14   Normally these will be transferred by delivery. However, in *Re Cole [1964] Ch 175* H bought and furnished a house whilst W and his family lived elsewhere. When W saw the house, H said 'It's all yours.' H went bankrupt. It was held that there had not been a gift of the chattels.

Declaration of trust

13.15   Instead of appointing trustees, the settlor can declare himself to be a trustee of trust property. However, the settlor must clearly show that he intends to become a trustee of the property. If this is not the case, the declaration will be ineffective. Two cases illustrate this point. In *Richards v Delbridge (1874) LR 18 Eq 11* Delbridge was the tenant of premises on which he carried on business as a bone manure merchant. He endorsed the following words on the lease:

> 'This deed and all thereto belonging I give to Edward Bennetto Richards from this time forth with all stock in trade.'

Delbridge then died. It was held that the lease and business passed under the will.

In *Jones v Lock (1865) 1 Ch App 25* Jones produced a cheque for £900 payable to himself, and said:

> 'Look you here, I give this to baby; it is for himself, and I am going to put it away for him, and will give him a great deal more along with it.'

He also said 'it is his own, and he may do what he likes with it'. It was held that there had been no effective gift, or declaration of trust.

PERPETUITIES AND ACCUMULATIONS

Perpetuities

13.16   Although the 'wait and see' rule has taken much of the sting out of the rules against perpetuities, practitioners should at least pay regard to them. Gifts must now vest within lives in being plus 21 years, or a period of years not exceeding 80 years. There are also some statutory presumptions about child-bearing:

- a male can have a child at the age of 14 years or over, but not under that age; and

- a female can have a child at the age of 12 years or over, but not under that age or over the age of 55 years.

A gift in a will to all my grandchildren contingent on them attaining the age of 25 might infringe the rule against perpetuities. The lives in being are the children and grandchildren living at the date of death of the testator, and it is possible that a grandchild born after the death of the testator might satisfy the contingency outside the period of lives in being at the date of death of the testator plus 21 years. The gift is not void at the outset – it would be necessary to wait and see if it vests within the perpetuity period. If it does, then it is valid. If it does not, then it is invalid. If the gift had been limited to those grandchildren living at the date of the death of the testator, there would not be a problem as the gift must then vest within the perpetuity period.

Accumulations

13.17   The trust must not infringe the accumulation periods permitted by the Law of Property Act 1925 and the Perpetuities and Accumulations Act 1964. The permitted periods are as follows:

- the life of the grantor or settlor;

- a term of 21 years from the death of the settlor;

- the duration of the minority or respective minorities of any person or persons living or en ventre sa mère at the death of the settlor;

- the duration of the minority or respective minorities of any person or persons who under the limitations of the instrument directing the accumulation would for the time being, if of full age, be entitled to the income directed to be accumulated;

- a term of 21 years from the making of the disposition; and

- the duration of the minority or respective minorities of any person or persons in being at that date.

There is no equivalent to the 'wait and see' rule as there is with perpetuities.

TAXATION OF SETTLEMENTS APART FROM IMMEDIATE POST DEATH INTERESTS, TRUSTS FOR BEREAVED MINORS AND TRUSTS FOR DISABLED PERSONS

13.18   The Finance Act 2006 has created three new types of trust – immediate post death interests, trusts for bereaved minors and trusts for disabled persons. The IHT treatment of these trusts is considered later.

Inheritance tax treatment of all settlements apart from immediate post death interests, trusts for bereaved minors and disabled persons

13.19   If a settlement is created inter vivos, this is a chargeable transfer, and if the settlor bears the IHT, grossing up may apply. The gift will also have to be cumulated with all the chargeable transfers made in the seven years before the gift in order to determine the rate of IHT. If IHT is payable, it will be at one-half of the rates applicable on death.

If the settlement is created by will, the settled assets will be part of the testator's estate, and will be subject to IHT in accordance with the normal principles; these are discussed in chapter 16.

Exemptions and reliefs

13.20

It may be possible to claim the following exemptions and reliefs:

(a)   Annual exemption. This is currently £3,000 per annum – in so far as it is not used in any one year, it can be carried forward to the next year.

(b)   Gifts in consideration of marriage. Transfers of value made by gifts in consideration of marriage are exempt to the extent that the values transferred by such transfers made by any one transferor in respect of any one marriage (calculated as values on which no tax is chargeable) do not exceed:

   (i)   in the case of a gift by a parent of a party to the marriage, £5,000;

   (ii)   in the case of grandparents and great-grandparents of a party to the marriage, £2,500;

   (iii)   in any other case, £1,000.

   (s 22 of the Inheritance Taxes Act 1984).

   Note that each parent can give £5,000, a possible total of £20,000. The marriage exemption is available on the creation of settlements, provided that the beneficiaries come within certain heads specified in s 22(4).

(c)   Gifts for the maintenance of the family. A disposition is not a transfer of value if it is made by one party to a marriage in favour of the other party or a child of either party and is:

   (i)   for the maintenance of the other party; or

   (ii)   for the maintenance, education or training of the child for a period ending not later than the year in which he attains the age of 18 or, after attaining that age, ceases to undergo full-time education and training.

   Similarly a disposition is not a transfer of value if it is made in favour of a child who is not in the care of a parent of his and is for his maintenance, education or training for a period ending not later than the year in which:

   (i)   he attains the age of 18; or

   (ii)   after attaining that age, he ceases to undergo full-time education or training.

      However, gifts to a person within (ii) are exempt only if before attaining that age the child has for substantial periods been in the care of the person making the disposition.

In addition, a disposition is not a transfer of value if it is made in favour of a dependent relative of the person making the disposition and is a reasonable provision for his care and maintenance. It will also not be a transfer of value if it is in favour of an illegitimate child of the person making the disposition and is for the maintenance, education or training of the child for a period ending not later than the year in which he attains the age of 18 or, after attaining that age, ceases to undergo full-time education or training.

'Maintenance' is not defined – could it include the transfer of capital assets?

'Dependent relative' is defined in s 11(6) as meaning in relation to any person:

(i) a relative of his, or of his spouse, who is incapacitated by old age or infirmity from maintaining himself; or

(ii) his mother or his spouse's mother, if she is widowed, or living apart from her husband, or a single woman in consequence of dissolution or annulment of marriage.

(d) Gifts of excluded property. No IHT is payable in respect of gifts of excluded property. Excluded property comprises the following:

(i) Property situated outside the UK if the person beneficially entitled to it is an individual domiciled outside the UK (s 6(1)).

(ii) A reversionary interest unless:

1 it has at any time been acquired (whether by the person entitled to it or by a person previously entitled to it) for a consideration in money or money's worth; or

II it is one to which the settlor or his spouse is or has been beneficially entitled (s 48(1)).

(iii) Section 48(3) provides that where property comprised in a settlement is situated outside the UK:

1 the property (but not a reversionary interest in the property) is excluded property unless the settlor was domiciled in the UK at the time when the settlement was made; and

II s 6(1) applies to a reversionary interest in the property, but does not otherwise apply in relation to that property.

(e) Variations and disclaimers. Beneficiaries under a will or the intestacy rules can vary the will so as to create settlements. If the variation is within two years of death, and the appropriate elections are made, then the deceased will be treated as having made the settlement.

(f)   Business property relief and agricultural property relief. Business property relief operates to reduce the value of the property by 100 per cent in the following cases:

   (i)   property consisting of a business or an interest in a business;

   (ii)   shares in or securities of a company which are unquoted and which (either by themselves or together with other such shares or securities owned by the transferor) gave the transferor control of the company immediately before the transfer;

   (iii)   any unquoted shares in a company.

   Relief of 50 per cent is available on the following:

   (i)   shares in or securities of a company which are quoted and which (either by themselves or together with other such shares or securities owned by the transferor) gave the transferor control of the company immediately before the transfer;

   (ii)   any land, or building, machinery or plant which, immediately before the transfer, was used wholly or mainly for the purposes of a business carried on by a company of which the transferor then had control or by a partnership of which he was then a partner;

   (iii)   any land or building, machinery or plant which, immediately before the transfer, was used wholly or mainly for the purposes of a business carried on by the transferor and was settled property in which he was then beneficially entitled to an interest in possession.

(s 105 of the Inheritance Tax Act 1984).

Shares are quoted if they are quoted on a recognised stock exchange (s 105(1ZA)).

Section 106 provides that property is not relevant business property in relation to a transfer of value unless it has been owned by the transferor throughout the two years immediately preceding the transfer.

Property qualifying for 100 per cent relief can be transferred to a settlement without incurring any charge to IHT. However, in order to claim the relief on death within seven years, the trustees must still own the property or replacement property, and the trustees will have to satisfy the qualifying conditions themselves before they can claim the reliefs.

Section 116 of the Inheritance Tax Act 1984 permits the value of agricultural property to be reduced by 100 per cent if:

   (i)   the interest of the transferor in the property immediately before the transfer carries the right to vacant possession or the right to obtain it within the next 24 months; or

(ii) it is notwithstanding the terms of the tenancy valued at an amount broadly equivalent to vacant possession value; or

(iii) the interest of the transferor in the property immediately before the transfer does not carry the right to vacant possession within 24 months because the property is let on a tenancy beginning on or after 1 September 1995 (see ESC F17).

In other cases the relief is 50 per cent.

Section 117 provides that relief is not available unless:

(i) it was occupied by the transferor for the purposes of agriculture throughout the period of two years ending with the date of transfer; or

(ii) it was owned by him throughout the period of seven years ending with that date and was throughout that period occupied (by him or another) for the purposes of agriculture.

A farmer who is an owner-occupier will qualify for 100 per cent relief if he has owned the land for two years.

If the land is let, it will still qualify for 100 per cent relief if the owner has owned it for seven years and can recover possession within 24 months, or the tenancy was granted after 1 September 1995.

(g) Section 146(6) provides that anything which is done in compliance with an order under the Inheritance (Provision for Family and Dependants) Act 1975 or occurs on the coming into force of such an order, and which would (apart from this subsection) constitute an occasion on which tax is chargeable under any provision, other than s 79, shall not constitute such an occasion; and where an order under the 1975 Act provides for property to be settled or for the variation of a settlement, and (apart from this subsection) tax would be charged under s 52(1) on the coming into force of the order, s 52(1) shall not apply.

(h) Use the nil rate band – if one spouse does not have the assets to do so, the other spouse should transfer sufficient assets to enable him or her to do so. However, care should be taken not to infringe the rules against associated operations. The property should not be transferred to the other spouse subject to any condition that it is to be transferred into a settlement.

The ten-yearly or principal charge

13.21 Section 64 imposes a charge on relevant property, which is defined by s 58(1) as settled property in which no qualifying interest in possession subsists. It also includes interests in possession if the following conditions are satisfied:

(a) an individual is beneficially entitled to the interest in possession,

(b) the individual became beneficially entitled to the interest in possession on or after 22 March 2006, and

(c) the interest in possession is not an immediate post death interest, not a disabled person's interest, and not a transitional serial interest.

The value charged is the value of the relevant property comprised in the settlement, less agricultural property relief and business property relief.

The settlement has its own cumulative total, which is defined in s 66(5) as the aggregate of:

(a) the values transferred by any chargeable transfers made by the settlor in the period of seven years ending with the day on which the settlement commenced; and

(b) the amounts on which any charges to tax were imposed under s 65 in respect of the settlement in the ten years before the anniversary concerned.

Section 65 imposes a charge to IHT inter alia when property leaves a settlement; it is discussed in the next section.

The rate of tax is 30 per cent of the rate which would be charged on a lifetime chargeable transfer (6 per cent).

The effect of these provisions is that on the tenth anniversary of the creation of every trust apart from immediate post death interests, trusts for disabled persons and trusts for bereaved minors, it is necessary to value all the property in the settlement. If any of the property qualifies for business property relief or agricultural property relief, the appropriate percentage of the value of that property can be deducted.

The next step is to determine the rate of tax. This is done by adding together the values transferred to any other discretionary trusts created in the seven years prior to the one which is the subject of the ten-year charge, to which must be added the value of any capital transferred to beneficiaries in the ten years prior to the anniversary concerned. Assuming that there are only two bands for IHT, if there is nothing left of the nil rate band, then the whole of the assets in the settlement will be subject to IHT at 6%. If there is anything left of the nil rate band, then it can be offset against the settlement.

Exit or proportionate charges

13.22 These arise in two situations:

(a)   where property comprised in a settlement ceases to be relevant property; and

(b)   if (a) does not apply, where the trustees of the settlement make a disposition as a result of which the value of relevant property comprised in the settlement is less than it would be but for the disposition.

(s 65(1)).

A termination of the settlement, or the distribution of some of the property to the beneficiaries, both fall within (a).

When (a) does not apply, (b) will catch any disposition by the trustees of the settlement which reduces the value of the relevant property comprised in the settlement.

Section 65(4) provides that there is no charge if the event in question occurs in a quarter beginning with the day on which the settlement commenced or with a ten-year anniversary. Thus there will be no charge if the event giving rise to the charge occurs within three months of the establishment of the settlement, or an anniversary charge.

Section 65(5) provides that tax will not be charged in respect of a payment of costs and expenses so far as fairly attributable to relevant property. Neither is tax payable if the payment is income of any person for the purposes of income tax.

The amount chargeable is the amount by which the value of the relevant property in the settlement is less immediately after the event in question than it would be but for the event (s 65(2)).

The rate of tax is a proportion of the rate charged on the last ten-year anniversary. The proportion is so many fortieths as there are complete successive quarters in the period beginning with the most recent anniversary and ending with the day before the occasion of the charge (s 69(4)). Thus, if four whole years have elapsed since the last ten-yearly charge, the rate of tax will be 16/40 of the rate charged on the last ten-year anniversary, 16 quarters having elapsed since the last ten-yearly charge.

Special rules apply to the calculation of the exit charge before the tenth anniversary.

Note that exit charges apply to all trusts apart from immediate post death interests, trusts for disabled persons and trusts for bereaved minors.

IHT ON IMMEDIATE POST DEATH INTERESTS, TRUSTS FOR BEREAVED MINORS AND TRUSTS FOR DISABLED PERSONS

13.23   The Finance Act 2006 substantially changed the rules with regard to the IHT treatment of trusts, and created two new types of trust, the immediate post death interest and the trust for bereaved minors, and amended the rules with regard to trusts for disabled persons.

What all this means is that if someone creates a trust in their lifetime and it is not a trust for a disabled person, then as far as IHT is concerned it will be taxed as described above. This means that inheritance tax will be payable on the creation of the trust at 20% on all assets transferred to the trust in excess of the nil rate band or what is left of the nil rate band. In addition, there will also be a charge to inheritance tax every ten years on the assets in the trust. There will also be an exit or proportionate charge to inheritance tax whenever the trustees hand out or transfer any capital to a beneficiary.

Trusts in wills will also be taxed as outlined above unless they come within the three exemptions, which are fairly narrowly targeted.

Immediate post death interest

13.24   In order for a settlement to qualify as an immediate post death interest, the following conditions must be satisfied:

(1)   The settlement must be effected by will or under the law relating to intestacy.

(2)   The life tenant must have become beneficially entitled to the interest in possession on the death of the testator or intestate.

(3)   Section 71A does not apply to the property in which the interest subsists or the interest is not a disabled person's interest.

(4)   Condition 3 has been satisfied at all times since the life tenant became beneficially entitled to the interest in possession.

The first condition requires that the settlement must arise on death, and so the settlement must either be created in a will, or it could arise under the intestacy rules. As no doubt readers are aware, if someone dies intestate leaving a spouse or civil partner and children and had a large enough estate, then the surviving spouse will get a life interest in one half of the residuary estate. That will be an immediate post death interest.

The second condition requires that the life tenant should become beneficially entitled to the interest on the death of the testator or intestate. This means that the life interest cannot be postponed until some future time, but a survivorship clause not exceeding six months would be in order.

Section 71A is concerned with trusts for bereaved minors. So if the trust is a trust for a bereaved minor, then it is not an immediate post death interest. In addition, if it is a trust for a disabled person, it is not an immediate post death interest.

If an immediate post death interest is created, the usual charging rules apply, so that if the death estate is above the nil rate band, or the nil rate band has been absorbed by inter vivos gifts in the seven years before death, IHT will be payable. If the spouse or civil partner of the deceased is the life tenant, and is domiciled in the United Kingdom, no IHT will be payable because of spouse exemption.

Trusts for disabled persons

13.25   The second exemption is concerned with trusts for disabled persons as set out in s 89 IHTA. To come within s 89, the beneficiary must be a disabled person as defined in the section. In effect they must be mentally incapable or in receipt of attendance allowance or disability living allowance. In addition, as originally drafted, the disabled person must be entitled to one half of any capital the trustees hand out.

If a settlor creates a trust in his lifetime for a disabled person, and complies with the rules in s 89(4) of the Inheritance Tax Act 1984, then it will not be taxed as if it was a trust without an interest in possession or a discretionary trust; instead it will be taxed as if the disabled person had a life interest. This means that there will be no charge to inheritance tax if the settlor creates one of these trusts during his or her lifetime. It will be a PET, and as long as the settlor survives for seven years, it will not have any adverse IHT consequences.

If the testator creates a trust for a disabled person in his will, then IHT will be payable on the death of the testator if the testator's estate is large enough, or the nil rate band has been absorbed by lifetime gifts in the seven years prior to death, in accordance with the normal rules about the taxation of estates on death. Again the disabled person will be deemed to have an interest in possession in the trust assets.

Whether the settlement is created in a will or is a lifetime creation, there will not be any ten-yearly or exit or proportionate charges, but IHT may be payable on the death of the disabled person as the settled assets will be aggregated with the disabled person's personal assets.

The definition of a trust for a disabled person has also been extended so as to include trusts where the disabled person has a life interest. This was not necessary under the old law as if a disabled person had a life interest, then the disabled person would be deemed to own the underlying trust assets as far as IHT was concerned. Under the new law such trusts will only be taxed as if the disabled person had a life interest if it was made in a will.

So a life interest trust for a disabled person will be taxed as if it was an immediate post death interest even if it was made during the lifetime of the settlor.

Under the existing law, a person who knew that they were going to become a disabled person could not create a trust for a disabled person for himself or herself.

Self settlements by disabled persons are now allowed, and will be taxed as if they were trusts with an interest in possession. The person will have to convince the Revenue that he or she had a condition which meant that they were likely to become a disabled person. So someone in the early stages of Alzheimer's disease who still retains mental capacity could create a trust for a disabled person. However, there must be no interest in possession, and if any of the assets are handed out, the disabled person must be entitled to everything. In effect a self settlement will have to take the form of a discretionary trust with the settlor within the class of beneficiaries. There would also have to be a term that if the trustees handed out anything, then the whole must go to the settlor, the disabled person.

Section 89(4) defines a disabled person as a person who, when the property was transferred into the settlement, was:

(a) incapable by reason of mental disorder within the meaning of the Mental Health Act 1983, of administering his property or managing his own affairs; or

(b) in receipt of an attendance allowance or disability living allowance by virtue of entitlement to the care component at the highest or middle rate.

Position of the life tenant under an immediate post death interest or the disabled person under a trust for a disabled person

13.26   For IHT purposes the life tenant is deemed to own the trust assets (s 49(1) of the Inheritance Tax Act 1984). As a consequence, the remainderman owns nothing – a reversionary interest is normally excluded property for IHT purposes (s 48 of the Inheritance Tax Act 1984). If a person is entitled to the income for a period less than life, he will still be deemed to own the trust assets. If there is more than one life tenant, they will be deemed to own the appropriate share of the trust fund, so if there are two life tenants equally entitled, they will be deemed to own one-half of the trust assets each (s 50(1) and (2) of the Inheritance Tax Act 1984). If the beneficiary is entitled to a fixed amount of income, and any left over is paid to another beneficiary, the first beneficiary will be deemed to be entitled to whatever proportion of the trust fund will yield the amount of income. As this could be used as a means of minimising IHT, there are anti-avoidance provisions in s 50(3) of the Inheritance Tax Act 1984.

The beneficiary under a disabled persons trust will also be deemed to own the underlying trust assets.

Death of the life tenant under an immediate post death interest or disabled person

13.27   On the death of the life tenant, or disabled person, for IHT purposes he is treated as being the owner of all the underlying trust assets (ss 5 and 49 of the Inheritance Tax Act 1984). The trust assets must be aggregated with the personal estate of the life tenant or the disabled person, and any IHT due must be apportioned between the trust assets and the personal estate in the proportions they bear to each other. The trustees are liable for the proportion of IHT due in respect of the trust property, and the deceased's personal representatives are liable for the IHT due in respect of the personal estate, if any.

Inter vivos termination by life tenant under an immediate post death interest

13.28   What happens if the life tenant assigns or surrenders his interest? An interest in possession may terminate during the life of the person entitled to the life interest, for example because the person entitled has a determinable interest, and the determining event occurs. This will be a PET provided that the property is held as:

(a)   a gift to another individual; or

(b)   a gift into a trust for a disabled person ; or

(c)   a gift into a bereaved minor's trust on the coming to an end of an immediate post death interest.

(ss 3A and 49(1) of the Inheritance Tax Act 1984 as amended).

If that is not the case, then there will be a chargeable disposal for IHT purposes – the life tenant will be deemed to have created a trust taxed as described in paras 13.19–13.22.

If the life tenant sells his interest, he will be making a PET of the value of the trust assets less any consideration received for the life interest (s 52(2)). The assignee of the life interest becomes a tenant pur autre vie, and there is a possibility of charge to IHT when the assignor dies. The assignee will then make a PET.

Frequently settlements contain an express power of advancement authorising the trustees to advance capital to a life tenant. An advancement to the life tenant will not normally result in a charge to IHT as the life tenant is already deemed to own the trust assets, and so there has been no reduction in the value of anyone's estate.

If the life tenant surrenders part or the whole of his life interest, and has not used the annual exemption or the gift in consideration of marriage exemption, the life tenant may give notice to the trustees that these exemptions are available, and the trustees can make use of them.

The same treatment will apply to trusts for disabled persons, although such a person would need the consent of the Court of Protection to any lifetime termination if they are mentally incapable.

Trusts for bereaved minors

13.29   It has been very common for testators to give legacies to children or grandchildren contingent on attaining a certain age –18, 21, 25. Strictly they should have been taxed as if they were trusts without an interest in possession or discretionary trusts. This meant that inheritance tax would have to be paid on their creation during someone's lifetime if the assets transferred were in excess of the nil rate band, or the nil rate band had been absorbed by other discretionary trusts in the seven years prior to the current one. In addition, there would be a charge to inheritance tax every ten years and also whenever any capital was paid out from the trust by the trustees.

Such trusts usually became accumulation and maintenance settlements, and received special treatment as far as IHT was concerned. The special treatment was that if they were created in a lifetime settlement it was not a chargeable disposal for inheritance tax purposes, but was treated as a PET. If the accumulation and maintenance settlement was created in a will, then the normal rules for the taxation of an estate on death applied. IHT was payable if the death estate was large enough, or if the NRB has been absorbed by lifetime gifts. However, once the accumulation and maintenance trust was going, there was no further charge to inheritance tax. There were no ten yearly charges or exit or proportionate charges.

This special treatment will now only apply to trusts for bereaved minors.

Various conditions have to be satisfied before a trust will be treated as a trust for bereaved minors. The most important points are that it is only parents who can create such a trust. In addition, the trust must be in a will. Furthermore, the children must become absolutely entitled to everything in the trust on attaining the age of 18. This means that they must be entitled to all capital in the trust, and any accumulated income.

So if grandparents create a trust for the benefit of grandchildren, the IHT treatment will be as outlined above in paras 13.19 – 13.22. It parents create a trust during their lifetime for the benefit of the children contingent on attaining the age of 18, then again the IHT treatment will be as outlined in those paras.

The statutory trusts which arise on intestacy will also qualify as a trust for a bereaved minor.

It is also possible to have 18 to 25 trusts. These are trusts where the contingency is attaining an age no greater than 25. This means that if there is a gift to a bereaved minor contingent on them attaining the age of 25, there will be a charge to IHT when the child attains 25. The rate of tax will be 4.2% in so far as the assets are in excess of the NRB. However, if the assets are within the NRB, there should be no problem. This treatment only applies to settlements created by parents for the benefit of their children. In addition, the settlement must be in a will. It does not apply to settlements created by grandparents.

EXISTING TRUSTS

13.30   If a beneficiary becomes absolutely entitled on the termination of a life interest, then the old regime applies.

If the trust does not terminate when the life interest ends, then the continuing trust will be taxed as if it was a trust without an interest in possession unless a transitional serial interest comes into existence.

In general terms a transitional serial interest is one where a life interest under a settlement created before 22 March 2006 terminates before 6 April 2008 and another life interest comes into existence, or where it terminates after 6 April 2008 and the spouse or civil partner is entitled to another life interest.

Existing accumulation and maintenance settlements where the beneficiary becomes absolutely entitled on attaining the age of 18 will be subject to the old regime. If that is not the case, then they will be taxed as if they were trusts without an interest in possession from 6 April 2008.

CAPITAL GAINS TAX

Lifetime creation of trust

13.31   This is a chargeable disposal for capital gains tax purposes, although holdover and taper relief may be available. CGT may be payable at 40 per cent depending on the rate of tax paid by the settlor. The settlor and the trustees are connected persons, and therefore any loss made on the creation of the settlement can only be offset against gains made on another disposal to the same settlement (s 18(3) of the Taxation of Chargeable Gains Act 1992). It cannot be offset against other losses incurred by the settlor.

A settlor could make a declaration of trust constituting himself the trustee. This will still be construed as a disposal of the whole property subject to the trust. Section 70 of the Taxation of Chargeable Gains Act 1992 provides that a transfer into a settlement, whether revocable or irrevocable, is a transfer of the entire property, thereby becoming settled property notwithstanding that the transferor has some interest as a beneficiary under the settlement and notwithstanding that he is a trustee, or the sole trustee, of the settlement.

Holdover relief is available whether or not the assets transferred are business assets (ss 165 and 260 of the Taxation of Chargeable Gains Act 1992). It may be claimed in respect of only part of the property transferred to trustees. However, holdover relief will be restricted to business assets if a trust for a disabled person is created. If the trust is a settler interested trust – one where the beneficiaries include the settlor, the settlor's spouse or civil partner or the infant children of the settlor who are not married or in a civil partnership – holdover relief is not available on any assets including business assets. In addition, if a settlement becomes a settlor interested settlement, when it was not one originally, then the holdover relief can be 'clawed back'.

Disposals by trustees

13.32   These are chargeable, and the gain is calculated in the same manner as for individuals (s 69 of the Taxation of Chargeable Gains Act 1992). The rate of tax applicable to the gain is 40 %. Trustees are entitled to a maximum of one-half the annual exemption available to individuals.

Transfers to beneficiaries or beneficiary becomes absolutely entitled otherwise than on death

13.33   If property is advanced to beneficiaries, or a beneficiary becomes absolutely entitled, there is a deemed disposal by the trustees (s 71(1)). Holdover relief will be available whatever the nature of the assets unless it is an immediate post death interest or a trust for a disabled person or a settlor interested trust. If it is an immediate post death interest or a trust for a disabled person, then holdover relief is limited to business assets. If it is a settlor interested trust, then holdover relief is not available.

With regard to trusts for bereaved minors, as far as capital gains tax is concerned, this will not be payable on the death of the testator.

When a child attains satisfies the contingency, there will be a deemed disposal at market value for capital gains tax purposes of all the assets in the trust to which the child is entitled provided the assets can be divided easily between the beneficiaries. If they cannot be easily divided, then the deemed disposal will not take place until the youngest child attains satisfies the contingency.

If those assets have increased in value, then there is a potential liability for capital gains tax on the trustees. However, if the trustees and child agree, then any gain can be held over whatever nature of the assets provided the assets can be easily divided between the beneficiaries.

If the assets cannot be easily divided, then the deemed disposal will not take place until the youngest child satisfies the contingency. Hold over relief will then be limited to business assets as far as the older children are concerned.

Since 16 June 1999, the only loss a beneficiary can take over is any notional loss on the deemed disposal which is not absorbed by gains made by the trustees in the same tax year as the transfer to the beneficiary and prior to the transfer. Such a loss can only be offset against gains made on a disposal by the beneficiary of the trust assets which have been transferred to him.

If the trustees distribute cash, there is no charge to CGT.

Death of the life tenant under an immediate post death interest or of a disabled person a trust for a disabled person

13.34   Normally there is no charge to CGT on death.

There is a deemed disposal and reacquisition by the trustees on the death of a life tenant, but no chargeable gain or allowable loss accrues (s 72(1)). If more than one beneficiary is entitled to the settled property, there will be a deemed disposal and reacquisition of the appropriate part of the fund. Thus, if on the death of the life tenant the trust assets have a market value of £900,000, the trustees will be deemed to dispose of those assets for £900,000. No chargeable gain or allowable loss will accrue to the trustees, and the remainderman will be deemed to acquire the trust assets at market value at the date of death of the life tenant.

Normally the costs of acquisition and disposal can be deducted from any gain, and any loss increased by such costs. However, Section 38(4) provides that any provision introducing the assumption that assets are sold and immediately reacquired shall not imply that any expenditure is incurred as incidental to the sale or reacquisition.

These provisions now only apply if the interest is an immediate post death interest or a trust for a disabled person where the disabled person has an interest in possession.

Death of the life tenant under a trust which is not an immediate post death interest

13.35   If there is a life interest under a trust, but it is not an immediate post death interest, for example because it has been created during the lifetime of the settlor, when the life tenant dies, there will be a deemed disposal of the assets in the trust at market value. If the assets have increased in value, then there is a potential liability for capital gains tax.

Disposal of beneficial interests

13.36   Section 76 of the Taxation of Chargeable Gains Act 1992 provides that no chargeable gain accrues when a beneficiary disposes of a life interest or a reversionary interest. However, a chargeable gain will accrue if the beneficiary has acquired the interest for a consideration in money or money's worth. Thus once an interest under a settlement has been purchased, whether or not for full consideration, any future disposal of that interest will give rise to a charge to CGT.

As a result of the Finance Act 2000, where a beneficiary disposes of an interest under a settlement for a consideration, and the settlor has an interest in the settlement, the trustees will be deemed to dispose of the assets and reacquire them at market value. Holdover relief is not available. Thus, if the settlor is entitled to the reversion, and the life tenant sells his life interest, the trustees are deemed to dispose of the trust assets, and to reacquire them at market value.

Section 76(2) provides that when a purchaser of a beneficial interest becomes absolutely entitled as against the trustees, he shall be treated as disposing of the interest in consideration of obtaining that settled property. This subsection would apply if the remainderman sells his interest. When the life tenant dies, the purchaser of the interest in remainder is deemed to dispose of his interest for CGT purposes.

Exemptions and reliefs

13.37
(a)   The annual exemption. Trustees are entitled to one-half of the exemption available to an individual. If the settlor creates more than one settlement,

the exemption is divided between them with a minimum of 10% of one-half of the annual exemption available to individuals.

(b)   Main residence exemption. Section 225 of the Taxation of Chargeable Gains Act 1992 provides that the main residence exemption is available if the main residence is settled property, and has been the only or main residence of a person entitled to occupy the property under the terms of the settlement. The exemption also applies if the trustees exercise a discretion and permit the beneficiary to occupy the property.

(c)   Holdover relief. The effect of the relief is to reduce the donee's acquisition cost to that of the donor plus indexation and any other allowable expenditure.

   This relief used to mean that there was no need to worry about CGT on inter vivos gifts. However, the relief was restricted to a limited class of assets in 1989. It is now confined to the following assets (ss 165 and 260 of the Chargeable Gains Act 1992 and Part I of Sch 7):

   (i)   it is, or is an interest in, an asset used for the purposes of a trade, profession or vocation carried on by:

      (1)   the transferor, or

      (2)   his personal company, or

      (3)   a member of a trading group of which the holding company is his personal company; or

   (ii)   it consists of shares or securities of a trading company, or of the holding company of a trading company, where:

      (1)   the shares or securities are neither quoted on a recognised Stock Exchange nor dealt with on the Unlisted Securities Market, or

      (2)   the trading company or holding company is the transferor's personal company;

   (iii)   agricultural property, or an interest in agricultural property, within the meaning of Chapter II of Part V of the Inheritance Tax Act 1984;

   'Personal company' in relation to an individual means a company the voting rights in which are exercisable, as to not less than 5 per cent, by the individual himself.

   If holdover relief has been claimed in respect of settled property, any held-over gain becomes chargeable on the death of the life tenant, but not any gain accruing since the date of the settlement (s 74 of the Taxation of Chargeable Gains Act 1992). This only applies now to life interest trusts created before 22 March 2006.

(d)   Trustees could also claim reinvestment relief in respect of acquisitions prior to 6 April 1998. This applied if the trustees owned shares in an unquoted trading company, sold the shares and reinvested the proceeds in a similar company (s 164A et seq of the Taxation of Chargeable Gains Act 1992).

(e)   Trustees may also claim deferral relief, provided that all the beneficiaries are individuals or charities. Deferral relief applies when a qualifying investment is made. A qualifying investment has to satisfy various conditions; in particular, the company issuing the shares must be a qualifying company for the purposes of Enterprise Investment Scheme income tax relief. The qualifying investment must be made within the qualifying time, which is one year before or three years after the gain arose.

(f)   There is also a form of deferral relief applying to reinvestments in venture capital trusts.

The effect of the reliefs described in (c)–(f) above (holdover relief; rollover relief; reinvestment relief; deferral relief) is not to exempt any gains, but to postpone payment of CGT until the asset is sold by the donee.

INCOME TAX

Where there is a beneficiary with an interest in possession – liability of trustees

13.38   Trustees are liable to income tax on all income received, but only pay basic rate tax.

Trustees are not liable if the income goes direct to a beneficiary who is not liable for income tax, for example because the beneficiary is a charity. In addition, trustees are not liable to income tax on any income deemed to be that of the settlor. Personal allowances and management expenses cannot be deducted.

If the trustees carry on business either on their own account or in partnership, a change in the trustees will not cause the discontinuance rules to apply.

Liability of a beneficiary who is entitled to the income

13.39   The beneficiary is subject to income tax, whether or not the trust income is paid to him. In the following circumstances the beneficiary will be liable to income tax at basic rate:

(a)   To A for life.

(b)   To B – B is 12. B has a vested interest, and although he cannot give a valid receipt for income, he is entitled to the income.

(c)   To C when he attains 25 – C is 21. On the assumption that s 31 of the Trustee Act 1925 applies, C will be entitled to the income at the age of 18.

(d)   To E but the income is to be accumulated for five years and then paid to E.

The beneficiary is entitled to a credit for the tax paid by the trustees. If the beneficiary is a higher rate taxpayer, extra tax will have to be paid; if the beneficiary has no other income, or is on a low income, the beneficiary may be able to obtain a refund from the Revenue.

If the beneficiary is a basic rate taxpayer, and the trust income paid to him does not take him into the higher rate tax band, no further income tax will be payable by the beneficiary.

Frequently, the trustees of a life interest trust mandate the income directly to the life tenant.

Expenses

13.40   The beneficiary is entitled to a credit for the amount of tax paid by the trustees in respect of that income. If management expenses have been deducted, the credit will not be for the full amount of tax paid by the trustees.

If the beneficiary is entitled to a refund of income tax, it is desirable to give the trustees power to charge the expenses to capital as otherwise the beneficiary will not be able to obtain a complete refund of the income tax paid by the trustees. Alternatively, the trustees could obtain an undertaking from the beneficiary to pay the management expenses. On the other hand, if the beneficiary is a higher rate taxpayer, it will be best if the expenses are paid out of income.

EXAMPLE (USING TAX RATES FOR 2006/2007)

Expenses deducted from income

A trust has rental income £3,000. The life tenant, B, has no other income.

The management expenses are £500.

If the management expenses are paid out of income, B will receive £3,000 – income tax of £660 and the expenses of £500 = £1,840.

The gross income of the beneficiary will be £1,840 x 100/78 = £2,358.97.

B will be able to recover the income tax of £518.97 (£2,358.97 – £1,840), so he will receive net £2,358.97.

If the expenses were paid out of capital, B would receive £2,340, and will be able to obtain a refund of the income tax of £660, and so will receive £3,000.

If B was a higher rate taxpayer, he will receive £2,358.97 gross. He will then have to pay an extra 18% = £424.61, and will not be able to recover the £518.97, leaving a net income of £1,415.39. The total income tax liability would be £943.58.

if the expenses were paid out of capital, he would receive £2,340. He will then have to pay income tax at 40% on the £3,000 = £1,200 less the £660 already paid leaving him with a net amount of £1,800.

Expenses refunded by the beneficiary

If the whole of the income is paid to B with no other income after the deduction of tax but without the deduction of management expenses, he will be able to recover £660. If he then refunds the management expenses to the trustees, he will be left with £2,500.

If B was a higher rate taxpayer, he will have to pay income tax at 40% on £3,000 = £1,200, plus the management expenses of £500, leaving a net income of £1,300.

Capital payments taxed as income

13.41   Normally income tax is not payable on payments to beneficiaries from capital, but according to *Revenue Law: Principles and Practice* (Tottel Publishing, 23rd edition, 2005) at page 250 it will be in the following situations:

(a)   if they are designed to augment income;

(b)   the trust deed authorises the trustees to apply the capital to maintain a beneficiary in the same degree of comfort as in the past;

(c)   the payments from capital amount to an annuity.

Where there is no beneficiary with an interest in possession

Rate applicable to trusts

13.42   Section 686 of the Income and Corporation Taxes Act 1988 imposes a charge on income in the case of settlements where there is power to accumulate income or where the trustees have a discretion as to whether income is distributed. More particularly, s 686(2) provides that income is accumulated or discretionary so far as:

(a)   it must be accumulated; or

(b)   it is payable at the discretion of the trustees or any other person.

However, income is not accumulated on discretionary income if before being distributed, it is the income of any person other than the trustees.

In *IRC v Berrill [1982] 1 All ER 867* a settlement directed trustees to hold the income of a trust fund on protective trusts. The trustees had power to accumulate the income. It was held that the income was subject to the additional rate tax (the predecessor of the rate applicable to trusts).

The expenses of the trust are deductible in computing the rate applicable to trusts. However, in *Carver v Duncan [1985] 2 All ER 645* trustees paid premiums on life insurance policies and the fees of an investment management company. The House of Lords held that these were not deductible in calculating the taxable income of the trustees, although they had been paid out of income as permitted by the trust document. Lord Templeman said at pages 654–655:

> 'In my opinion, s 16(2)(d) allows deduction of expenses properly chargeable to income, that is to say income expenses ... The natural construction of s 16(2)(d) seems to me to authorise the deduction of income applied in defraying income expenses but not income applied in defraying capital expenses.'

The rate of tax is the rate applicable to trusts, which is 40 per cent, or such other rate as Parliament may determine.

The rate of tax applicable to dividends, is 32.5 per cent. Dividends carry a tax credit of 10 per cent. This tax cannot be recovered. Trustees of a discretionary trust in receipt of dividend income therefore have to pay an extra 22.5 per cent tax in respect of the dividend. If trustees distribute the dividend income to beneficiaries, tax is charged at 40 per cent on the grossed up amount of the dividend.

EXAMPLE

Trustees of a discretionary trust receive a net dividend of £1,800. Tax of 10% has been deducted from the gross dividend of £2,000. This is irrecoverable.

The trustees will have to pay tax at 32.5% on the gross dividend, i.e. £650, less the 10% already paid (£200) = £450.

If the trustees distribute the net sum, it will have to be grossed up at 40%:
$$£1,350 \times \frac{100}{60} = £2,250.$$

The trustees will have to account to the Revenue for tax at 40% on £2,250 = £900.

Against this they will be able to offset the £450 already paid in respect of this dividend.

Discretionary beneficiaries

13.43   A discretionary beneficiary will be taxed on any income paid to him. If the trustees decide to retain income, it will be treated as capital. The beneficiary will have a tax credit for the income tax paid by the trustees, but if they are higher rate taxpayers, they will not have to pay any more; alternatively, the beneficiary may be able to obtain a refund of income tax depending on the beneficiary's circumstances.

The trustees should have power to distribute accumulated income as if it were income of the year in which it was distributed in order to utilise the credit for tax paid by the trustees.

The treatment of dividend income as far as trustees are concerned has been discussed in the previous section. If any income is paid to a beneficiary, the beneficiary will receive a tax credit for tax at 40%. However, the 10% paid in respect of dividends is not recoverable. This means that a basic rate taxpayer or a higher rate taxpayer will be worse off than if he had received the dividend direct. A non-taxpayer is in the same position as a person receiving the dividend direct.

What happens if the rates of income tax change between the date when the income arises and the date when it is paid out?

13.44   Section 687(2) uses the net amount paid in the earlier tax year. This then has to be grossed using the rate of tax applicable in the year of payment.

The gross figure is then taxed at the appropriate rate of tax for the year of payment, credit being given for the tax already paid.

BARE TRUSTS FOR MINORS

13.45 This is where trustees hold property on trust for infants who are absolutely entitled.

As far as IHT is concerned, if the infant dies under the age of 18, the trust property will form part of his death estate for IHT purposes, although there will not be a deemed disposal when the infant attains 18.

The infant will also be taxable on any capital gain made by the trustees.

As the minor cannot usually give a valid receipt, assuming s 31 of the Trustee Act applies, the trustees can retain the income, or they can apply it for the maintenance, education or benefit of the beneficiary. For income tax purposes, the income belongs to the infant. However, if the beneficiary is the infant unmarried child of the settlor, any income paid to the child will be deemed to belong to the parent.

PROTECTIVE TRUSTS

13.46 Protective trusts are where the beneficiary loses their interest if they become bankrupt or assign or charge their interest under the trust.

Strictly, they should be taxed as discretionary trusts, but they are treated as trusts with an interest in possession for IHT purposes. This treatment only applies now if the settlement is an immediate post death interest, which means that it must be created by will, and the life interest comes into immediate effect, or a disabled person's interest.

However, there is no special treatment as far as CGT and income tax is concerned. As these trusts can only be created by will, then there will be a free uplift to market value of all the assets which are the subject of the trust. If the principal beneficiary becomes bankrupt, there will be no charge. There will only be a charge when a beneficiary becomes absolutely entitled. When the principal beneficiary dies, there will be a free uplift to market value of all the assets in the trust. No chargeable gain will accrue to the trustees.

As far as income tax is concerned, whilst the principal beneficiary still has an interest in possession, the trustees will pay basic rate tax.

If the trust becomes a discretionary trust, then the trustees will pay the special rate applicable to trusts.

TRUST FOR VULNERABLE PERSONS

Income tax

13.47   The basic idea is to tax the income of the trustees as if it was the income of the beneficiary, the vulnerable person.

Section 26 provides that the trustees' liability to income tax for the tax year is to be reduced by an amount equal to:

TQTI – VTQI

Section 27 provides that the purpose of section 26 TQTI is the amount of income tax to which the trustees would be liable for the tax year in respect of the qualifying trust income were it not for the Act.

VQTI is an amount equal to TLV1 – TLV2.

TLV2 is the total amount of income tax and capital gains tax to which the vulnerable person would be liable for the tax year if his income tax liability were computed.

TLV1 is what it would be if the qualifying trust income arising or treated as arising to the trustees in the tax year in respect of which the trustees are liable to income tax were income of the vulnerable person for the tax year.

EXAMPLE

Assume that the beneficiary pays income tax at 20%, and that no allowances are available.

TQTI. Trustees of a trust for a vulnerable person have a rental income of £20,000.

Income tax liability of trustees is £8,000.

Vulnerable beneficiary has an income of £5,000.

TLV1. Calculate the income tax liability of the vulnerable beneficiary on the basis that the trust income has been paid to the vulnerable beneficiary – 20% of £25,000 = £5,000.

TLV2. Calculate the liability of the vulnerable beneficiary on the basis that the trust income has not been paid to the beneficiary – 20% of £5,000 = £1,000.

Deduct TLV2 from TLV1 = £4,000 – VQTI.

Deduct £4,000 VQTI from £8,000 TQTI = £4,000.

Trustees pay £4,000.

Beneficiary pays £1,000.

Capital gains tax

13.48   As far as CGT is concerned, the provision is simpler. The gains are treated as being the gains of the vulnerable person.

So if the trustees of a qualifying trust make a gain, the gain is taxed as if it had accrued to the vulnerable beneficiary.

OFFSHORE TRUSTS

13.49   Trusts are sometimes exported abroad, or established abroad. The taxation of such trusts is a complex subject, and what follows is only an outline of the provisions.

Inheritance tax

13.50   Usually the trust will still be subject to IHT; it is only if the settlor was domiciled outside the United Kingdom at the time the settlement was made that the trust will escape liability (s 48(3) of the Inheritance Taxes Act 1984).

Reversionary interests in the property are excluded property if the person beneficially entitled to it is domiciled outside the United Kingdom (s 48(3)(b)). This conflicts with s 48(1), which states that a reversionary interest is excluded property, subject to three exceptions. It has been suggested that there is no conflict in that a reversionary interest is excluded property wherever situated, and that s 48(3)(b) applies to the three exceptions, so that even if the reversionary interest is not excluded property because it comes within the exceptions, it will be if the person beneficially entitled to it is domiciled outside the United Kingdom (see *Revenue Law: Principles and Practice* (Tottel Publishing, 23rd edition, 2005, page 675).

Capital gains tax

13.51   There used to be a generous treatment of offshore trusts as far as capital gains tax was concerned. However, the law is now much more rigorous.

Section 80 of the Taxation of Chargeable Gains Act 1992 applies if the trustees of a settlement become at any time neither resident nor ordinarily resident in the United Kingdom. It provides that the trustees shall be deemed for all purposes of the Act:

(a)   to have disposed of the defined assets immediately before the relevant time, and

(b)   immediately to have reacquired them,

   at their market value at that time.

Section 83 provides for a similar deemed disposal if the trustees of a settlement, while continuing to be resident and ordinarily resident in the United Kingdom, become at any time trustees who fall to be regarded for the purposes of any double taxation relief arrangements:

(a)   as resident in a territory outside the United Kingdom, and

(b)   as not liable in the United Kingdom to tax on gains accruing on disposals of assets which constitute settled property of the settlement and fall within descriptions specified in the arrangements.

Normally no chargeable gain accrues on the disposal of an interest in settled property, but s 85 provides that if at the time of disposal the trustees are neither resident nor ordinarily resident in the United Kingdom, the person disposing of the interest is to be treated as having:

(a)   disposed of it immediately before the relevant time; and

(b)   immediately reacquired it,

   at its market value at that time.

Section 86 attributes gains to settlors who have interests in non-resident trusts. Before s 86 applies, the following conditions must be satisfied:

(a)   a person who is a settlor in relation to the settlement is domiciled in the United Kingdom at some time in the year and is either resident in the United Kingdom during any part of the year or ordinarily resident in the United Kingdom during any part of the year;

(b)   at any time during the year the settlor, the settlor's spouse or civil partner, any child of the settlor or the spouse or civil partner of the settlor, the spouse or civil partner of any such child, any grandchild of the settlor or of the settlor's spouse or civil partner, the spouse or civil partner of any such grandchild, a company controlled by any of these persons, or a company associated with such a company have an interest in the settlement.

The trustees must not be resident or ordinarily resident in the United Kingdom during any part of the year, or if they are, they must fall to be regarded for the purposes of any double taxation relief arrangements as resident in a territory outside the United Kingdom. If the section applies, gains accruing to the trustees are treated as accruing to the settlor, and form the highest part of the amount on which he is chargeable to capital gains tax for the year. This rule will also apply to trusts established after 17 March 1998 for grandchildren.

Section 87 attributes gains to beneficiaries. Section 87(1) provides that it applies to a settlement for any year of assessment during which the trustees are at no time resident or ordinarily resident in the United Kingdom.

Section 87(2) provides that there shall be computed in respect of every year of assessment the amount on which the trustees would have been chargeable to tax if they had been resident or ordinarily resident in the United Kingdom. Section 87(4) provides that the trust gains for a year of assessment shall be treated as chargeable gains accruing in that year to beneficiaries of the settlement who receive capital payments from the trustees in that year or have received such payments in an earlier year. Section 87(5) provides that the attribution of chargeable gains to beneficiaries shall be made in proportion to, but shall not exceed the amount of capital payments received by them. Section 87(7) provides that a beneficiary shall not be liable unless he is domiciled in the United Kingdom at some time in the year.

Section 97(1) provides that capital payment means any payment which is not chargeable to income tax on the recipient or, in the case of a recipient who is neither resident nor ordinarily resident in the United Kingdom any payment received otherwise than as income.

However it does not include a payment under a transaction entered into at arm's length if it is received on or after 19 March 1991.

Section 97(2) provides that references to a payment include references to the transfer of an asset and the conferring of any other benefit, and to any occasion on which settled property becomes property to which s 60 applies.

Income tax

13.52   Trustees resident abroad are not liable for income tax on income arising abroad; they will be liable for income tax on income arising in the United Kingdom.

Section 110 of Finance Act 1989 provides that if at least one trustee is resident abroad, and one is not, the trustees shall be treated as resident in the United Kingdom if the settlor is at any relevant time:

(a)   resident in the United Kingdom;

(b)   ordinarily resident there; or

(c)   domiciled there.

The relevant times in relation to a settlor are:

(a)   in the case of a settlement arising under a testamentary disposition of the settlor or on his intestacy, the time of his death; and

(b)   in the case of any other settlement, the time or, where there is more than one, each of the times when he has provided funds directly or indirectly for the purposes of the settlement.

If the trust is within s 686 of the Income and Corporation Taxes Act 1988 (the income is to be accumulated or is payable at the discretion of the trustees), the trustees will be liable to income tax at the rate applicable to trusts.

Beneficiaries resident and domiciled in the United Kingdom are subject to income tax on all the income received from the offshore trusts, and they may not be entitled to any allowance for tax already paid. However, ESC B 18 does permit certain reliefs if, in the case of discretionary trustees, income tax at the rate applicable to trustees has been paid.

ANTI-AVOIDANCE PROVISIONS

Inheritance tax

13.53   If the life tenant purchases the reversionary interest, there are anti-avoidance provisions in the Inheritance Tax Act 1984. Section 55(1) provides that where a person entitled to an interest (whether in possession or not) in any settled property acquires a reversionary interest expectant (whether immediately or not) on that interest, the reversionary interest is not part of his estate for the purposes of the Act. Furthermore, the exemption in s 10 for dispositions not intended to confer gratuitous benefit does not apply.

Section 52(3) provides that, where as a result of a transaction between the beneficiary or a person connected with a beneficiary and the trustees of a settlement, the value of the settled property is less than it would have been but for the transaction, a corresponding part of the interest shall be deemed for the purposes of this section to come to an end. A transaction lacking gratuitous intent is not a transfer of value. Thus if the trustees of a life interest settlement agree with the spouse of a beneficiary that the spouse can have the use of some land which they are holding as part of the trust assets rent-free, the life tenant will be deemed to have made a PET of the reduction in value of the trust assets – the difference in value between the land not occupied by the spouse of the beneficiary, and the value of the land when occupied by a beneficiary not paying any rent.

After 22 March, this section only applies if the interest in possession was an immediate post death interest or a disabled person's interest or a transitional serial interest.

There are anti-avoidance provisions in s 48(1) of the Inheritance Tax Act 1984 concerning reversionary interests. A reversionary interest is not excluded property:

(a)   if it has at any time been acquired (whether by the person entitled to it or by a person previously entitled to it) for a consideration in money or money's worth;

(b)   if it is one to which the settlor or his spouse has been beneficially entitled; or

(c)   if it is the interest expectant upon the termination of a lease which is treated as a settlement.

Income tax

13.54   Chapter 5 of the Income Tax (Trading and other Income) Act 2005 contains provisions deeming the income of trustees to be taxed as if it was the income of the settlor.

S 625 applies to trusts where the settlor retains an interest. A settlor is treated as having retained an interest if any property is payable to or applicable for the settlor or settlor's spouse or civil partner or will or may become so payable or applicable:

Note that a spouse of the settlor does not include:

(a)   a spouse or civil partner from whom the settlor is separated under an order of a court, or under a separation agreement or in such circumstances that the separation is likely to be permanent; or

(b)   the widow or widower or surviving civil partner of the settlor or;

(c)   a person to whom the settlor is not for the time being married but may later marry, or a person of whom the settlor is not the civil partner but of whom the settlor may later be a civil partner.

It could be argued that a settlor has an interest in the settled property even though it is highly unlikely that this will ever happen. This situation is dealt with in s 625(2) which provides that a settlor shall not be regarded as having an interest in property if and so long as none of that property, and no derived property, can become payable or applicable excepting in the event of:

(a)   the bankruptcy of some person who is or may become beneficially entitled to the property or any derived property, or

(b)   an assignment of or charge on the property or any derived property being made or given by some person, or

(c)   in the case of a marriage or civil partnership settlement, the death of both parties to the marriage or civil partnership and of all or any of the children of the marriage or civil partnership, or

(d)   the death of a child of the settlor who had become beneficially entitled to the property or any derived property at an age not exceeding 25.

Section 625(3) provides that a settlor shall not be regarded as having an interest in property if and so long as some person is alive and under the age of 25 during whose life that property, or any related property, cannot become payable or applicable as mentioned in subsection (1) except in the event of that person becoming bankrupt or assigning or charging his interest in the property or any related property.

Section 626 provides that the anti-avoidance rules do not apply to a settlement which includes an outright gift by one spouse to the other or one civil partner to the other to the other of property from which the income arises, if:

(a)   the gift carries a right to the whole of that income, or

(b)   the property given is not wholly or substantially a right to income.

A gift is not an outright gift if it is subject to conditions, or if the property given or any related property is or will or may become, in any circumstances whatsoever, payable to or applicable for the benefit of the donor.

Section 633 taxes capital payments to the settlor where there is undistributed income. The capital payment is regarded as income as far as it does not exceed the undistributed income in any year of assessment, and any excess is treated as the income of the settlor in subsequent years of assessment, again up to the undistributed income. Any capital so caught is treated as the income of the settlor. The sum is grossed up at basic and additional rates, and the settlor is entitled to a credit for the tax. However, he cannot obtain any repayment of the tax.

Section 634 defines capital sum as:

(i) any sum paid by way of loan or repayment of a loan; and

(ii) any other sum paid otherwise than as income, being a sum which is not paid for full consideration in money or money's worth.

Draftsmen should consider the inclusion of a provision forbidding the payment of capital sums to the settlor or the spouse.

There are also provisions deeming income payments to the settlor's infant unmarried child to be taxed as income of the settlor if in excess of £100 (s 629).

Capital gains tax

13.55 There are also anti-avoidance provisions in ss 77 and 78 of the Taxation of Chargeable Gains Act 1992 dealing with CGT. Section 77(1) provides that chargeable gains will be treated as accruing to the settlor in that year if the settlor has an interest in the settlement. Section 77(2) provides that a settlor has an interest in a settlement if:

(i) any property which may at any time be comprised in the settlement or any income which may arise under the settlement is, or will or may become applicable for the benefit of or payable to the settlor or the spouse of the settlor or civil partner or the infant children of the settlor who are not married or in a civil partnership in any circumstances whatsoever; or

(ii) the settlor, or the spouse of the settlor or the civil partner of the settlor or the infant children of the settlor who are not married or in a civil partnership, enjoy a benefit deriving directly or indirectly from any property which is comprised in the settlement or any income arising under the settlement.

The settlor can recover from the trustees any CGT paid, and can offset any losses incurred in a personal capacity against the gain. Losses incurred by the trustees are not taken over by the settlor; instead they are carried forward to be set off against future gains of the trustees.

SUMMARY

13.56
(1) Trusts can take various forms – fixed trusts, discretionary trusts, and accumulation and maintenance settlements are the ones most frequently encountered.

(2) Trusts should be completely constituted.

(3) Practitioners should have regard to the perpetuity period.

(4)   Practitioners should take care not to infringe the rule against accumulations.

All settlements apart from immediate post death interests, trusts for disabled persons, and trusts for bereaved minors

IHT

13.57   Inter vivos – payable on creation – rate 20% if in excess of NRB or NRB exhausted by other settlements.

On death – payable if estate large enough.

Ten-yearly or principal charge – 6%.

Exit or proportionate charge.

CGT

13.58   Inter vivos creation – deemed disposal by settler.

On death – no CGT.

Disposals by trustees chargeable.

Deemed disposal if beneficiary becomes absolutely entitled.

Holdover relief available whatever the nature of the assets unless it is a settlor interested trust.

Income tax

If no interest in possession

13.59   Rate applicable to trusts.

If income applied for benefit of beneficiary, beneficiary gets credit for tax paid by trustees.

Might be a trust for a vulnerable person.

If interest in possession

13.60   Trustees pay basic rate tax.

Beneficiary gets credit for whatever tax has been paid by the trustees.

Immediate post death interests, trusts for disabled persons and trusts for bereaved minors

IHT

13.61   Trust for disabled person created inter vivos – PET.

On death, IHT may be payable.

Life tenant deemed to own underlying trust assets.

Surrender of life interest by life tenant – PET.

Death of life tenant – deemed disposal of trust assets.

CGT

13.62   Inter vivos – deemed disposal by settler.

On death – no CGT.

Chargeable on disposal by trustees.

Deemed disposal at MV when beneficiary becomes absolutely entitled otherwise than on death of life tenant.

Income Tax

If no interest in possession

13.63   Rate applicable to trusts.

If income applied for benefit of beneficiary, beneficiary gets credit for tax paid by trustees.

Might be a trust for a vulnerable person.

If interest in possession

13.64   Trustees pay basic rate tax.

Beneficiary gets credit for whatever tax has been paid by the trustees.

PRACTICAL EXAMPLES

T makes a will transferring assets to A for life then to B

IHT

13.65   Taxed as if it was a trust with an interest in possession.

CGT

13.66   Not payable on death of life tenant.

Holdover relief limited to business assets.

Income tax

13.67   Taxed as if it was an interest in possession trust.

As far as inheritance tax is concerned, this trust will still be taxed as if it were a trust with an interest in possession.

This means that if T is married to A, and A is domiciled in the United Kingdom, spouse exemption will operate on the death of T and so no inheritance tax will be payable when he dies.

However when A dies, A will be deemed to dispose of all the assets in the trust for inheritance tax purposes, and they will be aggregated with A's personal estate.

As far as capital gains tax is concerned, there will be a free uplift to market value on the death of T and A.

Note that the trust must be in a will.

As far as income tax is concerned, it will be taxed as if it was an interest in possession trust, so the trustees will pay basic rate tax.

T transfers assets to trustees during his life to hold on trust for A for life then to B

IHT

13.68   Taxed as if it was a trust without an interest in possession.

CGT

13.69   Holdover relief for all assets, unless it is settlor interest trust.

Income tax

13.70–13.71 Taxed as if it was an interest in possession.

If it is a lifetime creation, then it will be taxed as if it was a trust without an interest in possession.

This means that inheritance tax will be payable on the initial creation of the trust if assets in excess of the nil rate band are transferred to the trustees.

In addition, there will be ten-yearly charges and exit or proportionate charges for inheritance tax.

With regard to capital gains tax, the transfer by T to the trustees will be a deemed disposal at market value of those assets, and if those assets have increased in value since T acquired them, there is a potential liability for capital gains tax.

However, holdover relief should be available whatever the nature of the assets.

When A dies, there will not be a free uplift to market value for capital gains tax purposes. Instead, there will be a deemed disposal at market value for capital gains tax purposes by the trustees of all the assets in the trust. However, if both the trustees and the beneficiary agree, then any gain can be held over whatever the nature of the assets.

Note that holdover relief does not apply if the settlement is a settlor interested trust.

As far as income tax is concerned, it will be taxed as if it was an interest in possession trust, so the trustees will pay basic rate tax. The trustees will have to pay the income to a beneficiary. The beneficiary will get a credit for the tax paid by the trustees. So if the beneficiary is a higher rate taxpayer, then the beneficiary will have to pay additional tax.

If the beneficiary is a basic rate taxpayer, and the income from the trust will not push them into the higher rate tax band, then there is no further tax liability.

T creates a discretionary trust either during T's lifetime or in a will the terms of the trust would have to require the trustees to apply one-half of the capital for the benefit of the disabled person, and there must be no interest in possession

IHT

13.72   Taxed as if it was a trust with an interest in possession.

CGT

13.73   Holdover relief limited to business assets.

Income tax

13.74   Taxed as if it was a trust without an interest in possession.

It could be taxed as a trust for a vulnerable person.

A trust for a disabled person is always treated as if it was a trust with an interest in possession. This means that if it was created during T's lifetime, T will be deemed to have made a PET of all the assets transferred to the trustees.

As far as capital gains tax is concerned, T would be deemed to dispose of all the assets transferred to the trustees at market value on the day of the transfer, and if the assets have increased in value since the date T acquired them, there is a potential liability for capital gains tax.

With regard to holdover relief, this will be limited to business assets as this type of trust is not classed as a trust without an interest in possession.

If this trust was created in a will, then the normal rule applies. If the death estate is in excess of the nil rate band, or the nil rate band has been absorbed by lifetime gifts, then inheritance tax will be payable.

However, there will not be any liability for capital gains tax on the death of T.

Whether the trust is created during the lifetime of T or in T's will, the disabled person will be deemed to have an interest in possession in the trust assets.

This means that there will not be any ten-yearly or exit or proportionate charges to inheritance tax, but instead inheritance tax will be payable on the assets in trust on the death of the disabled person.

When the disabled person dies, capital gains tax will not be payable.

As far as income tax is concerned, it will be taxed as if it was a discretionary trust.

So the trustees will pay the special rate applicable to trusts – 40% for all income apart from dividend income, 32.5% on dividend income.

However, it could be taxed as if it was a trust for a vulnerable person. This means that the trustees' liability for income tax and capital gains tax will be based on what rate the disabled person would have paid had the income been paid to the disabled person. So it assumes that the income has been paid to the disabled person, and if the disabled person is a basic rate taxpayer, then that is all the trustees will pay. If the disabled person is a higher rate taxpayer, then the trustees will pay higher rate tax.

It also assumes that any gain is taxed as if it was the top slice of the income of the disabled person.

T makes a will containing a gift to all my children contingent on them attaining the age of 18

IHT

13.75   Possibly payable on creation, but thereafter none.

CGT

13.76   Holdover relief for all assets.

Income tax

13.77   Taxed as if it was a trust without an interest in possession.

It could be taxed as a trust for a vulnerable person.

This trust will be a trust for bereaved minor.

As it is in a will, inheritance tax will be payable on the death of the testator if the death estate is large enough, or the nil rate band has been absorbed by lifetime gifts in the seven years prior to the death of the testator. However, it will not be taxed as if it were a trust without an interest in possession, so there will not be any ten-yearly or exit charges. There will be no charge to inheritance tax when the children attain 18.

As far as capital gains tax is concerned, this will not be payable on the death of the testator.

When a child attains 18, there will be a deemed disposal at market value for capital gains tax purposes of all the assets in the trust to which the child is entitled provided the assets can be divided easily between the beneficiaries. If they cannot be easily divided, then the deemed disposal will not take place until the youngest child attains 18.

If those assets have increased in value, then there is a potential liability for capital gains tax on the trustees. However, if the trustees and child agree, then any gain can be held over whatever nature of the assets provided the assets can be easily divided between the beneficiaries.

As far as income tax is concerned, this trust will be a trust for a vulnerable person.

This means that the trustees' liability for income tax and capital gains tax will be based on what rate the child would have paid had the income been paid to the child.

So it assumes that the income has been paid to the child, and if the child is a basic rate taxpayer, then that is all the trustees will pay. If the child is a higher rate taxpayer, then the trustees will pay higher rate tax. It also assumes that any gain is taxed as if it was the top slice of the income of the child.

T makes a lifetime settlement containing a gift to all my children contingent on them attaining the age of 18

IHT

13.78   Taxed as if it was a trust without an interest in possession.

CGT

13.79   Holdover relief probably not available.

Income tax

13.80   Taxed as if it was a trust without an interest in possession.

As it is a lifetime settlement, and not in a will, it will be taxed as if it was a discretionary trust.

This means that IHT will be payable on creation if assets in excess of the NRB are transferred to the trustees, or the NRB had been exhausted by other gifts in the seven years up to the date of this settlement. In addition there will be ten-yearly charges to IHT, and exit charges. So there will be an exit charge when a child attains 18 as far as that child's share is concerned.

As far as CGT is concerned, T will be deemed to dispose of the assets transferred to the trustees at market value. Holdover relief will not be available as it is probably a settlor interested trust – infant children of the settlor who are not married or in a civil partnership are probably within the class of beneficiaries.

When a child attains 18, there will be a deemed disposal of all the assets in the trust to which that child is entitled. Again holdover relief will not be available because it is a settllor interested trust.

As far as income tax is concerned, it will be taxed as if it was a discretionary trust. So the trustees will pay the special rate applicable to trusts – 40% for all income apart from dividend income, 32.5% on dividend income.

It would only be a trust for a vulnerable person if one or both parents were dead.

T makes a will containing a gift to all my grandchildren contingent on them attaining the age of 18

IHT

13.81   Taxed as if it was a trust without an interest in possession.

CGT

13.82   Holdover relief for all assets.

Income tax

13.83   Taxed as if it was a trust without an interest in possession.

As it is made by grandparents, it will be taxed as if it was a discretionary trust. This means that IHT will be payable on creation if assets in excess of the NRB are transferred to the trustees, or the NRB had been exhausted by other gifts in the seven years up to the date of death. In addition there will be ten-yearly charges to IHT, and exit charges. So there will be an exit charge when a grandchild attains 18 as far as that grandchild's share is concerned.

As far as CGT is concerned, none will be payable on the death of T. When a child attains 18, there will be a deemed disposal of all the assets in the trust to which that child is entitled. Holdover relief will be available whatever the nature of the assets.

If it was a lifetime creation, then again it would be taxed as if it was a trust without an interest in possession. This means that IHT would be payable on creation.

As far as CGT is concerned, it would be a deemed disposal at market value of all assets transferred to the trust. However, holdover relief would be available whatever the nature of the assets.

As far as income tax is concerned, it will be taxed as if it was a discretionary trust. So the trustees will pay the special rate applicable to trusts – 40% for all income apart from dividend income, 32.5% on dividend income.

It would only be a trust for a vulnerable person if one or both parents were dead.

SETTLEMENTS CREATED BEFORE 22 MARCH 2006

13.84   If a beneficiary becomes absolutely entitled on the termination of a life interest, then the old regime applies.

If the trust does not terminate when the life interest ends, then the continuing trust will be taxed as if it was a trust without an interest in possession unless a transitional serial interest comes into existence.

In general terms a transitional serial interest is one where a life interest under a settlement created before 22 March 2006 terminates before 6 April 2008 and another life interest comes into existence, or where it terminates after 6 April 2008 and the spouse or civil partner of the life tenant is entitled to another life interest.

Existing accumulation and maintenance settlements where the beneficiary becomes absolutely entitled on attaining the age of 18 will the subject to the old regime. If that is not the case, then they will be taxed as if they were trusts without an interest in possession from the 6th April 2008

To A for life, then to B absolutely

13.85   The old treatment will continue.

A will be deemed to own all the trust assets so when A dies A will be deemed to dispose of all the assets in the trust, and those assets will be aggregated with A's personal estate.

There will also be a free uplift to market value of all the assets in the trust.

To A for life, then to B for life, then to C absolutely

13.86   As far as A is concerned, the treatment is the same as above.

A will be deemed to own all the trust assets so when A dies A will be deemed to dispose of all the assets in the trust, and those assets will be aggregated with A's personal estate.

Unless a transitional serial interest comes into existence, the trust will then be taxed as if it was a discretionary trust. This means that there will be a charge to IHT every ten years, and also exit or proportionate charges whenever the trustees hand out any capital.

If a transitional serial interest comes into existence, then the trust will still be taxed as if it was an interest in possession trust.

So IHT will be payable on B's death, and there will be a free uplift to market value on the death of B for all the assets in the trust as far as CGT is concerned.

It will be a transitional serial interest if A dies before 6 April 2008, or if after that, A and B are married or become civil partners.

To all my grandchildren contingent on them attaining the age of 25

13.87   This is an accumulation and maintenance settlement.

If all the grandchildren will attain 25 before 6 April 2008, then it will continue to be taxed as if it was an accumulation and maintenance settlement. This means that there will be no ten-yearly charge to inheritance tax and no charge to inheritance tax when a beneficiary attains 25.

If all the grandchildren will not attain 25 before 6 April 2008, then if the trustees do nothing, it will be taxed as if it was a discretionary trust or a trust without an interest in possession as from that date.

Chapter 14

Charities

CHARITIES BILL

14.1   The Charities Bill is at present before Parliament. The changes proposed have been incorporated in the text.

One change is the abolition of the office of Charity Commissioner. Instead the Charity Commissioners will be replaced by the Charity Commission, which will be a body corporate. The Commission must consist of a chairman and at least four but not more than eight members, and at least two members must have a seven-year general qualification within the meaning of s 71 of the Courts and Legal Services Act 1990. The Commissioners must appoint a chief executive.

Another change is the creation of a Charity Tribunal. This will have a President, who must have a seven-year general qualification within the meaning of s 71 of the Courts and Legal Services Act 1990. The Tribunal will sit in panels at such times and places as the President may direct. The Act has a table of matters which the Tribunal can deal with; the first matter is a decision of the Commission to enter or not to enter an institution in the register of charities, or to remove or not remove an institution from the register. The table also specifies who can appeal in addition to the Attorney General. There is a further appeal to the High Court on a point of law with the permission of the Tribunal or the High Court.

The Bill also confers powers on the Commission to suspend or remove trustees from membership of the charity, to give specific directions for the protection of the charity and to direct application of charity property, to give advice and assistance, and to enter premises and seize documents.

Until the Charities Bill the courts relied on the definition in *Commission of Income Tax v Pemsel [1891] AC 531* where Lord Macnaghten said at page 583:

> 'Charity in its legal sense comprises four principal divisions: trusts for the relief of poverty; trusts for the advancement of education; trusts for the advancement of religion; and trusts for other purposes beneficial to the community, not falling under any of the preceding heads.'

The Charities Bill defines charity as an institution which:

(a)   is established for charitable purposes only, and

(b)   falls to be subject to the control of the High Court in the exercise of its jurisdiction with respect to charities (s1(1)).

Clause 1(2) provides that this definition does not apply if any other enactment contains a different definition of charity for the purposes of that enactment or any other enactment.

The Charitable Uses Act 1601 contains a definition of charity, and clause 1(3) provides that a reference to any enactment or document or to a charity within the meaning of the Charitable Uses Act or the preamble to it is to be construed as a reference to a charity as defined by subsection (1).

Clause 2 defines what is meant by a charitable purpose. It is a purpose which falls within clause 2(2) and is for the public benefit as defined in clause 3. Clause 2(2) provides that a purpose is charitable if it falls within any of the following descriptions of purposes:

(a)   the prevention or relief of poverty;

(b)   the advancement of education;

(c)   the advancement of religion; religion is defined in clause 2(3) as including a religion which involves belief in more than one god, and a religion which does not involve belief in a god;

(d)   the advancement of health or the saving of lives; clause 2(3) provides that this includes the prevention of or relief of sickness, disease or human suffering;

(e)   the advancement of citizenship or community development; clause 2(3) provides that this includes rural or urban regeneration, and the promotion of civic responsibility, volunteering, the voluntary sector or the effectiveness or efficiency of charities;

(f)   the advancement of arts, culture, heritage or science;

(g)   the advancement of amateur sport; clause 2(3) provides that sport means a sport which involves physical skill and exertion; is the sport of darts included? Presumably, although it involves skill, it would not be included as it does not involve physical exertion;

(h)   the advancement of human rights, conflict resolution or reconciliation or the promotion of religious or racial harmony or equality and diversity;

(i)   the advancement of environmental protection or improvement;

(j)   the relief of those in need by reason of youth, age, ill-health, disability, financial hardship or other disadvantage; this includes relief given by the provision of accommodation or care to the persons mentioned in this paragraph (clause 2(3));

(k)   the advancement of animal health;

(l)   the promotion of the efficiency of the armed forces of the Crown;

(m)   any other purpose within subsection (4). Clause 2(4) provides that the purposes within that subsection are:

    (i)   any purpose not within paragraphs (a) to (l) of subsection (2) but recognised as charitable purposes under existing charitable law or by virtue of s 1 of the Recreational Charities Act 1958;

    (ii)   any purposes that may reasonably be regarded as analogous to, or within the spirit of, any purposes falling within any of those paragraphs or paragraph (a); and

    (iii)   any purposes that may reasonably be regarded as analogous to, or within the spirit of, any purposes which have been recognised under charity law as falling within paragraph (b) above or this paragraph.

As the Charities Bill is not yet law, it is necessary to consider the present classification of charitable trusts. As stated above, the courts rely on the definition in *Commission of Income Tax v Pemsel [1891] AC 531* where Lord Macnaghten said at page 583:

'Charity in its legal sense comprises four principal divisions: trusts for the relief of poverty; trusts for the advancement of education; trusts for the advancement of religion; and trusts for other purposes beneficial to the community, not falling under any of the preceding heads.'

Presumably the old law as to what is meant by trusts for the relief of poverty, the advancement of education or the advancement of religion will apply.

Poverty

14.2   This deals with the law prior to the Charities Bill.

It is very hard to frame a definition of poverty, and the courts have not sought to do so. It is clear that it does not mean only someone who is living on the breadline. In *Re Coulthurst [1951] Ch 661* at pages 665–666 Evershed MR said:

'It is quite clearly established that poverty does not mean destitution; it is a word of wide and somewhat indefinite import; it may not be unfairly paraphrased for present purposes as meaning persons who have to "go short" in the ordinary acceptation of that term, due regard being had to their status in life, and so forth.'

A rich man may thus be considered to be living in poverty, when in similar circumstances a poor man would be living in luxury. Thus trusts for distressed gentlefolk are charitable. However, a trust which can benefit both rich and poor will not be charitable. In *Re Gwyon [1930] 1 Ch 255* a will established a trust for the provision of knickers for boys of Farnham and district. It was held that this was not charitable as it could benefit boys who were not poor.

In recent years funds have been established to relieve the victims of disasters. These funds are often not charitable as many victims would not be classified as poor.

Education

14.3   This deals with the law prior to the Charities Bill.

This head clearly includes schools and universities, but it is also wider. It can include trusts for the promotion of choral singing in London, and bodies such as the royal medical colleges, and the Incorporated Council of Law Reporting. However, there are limits.

Charitable trusts for the promotion of sport are valid, at any rate if the beneficiaries are young people. In *IRC v McMullen [1981] AC 1* the objects of a trust were the organisation or provision of facilities to enable and encourage pupils of schools and universities to play Association football or other games and sports. It was held that this was charitable. Lord Hailsham said at page 18:

> 'We are not dealing with adult education, physical or otherwise, as to which some considerations may be different ... the picture of education ... is the picture of a balanced and systematic process of instruction, training and practice containing, to borrow from section 7 of the 1944 Act, both spiritual, moral, mental and physical elements, the totality of which, in any given case, may vary with, for instance, the availability of teachers and facilities, and the potentialities, limitations and the individual preferences of pupils. But the totality of the process consists as much in the balance between each of the elements as of the enumeration of the thing learned or the places in which the activities are carried on.'

There were doubts as to whether a trust for research could be charitable, but these have been settled to a large extent by the case of *Re Hopkins' Will Trusts [1965] Ch 669* where a will established a trust for the Francis Bacon Society Inc., of 50A Old Brompton Road, London SW7 'to be earmarked and applied towards finding the Bacon – Shakespeare manuscripts ...'. This was held to be a valid charitable trust, and Wilberforce J said at page 680:

' ... in order to be charitable, research must either be of educational value to the researcher or must be so directed as to lead to something which will pass into the store of educational material, or so as to improve the sum of communicable knowledge in an area which education may cover – education in this last context extending to the formation of literary taste and appreciation ...'.

In *McGovern v Att-Gen [1982] Ch 321* at page 352 Slade J stated:

'(1) A trust for research will ordinarily qualify as a charitable trust if, but only if (a) the subject matter of the proposed research is a useful subject of study; and (b) it is contemplated that knowledge acquired as a result of the research will be disseminated to others; and (c) the trust is for the benefit of the public or a sufficiently important section of the public. (2) In the absence of a contrary context, however, the court will be readily inclined to construe a trust for research as importing subsequent dissemination of the results thereof. (3) Furthermore, if a trust for research is to constitute a valid trust for the advancement of education, it is not necessary either (a) that a teacher/pupil relationship should be in contemplation, or (b) that the persons to benefit from the knowledge to be acquired should be persons who are already in the course of receiving "education" in the conventional sense.'

Religion

14.4   This deals with the law prior to the Charities Bill.

Trusts for the advancement of religion are charitable. It does not matter that the religion which is being promoted is not the Christian religion, but there must be a religious purpose. In *Re South Place Ethical Society [1980] 3 All ER 918* the objects of the society were 'the study and dissemination of ethical principles' and 'the cultivation of a rational religious sentiment'. It was held that the society was not a religious charity. Dillon J said at page 924:

'Religion, as I see it, is concerned with man's relations with God, and ethics are concerned with man's relations with man. The two are not the same, and are not made the same by sincere inquiry into the question, "What is God?" If reason leads people not to accept Christianity or any known religion, but they do believe in the excellence of qualities such as trust, beauty and love, or believe in the Platonic concept of the ideal, their beliefs may be to them the equivalent of a religion, but viewed objectively, they are not a religion.'

223

In *Gilmour v Coats [1949] AC 426* there was a trust for a Carmelite convent. The nuns spent all their time in prayer and meditation, and did not help people outside the convent. It was held that the trust was not charitable.

Trusts for objects closely associated with religion have been held to be charitable. For example, trusts for the maintenance of churches or parts of churches have been held to be charitable, although not a trust for the maintenance of individual tombs (*Lloyd v Lloyd (1852) 2 Sim (NS) 225*).

Other purposes beneficial to the community

14.5   This deals with the law prior to the Charities Bill. It encompasses many of the charitable purposes mentioned in clause 2(2).

This head is wide enough to encompass many purposes, and the courts and the Charity Commissioners have not imposed rigid guidelines in deciding whether or not a purpose is charitable. The head has its foundation in the preamble to the Statute of Charitable Uses Act 1601, and over the years the courts have gradually extended the purposes specifically mentioned. For example, the preamble specifically states that trusts for the 'relief of aged, impotent and poor people' are charitable. It has never been the case that potential beneficiaries had to be aged *and* impotent *and* poor in order to qualify, and it has been held that a gift to a private hospital is charitable (*Re Resch's Will Trust [1969] 1 AC 514*).

It is well established that trusts for the benefit of animals are charitable. The reasoning behind these cases was explained in *Re Wedgwood [1915] 1 Ch 113* by Swinfen Eady LJ at page 122 where he said:

> 'A gift for the benefit and protection of animals tends to promote and encourage kindness towards [animals], and to ameliorate the condition of the brute creation, and thus to stimulate humane and generous sentiments in man towards the lower animals, and by this means to promote feelings of humanity and morality generally, repress brutality, and thus elevate the human race.'

However, not all trusts concerned with animals will be charitable. In *National Anti-Vivisection Society v IRC [1948] AC 31* the object of the society was the abolition of vivisection. It was held that this object was not charitable. Lord Simonds said at pages 60–61:

> 'The second point is fundamental ... . It is whether the court, for the purposes of determining whether the object of the society is charitable may disregard the finding of fact that any assumed public benefit in the direction of the advancement of public morals and education is

far outweighed by the detriment to medical science and research and consequently to the public health which would result if the society succeeded in achieving its object, and that on balance, the object of the society, so far from being for the public benefit, was gravely injurious thereto. The society says that the court must disregard this fact, arguing that evidence of disadvantages or evils which would or might result from the stopping of vivisection is irrelevant and inadmissible.'

It may be that trusts which do not qualify as charitable under some other head may be charitable under this head; an example of this is provided by the case of *Re South Place Ethical Society* where although the objects of the society were held not to be for the advancement of religion, they were charitable as being for other purposes beneficial to the community.

There were problems with the charitable status of recreational trusts, as a result of which the Recreational Charities Act was passed in 1958. Section 1(1) of the Act provides that it shall be and be deemed always to have been charitable to provide, or assist in the provision of, facilities for recreation or other leisure-time occupation, if the facilities are provided in the interests of social welfare. Section 1(2) as amended by the Charities Bill provides that the requirement that the facilities are provided in the interests of social welfare shall not be treated as satisfied unless the basic conditions are met. Section 1(2)(A) provides that the basic conditions are:

(a) the facilities are provided with the object of improving the conditions of life for the persons for whom the facilities are primarily intended; and

(b) that either:

   (i)   those persons have need of the facilities by reason of their youth, age, infirmity or poverty or social and economic circumstances; or

   (ii) the facilities are to be available to the members of the public at large or to male, or to female, members of the public at large.

Section 1(3) provides that subsection (1) applies in particular to the provision of facilities at village halls, community centres and women's institutes, and to the provision and maintenance of grounds and buildings to be used for the purposes of recreation and leisure-time occupation and extends to the provision of facilities for those purposes by the organising of any activity.

The House of Lords has now approved a liberal interpretation of the requirement of 'social welfare'. In *Guild v IRC [1992] 2 AC 310* Lord Keith said at page 322:

'I would therefore reject the argument that the facilities are not provided in the interests of social welfare unless they are provided with the object of improving the conditions of life for persons who suffer from some form of social disadvantage. It suffices if they are provided with the object of improving the conditions of life for members of the community generally.'

Political purposes

14.6 Trusts for the benefit of a political party are not charitable, and similarly trusts advocating a change in the law are not charitable. In *McGovern v Attorney General [1981] 3 All ER 493* the question of whether Amnesty International was a charity was at issue. It was held that it was not. Slade J said at page 507:

'The mere fact that the trust was intended to be carried out abroad would not by itself necessarily deprive it of charitable status ... . The point with which I am at present concerned is whether a trust of which a direct and main object is to secure a change in the laws of a foreign country can ever be regarded as charitable under English Law. Though I do not think that any authority cited to me precisely covers the point, I have come to the conclusion that it cannot.'

However, whilst charitable trusts for political purposes are not permitted, it is permissible for a charity to engage in political activities in furtherance of its charitable objects. Charities may wish to make representations to government on matters concerning the objects of the charity. The Charity Commission has provided some guidance as to what is permissible. It is permissible for a charity to help the government reach a decision on a particular issue by providing information and argument, but the emphasis must be on rational persuasion. Whilst a charity may support or oppose a Bill before Parliament which is concerned with its charitable objects, it would not be permissible for a charity to campaign for a political party.

Requirement of public benefit

14.7 Before the Charities Bill, with one exception, a trust had to be for the public benefit in order to be charitable. The exception is trusts for the relief of poverty, where trusts for the benefit of a limited class of persons are valid, although a trust for the benefit of specified individuals is not valid. In *Dingle v Turner [1972] 1 All ER 878* Lord Cross said at page 507:

'His (counsel for the appellant) submission was that while the "poor relations" cases might have to be left as long-standing anomalies there was no good reason for sparing the "poor employees" cases which only date from *Re Gosling (1900) 48 WR 300* decided in 1900 and which have been under suspicion ever since the decision in *Re Compton* in 1945. But the "poor members" and the "poor employees" decisions were a natural development of the "poor relations" decisions and to draw a distinction between the different sort of poverty trusts would be quite illogical and could certainly not be said to be introducing greater harmony into the law of charity.'

Clause 2(1)(b) of the Charities Bill preserves the public benefit test. Clause 3 provides that in determining whether the requirement of public benefit is satisfied in relation to any such purpose, there is no presumption that a purpose of a particular description is for the public benefit. So the mere fact that a charity has one of the purposes mentioned in clause 2(2) does not mean that is for the public benefit. Clause 3(3) provides that any reference to the public benefit is a reference to the public benefit as understood for the purposes of the law relating to charities in England and Wales. Thus the old law is still relevant, but clause 4(1) imposes a duty on the Charity Commission to issue guidance as to the operation of the public benefit requirement.

Public benefit and educational trusts

14.8   A trust for educational purposes must benefit a section of the community in order to be charitable. In *Oppenheim v Tobacco Securities Trust Co Ltd [1951] AC 297* a trust was established to apply the income for the education of children of employees and former employees of the British-American Tobacco Co Ltd, or any of its subsidiaries or allied companies. It was held that the trust was not charitable. Lord Simonds at page 306 said:

'These words "section of the community" have no special sanctity, but they conveniently indicate first that the possible ... beneficiaries must not be negligible, and secondly that the quality which distinguishes them from other members of the community, so that they form by themselves a section of it, must be a quality which does not depend on their relationship to a particular individual ... A group of persons may be numerous, but if the nexus between them is their personal relationship to a single propositus, or to several propositi, they are neither the community nor a section of the community for charitable purposes.'

However, it may be possible to create a charitable trust to provide education for the children of the employees of a company. In *Re Koettgen's Will Trust [1954] Ch 252* there was an educational trust, but there was a direction that a maximum of 75 per cent of the income should be applied for the education of the families of employees of a named company. It was held that this was a valid charitable trust. It should be noted that this case may have been incorrectly decided.

Public benefit and trusts for the advancement of religion

14.9   It appears that the test is the same as for trusts for the advancement of education.

Public benefit and trusts for other purposes beneficial to the community

14.10   These trusts will not be charitable if there is a personal nexus between the beneficiaries. In *IRC v Baddeley [1955] AC 572* Viscount Simonds said at page 590 that it is possible that a different degree of public benefit is requisite according to the class in which the charity is said to fall. At page 592 he said:

> 'I should in the present case conclude that a trust cannot qualify as a charity within the fourth class … if the beneficiaries are a class of persons not only confined to a particular area but selected from within it by reference to a particular creed.'

THE CY-PRÈS DOCTRINE

14.11   The cy-près doctrine means that if a charitable purpose fails for some reason, the assets may be applied for similar charitable purposes. If the charitable trust fails at the outset, a general charitable intention must be displayed before the cy-près doctrine will apply. If there is a subsequent failure, no such general charitable intention is required.

What is meant by general charitable intention? In *Re Lysaght [1966] Ch 191* at page 202 Buckley J said:

> 'A general charitable intention … may be said to be a paramount intention on the part of the donor to effect some charitable purpose which the court can find a method of putting into operation, notwithstanding that it is impracticable to give effect to some direction by the donor which is not an essential part of his true intention – not, that is to say, of his paramount intention.
>
> In contrast, a particular charitable intention exists when the donor means his charitable disposition to take effect if, but only if, it can be carried into effect in a particular specified way, for example, in connection with a particular place, or by establishing a home in a particular house … .'

The courts may also be able to find a general charitable intention when the charity has never existed. In *Re Harwood [1936] Ch 285* a will contained gifts in favour of the Wisbech Peace Society, the Peace Society of Belfast, and the Peace Society of Dublin. There was evidence that the first society had ceased to exist before the death of the testatrix, but it appeared that the second and third societies had never existed. It was held that the cy-près doctrine could be applied to the second and third gifts, but not to the first.

The cy-près doctrine can apply if a charity has ceased to exist at the date when the gift comes into operation. However, in *Re Rymer [1895] 1 Ch 19* a will contained a legacy to the rector for the time being of St Thomas's seminary for the education of priests for the diocese of Westminster. When the testator had died, the seminary was not in existence. It was held that this did not show any general charitable intention. Lindley LJ said at page 35:

> ' … when once you arrive at the conclusion that a gift to a particular seminary or institution, or whatever you may call it, is "for the purposes thereof", and for no other purpose – if you once get to that, and it is proved that that institution or seminary, or whatever it is, has ceased to exist in the lifetime of the testator, you are driven to arrive at the conclusion that there is a lapse, and then the doctrine of cy-près is inapplicable.'

In *Re Woodhams [1981] 1 WLR 493* there was a bequest to two colleges to 'found a scholarship to be known as the Herbert G. Woodham's scholarship for the complete musical education of a promising boy who is an absolute orphan and only of British nationality and birth from any one of the Dr. Barnardo's homes or the Church of England Children's Society homes'. The colleges were not prepared to accept the limitations on the gift. It was held that the gifts were valid, but the matter was referred to the Charity Commission for the settlement of a scheme.

Many charities operate as companies these days. What is the effect of a gift to such a charity? In *Re Vernon's Will Trust [1972] Ch 300* Buckley J said at page 303:

> 'A bequest to a corporate body … takes effect simply as a gift to that body beneficially, unless there are circumstances which show that the recipient is to take the gift as a trustee. There is no need in such a case to infer a trust for any particular purpose. The objects to which the corporate body can properly apply its funds may be restricted by its constitution, but this does not necessitate inferring as a matter of construction of the testator's will a direction that the bequest is to be held in trust to be applied for those purposes: the natural construction is that the bequest is made to the corporate body as part of its

general funds, that is to say, beneficially and without the imposition of any trust.'

In *Re ARMS (Multiple Sclerosis Research) Ltd, Alleyne v Attorney-General and Another [1997] 2 All ER 679* a charitable company had gone into insolvent liquidation, but had not yet been formally dissolved. The question arose as to whether bequests made to the company since it had been compulsorily wound up could be applied to pay the company's creditors. It was held that they could be so applied in the absence of any limitation or trust. It was also held that the mere fact that a bequest was made to a charitable company did not imply any intention that the bequest should be applied solely for charitable purposes.

A gift to a company which does not exist will be applied cy-près if there is a general charitable intention. In *Re Finger's Will Trust [1972] Ch 286* there was a gift in a will to a corporate charity which did not exist at the date of the death of the testator. It was held that the gift could not be applied cy-près 'unless there is a context in the will to show that the gift was intended to be on trust for that purpose and not an absolute gift to the corporation' (Goff J at page 297). However, the will showed a general charitable intention, and the gift was applied cy-près.

Charities also amalgamate, and sometimes change the trusts under which they operate. In these circumstances, the courts will readily construe the gift as being to the amalgamated charity, or direct that the assets should be held on the new trusts.

Subsequent failure

14.12   Once a charitable trust has come into effect, the assets will be applied cy-près in the event of subsequent failure. This will happen even if the gift to the charity did not take effect until some time in the future; as long as the gift has come into effect, it does not matter that there is a prior interest. In *Re Wright [1954] Ch 347* a residuary estate was subject to a life interest, and thereafter to a trust for a convalescent home. The testatrix had died in 1933, and in 1952 the Master certified that it was not then possible to carry out the trusts. It was held that the gift was still effective. Romer LJ said at pages 362–363:

'Once money is effectually dedicated to charity, whether in pursuance of a general or particular charitable intent, the testator's next of kin or residuary legatees are forever excluded and no question of subsequent lapse, or of anything analogous to lapse, between the date of the testator's death and the time when the money becomes available for actual application to the testator's purpose can affect the matter so far as they are concerned.'

Charities Act 1993, s 13

14.13   Section 13 of the Charities Act 1993 as amended by the Charities Bill permits the Charity Commission to make schemes permitting charity assets to be applied in the following circumstances:

(a)   where the original purposes, in whole or in part:

  (i)   have been as far as may be fulfilled; or

  (ii)   cannot be carried out, or not according to the directions given or to the spirit of the appropriate considerations; appropriate considerations are defined in clause 13(1)(1A) of the Charities Bill as meaning on the one hand the spirit of the gift concerned and on the other hand the social and economic circumstances prevailing at the time of the proposed alteration of the original purposes; or

(b)   where the original purposes provide a use for part only of the property available by virtue of the gift; or

(c)   where the property available by virtue of the gift and other property applicable for similar purposes can be more effectively used in conjunction, and to that end can suitably, regard being had to the spirit of the gift, be made applicable to common purposes; or

(d)   where the original purposes were laid down by reference to an area which then was but has since ceased to be a unit for some other purpose, or by reference to a class of persons or to an area which has for any reason ceased to be suitable, regard being had to the spirit of the gift, or to be practical in administering the gift; or

(e)   where the original purposes, in whole or in part, have since they were laid down:

  (i)   been adequately provided by other means; or

  (ii)   ceased, as being useless or harmful to the community or for other reasons, to be in law charitable; or

  (iii)   ceased in any other way to provide a suitable and effective method of using the property available by virtue of the gift, regard being had to the spirit of the gift.

Section 13(2) provides that the other conditions for the application of the cy-près doctrine must be satisfied; the effect of subsection (1) is to relax the requirement as to the failure of the original purpose.

In *Varsani and others v Jesani and others [1983] 3 All ER 273* a charitable trust had been established for the purpose of promoting the faith of a particular Hindu sect. The sect split into two groups. It was held that the court had power to order a scheme under s 13(1)(e).

231

Section 14B as inserted by the Charities Bill contains provisions as to how the court or the Commission should exercise its powers to make schemes for the application of property cy-près. Section 14B(2) provides that where any property given for charitable purposes is applicable cy-près, the court or the Commission may make a scheme providing for the property to be applied:

(a)   for such charitable purposes, and

(b)   (if the scheme provides for the property to be transferred to another charity) by or on trust for such charity

as it considers appropriate, having regard to the matters set out in subsection (3).

Section 14B(3) provides that the matters are:

(a)   the spirit of the original gift;

(b)   the desirability of securing that the property is applied for charitable purposes which are close to the original purposes, and

(c)   the need for the relevant charity to have purposes which are suitable and effective in the light of current social and economic circumstances.

Appeals and collections

14.14   What happens if there is an appeal or collection for a particular charitable purpose which fails? Section 14(1) of the Charities Act 1993 deals with this problem and provides that such property shall be applied cy-près as if given for charitable purposes generally, where it belongs:

(a)   to a donor who, after:

  (i)   the prescribed advertisements and inquiries have been published and made; and

  (ii)   the prescribed period beginning with the publication of those advertisements has expired,

  cannot be identified or cannot be found; or

(b)   to a donor who has executed a disclaimer in the prescribed form of his right to have the property returned.

Section 14(3) provides that property shall be conclusively presumed without any advertisement or inquiry to belong to donors who cannot be identified, in so far as it consists:

(a)   of the proceeds of cash collections made by means of collecting boxes or by other means not adapted for distinguishing one gift from another; or

(b)   of the proceeds of any lottery, competition, entertainment, sale or similar money-raising activity, after allowing for property given to provide prizes or articles for sale or otherwise to enable the activity to be undertaken.

These subsections effectively deal with the problem of a collection for some charitable purpose which is never implemented. It may be that some money will have been raised by means of collecting boxes, which will come within s 14(3); other money may have been contributed by donors who can be found. Such donors will have to be asked to execute a disclaimer if the property is to be applied cy-près.

Section 14(4) provides that the court may by order direct that property not falling within subsection (3) shall be treated (without any advertisement or inquiry) as belonging to donors who cannot be identified, where it appears to the court or the Commission either:

(a)   that it would be unreasonable, having regard to the amounts likely to be returned to the donors, to incur expense with a view to returning the property; or

(b)   that it would be unreasonable, having regard to the nature, circumstances and amounts of the gifts, and to the lapse of time since the gifts were made, for the donors to expect the property to be returned.

Section 14A as inserted by the Charities Bill provides that if property is given for specific charitable purposes, and the solicitation was accompanied by a statement to the effect that property given in response to it, will, in the event of those specific charitable purposes failing, be applicable cy-près as if given for charitable purposes generally, unless the donor makes a relevant declaration at the time of the gift. Section 14A(3) provides that a relevant declaration is a declaration in writing by the donor to the effect that, in the event of the specific charitable purposes failing, he wishes the trustees holding the property to give him the opportunity to request the return of the property in question or a sum equal to the value at the time of the gift. If this provision applies, the trustees must contact the donor to see if the donor wishes the property or the equivalent value to be returned. If the donor does not respond, or cannot be found, the trustees can then apply the property cy-près.

SMALL CHARITIES

14.15   Section 74 empowers small charities to transfer all property or to modify the objects of the charity. Section 74(1) provides that the section applies to a charity if:

(a)   its gross income in its last financial year did not exceed £5,000; and

(b)   it does not hold any land on trusts which stipulate that the land is to be used for the purposes, or any particular purposes, of the charity,

and it is neither an exempt charity nor a charitable company.

The trustees of such a charity can resolve:

(a)   that all the property of the charity should be transferred to such other charity as is specified in the resolution, being either a registered charity or a charity which is not required to be registered; and

(b)   that all the property of the charity should be divided, in such manner as is specified in the resolution, between such two or more other charities as are so specified, being in each case either a registered charity or a charity which is not required to be registered.

Before exercising this power, the trustees of the charity must be satisfied:

(a)   that the existing purposes of the transferor charity have ceased to be conducive to a suitable and effective application of the charity's resources; and

(b)   that the purposes of the charity or charities specified in the resolution are as similar in character to the purposes of the transferor charity as is reasonably practicable.

In addition, the trustees of those charities to which the property is to be transferred must have confirmed in writing that they are prepared to accept a transfer of property under this section.

The trustees can also resolve that the trusts of the charity should be modified by replacing all or any of the purposes of the charity with such other purposes, being in law charitable, as are specified in the resolution provided the trustees are satisfied:

(a)   that the existing purposes of the charity (or, as the case may be, such of them as it is proposed to replace) have ceased to be conducive to a suitable and effective application of the charity's resources; and

(b)   that the purposes specified in the resolution are as similar in character to those existing purposes as is practicable in the circumstances (s 74(2) and (5)).

The trustees can also resolve that any provisions of the trusts of the charity:

(i)   relating to any of the powers exercisable by the charity trustees in the administration of the charity; or

(ii)   regulating the procedure to be followed in any respect in connection with its administration,

should be modified (s 74(2)(d)).

Section 74(3) provides that any resolution must be passed with a majority of not less than two-thirds of such charity trustees as vote on the resolution.

Section 74(6) provides that when charity trustees have passed a resolution under subsection (2), they must give public notice of the resolution in such manner as they think reasonable in the circumstances. They must also send a copy of the resolution to the Commission, together with a statement of their reasons for passing it. The Commission then have three months in which to approve or reject the resolution.

Section 75(2) permits charity trustees to pass a resolution that the charity ought to be freed from the restrictions with respect to the expenditure of capital to which its permanent endowment is subject if they are of the opinion that the property of the charity is too small for any useful purpose to be achieved by the expenditure of income alone. Note that this only applies to a charity if:

(a)   it has a permanent endowment which does not consist of or comprise any land; and

(b)   its gross income in its last financial year did not exceed £1,000.

Section 75(4) provides that before passing any resolution the charity trustees must consider whether any reasonable possibility exists of effecting a transfer or division of all the charity's property under s 74 (disregarding any such transfer as would, in their opinion, impose on the charity an unacceptable burden of costs).

There are similar requirements with regard to notices and the majority required to pass a resolution as appears in s 74.

PERPETUITIES

14.16   Charities are subject to the normal rules about perpetuities as far as the actual vesting of the gift is concerned. However, once a charitable trust is established it can last indefinitely. One consequence is that a gift from one charity to another is not subject to the rule against perpetuities, and so it is in order for there to be a gift from one charity to another outside the perpetuity period (*Christ's Hospital v Grainger (1849) 1 Mac & G 460*). However, a gift from a charity to an individual and an individual to a charity to take effect in the future is subject to the rule against perpetuities, although it is now possible to wait and see if the gift vests outside the perpetuity period (s 12 of the Perpetuities and Accumulations Act 1964).

POWERS AND DUTIES OF CHARITY TRUSTEES

14.17 The trustees of charities are under the same duties as trustees of a private trust.

Section 26(1) authorises the Charity Commissioners to sanction action, whether or not it would otherwise be within the powers exercisable by the charity trustees in the administration of the charity, if it appears to the Commissioners that the action is expedient in the interests of the charity.

Powers of investment

14.18 In the absence of any express power, the powers of investment are contained in the Trustee Act 2000 (see chapter 2 above).

In *Harries v Church Commission for England [1992] 1 WLR 1241* the duties of the Church Commission with regard to investment were considered. Sir Donald Nicholls V-C said at page 1246:

> 'It is axiomatic that charity trustees, in common with all other trustees, are concerned to further the purpose of the trust of which they have accepted the office of trustee ... .
>
> In other words, property held by trustees as an investment. Where property is so held, *prima facie* the purpose of the trust will be best served by the trustees seeking to obtain therefrom the maximum return, whether by way of income or capital growth, which is consistent with commercial prudence ... .
>
> In most cases the best interests of the charity require that the trustees' choice of investments should be made solely on the basis of well-established investment criteria, having taken expert advice where appropriate and having due regard to such matters as the need to diversify, the need to balance income against capital growth, and the need to balance risk against return ... .
>
> There will be some cases, I suspect comparatively rare, when the objects of the charity are such that investments of a particular type would conflict with the aims of the charity. Much cited examples are those of cancer research companies and tobacco shares ... .'

Moral obligations

14.19   It may be that charity trustees consider that they have a moral obligation to make a payment, but strictly this may not be permissible. Section 27(1)
authorises the Commissioners to exercise the same power as is exercisable by
the Attorney-General to authorise the charity trustees of a charity:

(a)   to make any application of property of the charity; or

(b)   to waive to any extent, on behalf of the charity, its entitlement to receive
       any property;

      in a case where the charity trustees:

    (i)   (apart from this section) have no power to do so, but

    (ii) in all the circumstances regard themselves as being under a moral
      obligation to do so.

Section 27(2) provides that these powers must be exercised under the supervi-
sion of, and in accordance with such directions as may be given by, the
Attorney-General. The Attorney-General may require the Commissioners:

(a)   to refrain from exercising that power;

(b)   to consult the Attorney-General before exercising it.

Official Custodian for Charities

14.20   The Official Custodian for Charities is required by the Charities
Act 1993 to divest himself of charity property apart from two exceptions, one of
which is land. With regard to land, s 22(2) provides that the charity trustees shall
have power in his name and on his behalf to execute and do all assurances and
things which they could properly execute or do in their own name and on their
own behalf if the land were vested in them.

REGISTRATION OF CHARITIES

14.21   Section 3 of the Charities Act 1993 as amended by the Charities Bill
obliges the Charity Commission to keep a register of charities. Every charity
must be entered on the register, although there are the following exceptions:

●   the charities specified in Sch 2 – for example the universities of Oxford
     and Cambridge, grant-maintained schools, and higher education corpora-
     tions;

- any charity excepted by order or regulation;

- any charity which is permanently or temporarily excepted by order of the Commission, and complies with any conditions of the exception; the gross income of the charity must not exceed £100,000;

- any charity which is, or is of a description, permanently or temporarily excepted by regulations made by the Secretary of State, and which complies with any conditions of the exception and whose gross income does not exceed £100,000;

- any charity whose gross income does not exceed £5,000 (s 3A of the Charities Act 1993 as amended by the Charities Bill.

Clause 3B(1) imposes a duty on charity trustees to apply for registration unless the charity is excepted from that requirement. Clause 3B(2) imposes a duty on charity trustees to supply copies of its trusts, and such other documents and information as may be prescribed in regulations. Section 3(7) imposes a duty on charity trustees to apply for registration unless the charity is excepted from that requirement.

If the charity ceases to exist, or if there is any change in its trusts, or of any particulars entered on the register, the charity trustees must notify the Commission (Clause 3B(32)).

Section 4(1) of the 1993 Act provides that an institution shall be conclusively presumed to have been a charity at any time when it is or was on the register of charities. Provision is made for objections to the registration of the charity, and there is a right of appeal against the decisions of the Commission to the Charity Tribunal.

Notification of status as a registered charity

14.22   Section 5 of the 1993 Act applies to a registered charity where the gross income in its last financial year exceeded £10,000. It requires the fact that it is a registered charity to be stated in English in legible characters:

(a)   in all notices, advertisements, and other documents issued by or on behalf of the charity and soliciting money or other property for the benefit of the charity;

(b)   in all bills of exchange, promissory notes, endorsements, cheques and orders for money or goods purporting to be signed on behalf of the charity; and

(c)   in all bills rendered by it and in all its invoices, receipts, and letters of credit.

POWERS OF THE CHARITY COMMISSION

14.23   Section 16(1) of the 1993 Act provides that the Commissioners may by order exercise the same jurisdiction and powers as are exercisable by the High Court in charity proceedings for the following purposes:

(a)   establishing a scheme for the administration of the charity;

(b)   appointing, discharging or removing a charity trustee or trustee for a charity, or removing an officer or employee;

(c)   vesting or transferring property or requiring or entitling any person to call for or make any transfer of property or any payment.

Section 97(1) defines charity trustees as the persons having the general control and management of the administration of a charity.

Section 17 empowers the Commission to make a scheme which would result in the modification of an Act of Parliament; s 17(2) provides that any such scheme may be given effect to by order of the Secretary of State.

Common investment funds

14.24   Section 24 authorises the Commissioners to make schemes for the establishment of common investment funds under trusts which provide:

(a)   for property transferred to the fund by or on behalf of a charity participating in the scheme to be invested under the control of trustees appointed to manage the fund; and

(b)   for the participating charities to be entitled (subject to the provisions of the scheme) to the capital and income of the fund in shares determined by reference to the amount or value of the property transferred to it by or on behalf of each of them and to the value of the fund at the time of the transfers.

Section 25 permits the Commissioners to establish common deposit funds.

Under both ss 24 and 25 the powers of investment of every charity are deemed to include the power to participate in common investment schemes and common deposit funds unless the power is specifically excluded by a provision specifically referring to common investment schemes or common deposit funds in the trusts of the charity.

Dormant bank accounts

14.25   Charities may cease to function, in which event banks may find that they hold dormant accounts. In these circumstances, s 28 empowers the Commissioners to give directions about the account.

Solicitors' costs

14.26   Solicitors employed by charity trustees are of course entitled to be paid for the work carried out for the charity trustees. Section 31 empowers the Charity Commission to order that such a bill should be taxed by a taxing office in the High Court, or another court. However, once the bill has been paid, taxation cannot be ordered unless the Commission are of the opinion that it contains exorbitant charges. In addition, no order for taxation can be made if the costs are not subject to taxation on an order of the High Court by reason either of an agreement as to the solicitor's remuneration or the lapse of time since the payment of the solicitor's bill.

Litigation by charities

14.27   Section 32(1) confers on the Commissioners the same powers with respect to the taking of legal proceedings or the compromise of claims as are exercisable by the Attorney-General acting ex officio.

Section 33(1) authorises charity proceedings to be taken with reference to a charity either by the charity, or by any of the charity trustees, or by any person interested in the charity, or by any two or more inhabitants of the area of the charity if it is a local charity, but not by any other person.

Section 33(2) provides that no charity proceedings relating to a charity (other than an exempt charity) shall be entertained or proceeded with in any court unless the taking of the proceedings is authorised by order of the Commissioners. If the Commissioners refuse to authorise the taking of the proceedings, leave can be obtained from one of the judges of the High Court attached to the Chancery Division. Section 33(8) defines 'charity proceedings' as proceedings in any court in England and Wales brought under the court's jurisdiction with respect to charities, or brought under the court's jurisdiction with respect to trusts in relation to the administration of a trust for charitable purposes.

In *Muman and others v Nagasena [1999] 4 All ER 178* premises used as a temple by a Buddhist charity were vested in the Official Custodian for Charities. The charity trustees brought possession proceedings against the defendant who had been named in the charity's constitution as the charity's patron or resident monk. The defendant alleged that, after the commencement of proceedings, the plaintiffs had been removed as trustees. It was held that trustees of a charity were entitled to bring proceedings in their own name to recover possession of property for the charity's purposes without obtaining the consent of the Official Custodian for Charities, or joining him in the proceedings. However, it was held that the dispute was an internal or domestic dispute and therefore constituted charity proceedings within the meaning of s 33 of the Charities Act 1993, and such proceedings required the consent of the Charity Commissioners or a judge of the Chancery Division under s 33 of the Charities Act.

LAND HELD BY OR FOR CHARITIES

14.28   Section 36(1) provides that no land held by or in trust for a charity shall be conveyed, transferred, leased or otherwise disposed of without an order of the court or of the Commission. Section 36(2) provides that s 36(1) shall not apply to a disposition of such land if the disposition is made to a person who is not:

(i)   a connected person, or

(ii) a trustee for, or nominee of, a connected person.

Schedule 5 to the Act defines 'connected person' as:

(a)   a charity trustee or trustee for the charity;

(b)   a person who is the donor of any land to the charity (whether the gift was made on or after the establishment of the charity);

(c)   a child, parent, grandchild, grandparent, brother or sister of any such trustee or donor;

(d)   an officer, agent or employee of the charity;

(e)   the spouse or civil partner of any person falling within any of sub-paragraphs (a) to (d) above;

(f)   an institution which is controlled:

   (i)   by any person falling within sub-paragraphs (a) to (e) above, or

   (ii) by two or more persons, such persons taken together; or

(g)   a body corporate in which:

   (i)   any connected person falling within any of sub-paragraphs (a) to (e) above has a substantial interest; or

   (ii) two or more such persons, taken together, have a substantial interest.

'Child' includes a stepchild and an illegitimate child; a person living with another as that person's husband or wife is to be treated as that person's spouse. There is also a definition of 'substantial interest in a body corporate'.

In addition, before entering into an agreement for the sale, or (as the case may be) for a lease or other disposition of the land, the charity trustees must:

(a) obtain and consider a written report on the proposed disposition from a qualified surveyor instructed by the trustees and acting exclusively for the charity;

(b) advertise the proposed disposition for such period and in such manner as the surveyor has advised in his report (unless he has there advised that it would not be in the best interests of the charity to advertise the proposed disposition); and

(c) decide that they are satisfied, having considered the surveyor's report, that the terms on which the disposition is proposed to be made are the best that can reasonably be obtained for the charity (s 36(3)).

Section 36(4) provides that a person is qualified as a surveyor if:

(a) he is a fellow or professional associate of the Royal Institution of Chartered Surveyors or of the Incorporated Society of Valuers and Auctioneers or satisfies such other requirement(s) as may be prescribed by regulations made by the Secretary of State; and

(b) he is reasonably believed by the charity trustees to have ability in, and experience of, the valuation of land of the particular kind, and in the particular area, in question.

Section 36(5) permits charity trustees to grant a lease for not more than seven years if no fine is paid for the grant of the lease. However, before entering into an agreement for the lease, the charity trustees must:

(a) obtain and consider the advice on the proposed disposition of a person who is reasonably believed by the trustees to have the requisite ability and practical experience to provide them with competent advice on the proposed disposition; and

(b) decide that they are satisfied, having considered that person's advice, that the terms on which the disposition is proposed to be made are the best that can reasonably be obtained for the charity.

Section 36(6) deals with the situation where land is held in trust for the charity, and the trusts on which it is so held stipulate that it is to be used for the purposes, or any particular purposes, of the charity. Such land cannot be conveyed, transferred, leased or otherwise disposed of unless the charity trustees have previously:

(i) given public notice of the proposed disposition inviting representations to be made to them within a time specified in the notice, being not less than one month from the date of the notice; and

(ii) taken into consideration any representations made to them within that time about the proposed disposition.

These requirements do not have to be complied with if:

(a)   the disposition is to be affected with a view to acquiring by way of replacement other property which is to be held on the trusts referred to in s 36(6)(b); or

(b)   the disposition is the granting of a lease for a term ending not more than two years after it is granted (other than one granted wholly or partly in consideration of a fine);

(s 36(7)).

Section 36(9) provides that the restrictions on dispositions imposed by the section apply notwithstanding anything in the trusts of the charity; but nothing in this section applies:

(a)   to any disposition for which general or special authority is expressly given (without the authority being made subject to the sanction of an order of the court) by any statutory provisions contained in or having effect under an Act of Parliament or by any scheme legally established; or

(b)   to any disposition of land held by or in trust for a charity which:

  (i)   is made to another charity otherwise than for the best price that can reasonably be obtained, and

  (ii)   is authorised to be so made by the trusts of the first mentioned charity; or

(c)   to the granting, by or on behalf of a charity and in accordance with its trusts, of a lease to any beneficiary under those trusts where the lease:

  (i)   is granted otherwise than for the best rent that can reasonably be obtained; and

  (ii)   is intended to enable the demised premises to be occupied for the purposes, or any particular purposes, of the charity.

Protection of purchasers

14.29   Section 37(1) provides that any contract for the sale, or for a lease or other disposition, of land which is held by or in trust for a charity, and any conveyance, transfer, lease, or other instrument effecting a disposition of such land must state *inter alia*:

 (i)   that the land is held by or in trust for a charity;

 (ii)   whether the charity is an exempt charity and whether the disposition is one falling within paragraph (a), (b), or (c) of s 36(9); and

(iii)   that the land is land to which the restrictions on disposition imposed by that section apply.

Section 37(2) provides that if the disposition is within s 36(1) the charity trustees must certify in the instrument by which the transaction is effected that the disposition has been sanctioned by an order of the court or of the Commissioners. If the transaction is within s 36(2), the trustees must certify that they have power under the trusts of the charity to effect the disposition and that they have complied with the provisions of that section so far as applicable to it. Section 37(3) provides that where s 37(2) has been complied with, it is to be conclusively presumed that the facts were as stated in the certificate in favour of a person who (whether under the disposition or afterwards) acquires an interest in the land for money or money's worth.

Section 37(4) provides that if s 36(2) is not complied with, then in favour of a person who (whether under the disposition or afterwards) in good faith acquires an interest in the land for money or money's worth, the disposition shall be valid whether or not:

(i)   the disposition has been sanctioned by an order of the court or of the Commissioners; or

(ii) the charity trustees have power under the trusts of the charity to effect the disposition and have complied with the provisions of that section so far as applicable to it.

Mortgaging

14.30   Section 38(1) forbids the granting of a mortgage by charity trustees unless it has been authorised by the court or the Commissioners. Section 38(2) provides that this does not apply where the charity trustees have obtained and considered proper advice in writing on the following matters:

(a)   whether the proposed loan is necessary in order for the charity trustees to be able to pursue the particular course of action in connection with which the loan is sought by them;

(b)   whether the terms of the proposed loan are reasonable having regard to the status of the charity as a prospective borrower; and

(c)   the ability of the charity to repay on those terms the sum proposed to be borrowed.

'Proper advice' is defined in s 38(4) as the advice of a person:

(a)   who is reasonably believed by the charity trustees to be qualified by his ability in and practical experience of financial matters; and

(b)   who has no financial interest in the making of the loan in question.

Such advice may constitute proper advice even though the person giving it does so in the course of his employment as an officer or employee of the charity or the charity trustees.

Manner of executing instruments

14.31   Section 82(1) authorises charity trustees to confer on at least two of their number authority to execute in the names and on behalf of the trustees assurances or other deeds for giving effect to transactions to which the trustees are a party. Section 82(2) provides that such an authority shall suffice for any deed or instrument if it is given in writing or by resolution of a meeting of the trustees, notwithstanding the want of any formality that would be required in giving an authority apart from subsection (1).

The authority may be given so as to make the powers conferred exercisable by any of the trustees, or may be restricted to named persons or in any other way (s 82(2)(b)). The authority continues until it is revoked notwithstanding any change in the trustees of the charity.

Section 82(3) provides that if such an authority is given, there is also an implied authority to execute it for them in the name and on behalf of the Official Custodian or of any other person.

Section 82(4) protects purchasers, and provides that where a deed or instrument purports to be executed in pursuance of this section, then in favour of a person who (then or afterwards) in good faith acquires for money or money's worth an interest in or charge on property or the benefit of any covenant or agreement expressed to be entered into by the charity trustees, it shall be conclusively presumed to have been duly executed by virtue of this section.

As will be seen later, charity trustees can incorporate. If this occurs, s 60(2) provides that if an incorporated body has a common seal, it may execute a document by affixing its common seal. Section 60(3) provides that a document may be executed by an incorporated body (regardless of whether it has a common seal) either:

(a)   by being signed by a majority of the trustees of the relevant charity and expressed (in whatever form of words) to be executed by the body; or

(b)   by being executed in pursuance of an authority given under subsection (4).

Subsection (4) permits the trustees of an incorporated charity to confer on any two or more of their number:

(a)   a general authority, or

(b)   an authority limited in such manner as the trustees think fit to execute, in the name and on behalf of the body, documents for giving effect to transactions to which the body is a party.

Section 60(5) provides that an authority under subsection (4) shall suffice if it is given in writing or by resolution of a meeting of the trustees of the relevant charity, notwithstanding the want of any formality that would be required in giving an authority apart from that subsection. The authority may be given so as to make the powers conferred exercisable by any of the trustees, or may be restricted to named persons or in any other way (s 60(5)(b)). The authority continues until it is revoked notwithstanding any change in the trustees of the charity.

Section 60(6) provides that if an authority is granted under subsection (4), there is implied authority to execute it for the body in the name and on behalf of the Official Custodian or of any other person in any case where the trustees could do so.

Section 60(7) provides that a document duly executed by an incorporated body, which makes it clear on its face that it is intended by the persons making it to be a deed, has effect, upon delivery, as a deed. It is also to be presumed that it is delivered on being so executed.

Section 60(8) provides that in favour of a purchaser a document shall be deemed to have been duly executed by an incorporated body if it purports to be signed:

(a)   by a majority of the trustees of the relevant charity; or

(b)   by such of the trustees of the relevant charity as are authorised by the trustees of that charity to execute it in the name and on behalf of the body.

Where a document makes it clear on its face that it is intended by the person or persons making it to be a deed, it shall be deemed to have been delivered on its being executed. For the purposes of s 60(8) 'purchaser' is defined as a purchaser in good faith for valuable consideration and includes a lessee, mortgagee or other person who for valuable consideration acquires an interest in property.

Transfer and evidence of title

14.32   Frequently charity trustees can be appointed or discharged by resolution of the charity trustees, members or other persons. In these circumstances, s 83(1) provides that a memorandum declaring a trustee to have been so appointed or discharged shall be sufficient evidence of that fact if the memorandum is signed either at the meeting by the person presiding or in some other manner directed by the meeting and is attested by two persons present at the meeting. Section 83(2) provides that such a memorandum, if executed as a deed, shall have the same effect as a deed executed under s 40 of the Trustee Act 1925 (this provides for the vesting of trust property in new or continuing trustees). Section 83(3) provides that where a document purports to have been signed and attested as mentioned in subsection (1), then on proof (whether by evidence or as a matter of presumption) of the signature, the document shall be presumed to have been so signed and attested, unless the contrary is shown.

ACCOUNTS, REPORTS AND RECORDS

14.33   Section 41(1) requires charity trustees to ensure that accounting records are kept in respect of the charity which are sufficient to explain all the charity's transactions, and which are such as to:

(a)   disclose, at any time with reasonably accuracy, the financial position of the charity at that time; and

(b)   enable the trustees to ensure that, where any statements of accounts are prepared by them under s 42(1) (see below), those statements of accounts comply with the requirements of regulations under that provision.

The accounting records must contain entries showing from day to day all sums of money received and expended by the charity, and the matters in respect of which the receipt and expenditure took place. The accounts must also contain a record of the assets and liabilities of the charity.

Section 41(3) provides that charity trustees of a charity must preserve any accounting records made for the purpose of the section in respect of the charity for at least six years from the end of the financial year of the charity in which they are made.

Section 42(1) obliges charity trustees to prepare in each financial year a statement of accounts in accordance with regulations made by the Secretary of State. Section 42(3) provides that where the gross income of a charity does not exceed £100,000 in any one financial year, the charity trustees need not comply with s 42(1), and instead they may elect to prepare the following:

(a)   a receipts and payments account;

(b)   a statement of assets and liabilities.

Section 43 as amended by the Charities Bill requires the accounts of a charity to be audited if the charity's gross income or total expenditure in the year in question, or the previous or subsequent year, exceeds £2500,000, or the charity's gross income in that year exceeds the accounts threshold and at the end of the year the aggregate value of the assets before deduction of liabilities exceeds

£2.8m. The accounts threshold at the moment is £100,000. The auditor must be a person who is eligible for appointment as a company auditor, or who is a member of a body for the time being specified in regulations made under s 44, and is eligible under the rules of that body for appointment as auditor of the charity.

The accounts of other charities, if the gross income or total expenditure in that year exceeds £10,000, can either be audited, or examined by an independent examiner who must have the appropriate qualifications.

Section 45 obliges charity trustees to prepare an annual report, and to send it to the Commissioners within ten months from the end of any financial year. The report must have attached to it the statement of accounts prepared for the financial year in question.

Section 46(1) provides that ss 41 to 45 do not apply to any exempt charities. However, the charity trustees of an exempt charity are required to keep proper books of account with respect to the affairs of the charity, and if not required to prepare periodical statements of account, they must prepare consecutive statements of account consisting on each occasion of an income and expenditure account relating to a period of not more than 15 months and a balance sheet relating to the end of that period.

Section 48(1) obliges every registered charity to lodge with the Commission a return containing such information as may be prescribed by the Commission.

These sections are modified if the gross income or the total expenditure does not exceed £10,000 in the year in question.

INCORPORATION OF TRUSTEES OF A CHARITY

14.34   Section 50(1) authorises charity trustees to apply for a certificate of incorporation of the trustees as a body corporate. The Commissioners may grant such a certificate if they consider that it is in the interests of the charity. If the certificate is granted, the trustees become a body corporate by such name as is specified in the certificate (s 50(3)). After incorporation, the trustees may sue and be sued in their corporate name, and have the same powers and are subject to the same restrictions and limitations as regards the holding, acquisition and disposal of property for or in connection with the purposes of the charity as they had or were subject to whilst unincorporated (s 50(4)). A body incorporated under the section need not have a common seal.

Section 51 provides that the certificate of incorporation vests in the body corporate all real and personal estate, of whatever nature or tenure, belonging to or held by any person(s) in trust for the charity, and thereupon any person(s) in whose name any stocks, funds or securities are standing in trust for the charity shall transfer them into the name of the body corporate. This provision does not apply to property vested in the Official Custodian.

Section 52 prescribes that every application for a certificate of incorporation must be in writing and signed by the trustees of the charity. It must also be accompanied by such documents or information as the Commission may require.

Section 54 provides that trustees have the same duties as if no incorporation had taken place.

Section 61(1) empowers the Commissioners to dissolve an incorporated body on various grounds, for example that the incorporated body has no assets or does not operate.

CHARITABLE COMPANIES

14.35   Section 63(1) permits the Attorney-General to present a petition to the High Court for the winding up of a charitable company.

Section 64(1) provides that a charitable company cannot exercise any power to alter the instruments establishing or regulating it so that it ceases to be a charity so as to affect the application of:

(a)   any property acquired under any disposition or agreement previously made otherwise than for full consideration in money or money's worth, or any property representing property so acquired;

(b)   any property representing income which has accrued before the alteration is made; or

(c)   the income from any such property as aforesaid.

Where the charity is a company, any alteration by it:

(a)   of the object's clause in its memorandum of association, or

(b)   of any other provision in its memorandum of association, or of any provision in its articles of association, which is a provision directing or restricting the manner in which the property of the company may be used or applied,

is ineffective without the prior written consent of the Commissioners.

Section 68(1) provides that if a company is a charity and its name does not include the word 'charity' or the word 'charitable', the fact that the company is a charity shall be stated in legible characters:

(a)   in all business letters of the company;

(b)   in all its notices and other official publications;

(c)   in all bills of exchange, promissory notes, endorsements, cheques, and orders for money or goods purporting to be signed on behalf of the company;

(d)   in all conveyances, purporting to be executed by the company; and

(e)   in all bills rendered by it and in all its invoices, receipts, and letters of credit.

Section 68(2) provides that 'conveyance' means any instrument creating, transferring, varying or extinguishing an interest in land.

DISQUALIFICATION FROM ACTING AS A TRUSTEE

14.36   Section 72(1) provides that a person shall be disqualified from being a charity trustee on various grounds; these include that the person has been convicted of any offence involving dishonesty or deception, or the person has been adjudged bankrupt or sequestration of his estate has been made and in either case he has not been discharged, or the person has made a composition or arrangement with, or granted a trust deed for, his creditors and has not been discharged in respect of it.

NOTICES WITH REGARD TO CHARITY MEETINGS

14.37   Section 81(1) provides that all notices which are required or authorised by the trusts of a charity to be given to a charity trustee, member or subscriber may be sent by post, and if sent by post, may be addressed to any address given as his in the list of charity trustees, members or subscribers for the time being in use at the office or principal offices of the charity.

GIFTS TO UNINCORPORATED NON-CHARITABLE ASSOCIATIONS

14.38   Reference has already been made in chapter 5 to some of the problems associated with non-charitable unincorporated associations.

A donor or testator may wish to give property to an unincorporated non-charitable association. There are many such associations in existence – gardening clubs, sports clubs, and other clubs associated with leisure activities. What is the effect of a gift to one of these societies? In *Neville Estates Ltd v Madden [1962] Ch 832* Cross J said at page 849:

> 'Such a gift [to an unincorporated association] may take effect in one or other of three different ways. In the first place, it may, on its true construction, be a gift to the members at the relevant date as joint tenants, so that any member can sever his share and claim it whether or not he continues as a member of the association. Secondly, it may be a gift to the existing members not as joint tenants, but subject to their respective contractual rights and liabilities towards one another as members of the association. In such a case a member cannot sever his share. It will accrue to other members on his death or resignation, even though such members include persons who became members after the gift took effect … .

> Thirdly, the terms or circumstances of the gift or the rules of the association may show that the property in question is to be at the disposal of the members for the time being, but is to be held in trust for or applied for the purposes of the association as a quasi-corporate entity. In this case the gift will fail unless the association is a charitable body.'

It is suggested that the most satisfactory way of dealing with this problem is the contractual solution. The rules of an association should be drafted on this basis at the outset as it may be difficult to amend the rules at a later date.

FOREIGN CHARITIES

14.39   In *Gaudiya Mission and others v Brahmachary and others [1997] 4 All ER 957* the plaintiff mission was registered as a body corporate in India. It enjoyed charitable status there. Proceedings were commenced in England concerning the charity without obtaining the consent of the Charity Commissioners as required by s 33(2) of the Charities Act 1993. It was held that the Charities Act applied only to institutions established for charitable purposes under English law, and accordingly the consent of the Charity Commissioners in this case was not required.

CRIMINAL OFFENCES

14.40   It should be noted that some sections of the Charities Act (e.g. ss 5 and 11) create criminal offences. Section 94(1) provides that no proceedings for an offence to which this section applies shall be instituted except by or with the consent of the Director of Public Prosecutions.

TAXATION OF CHARITIES

Inheritance tax

14.41 Section 23(1) of the Inheritance Tax Act 1984 provides that gifts to charities are exempt from inheritance tax. Section 23(3) provides that this exemption does not apply if the gift is of an interest in other property, and that interest is less than the donor's, or the property is given for a limited period only. Section 23(4) provides that if the gift is of land or buildings, the gift will not be exempt if the donor, or the donor's spouse, or any person connected with him, can occupy the property rent-free or at a rent less than that which might be expected to be obtained in a transaction at arm's length between persons not connected with each other. There are similar provisions with regard to property other than land.

Capital gains tax

14.42 Section 257(2) of the Taxation of Chargeable Gains Act 1992 provides that if the disposal is a gift or for a consideration less than the deductible expenditure, it is to be treated as being made for such consideration as to secure that neither a gain nor a loss accrues on the disposal.

Income tax

Covenants in favour of charities

14.43 Covenants in favour of charities were very common, and now qualify for gift aid relief, which is discussed below.

Payroll deduction scheme

14.44 This applies to employees whose employers operate a scheme approved by the Board of the Inland Revenue, or which is of a kind approved by the Board. If the requirements are satisfied, the employer withholds part of the salary of the employee; that part withheld is deductible in calculating the tax liability of the employee. The scheme must provide for payments to an agent approved by the Board, who pays them to a charity or charities. In addition, the employer can pay the sums withheld direct to a charity or charities. The sums must be withheld in accordance with a request by the employee that they be paid to a charity or charities in accordance with a scheme approved by the Board. Furthermore, the sums must constitute gifts to the charity, and must not be paid under a deed of covenant. There is now no limit on the amount which can be given.

A statutory instrument has been made in order to implement the section (SI 1986 No 2211).

Gift aid

14.45   Section 25 of Finance Act 1990 as amended provides tax relief on individual gifts to charity. The following conditions must be satisfied in respect of the gift (s 25(2)):

(a)   it must take the form of a payment of a sum of money;

(b)   it must not be subject to a condition as to repayment;

(c)   it must not constitute a sum falling within s 713(3) of the Income Tax (Earnings and Pensions) Act 2003 (payroll deduction scheme);

(d)   neither the donor nor any person connected with him must receive a benefit in consequence of making it or, where the donor or a person connected does receive a benefit in consequence of making it, the relevant value in relation to the gift does not exceed two and a half per cent of the amount of the gift if the value of the gift is £1,000 or more. If the gift is of a sum between £100 and £1,000 the value of the benefit must not exceed £25. If the gift is less than £100, the value of the benefit must not exceed 25 per cent of the amount of the gift. There is an overall maximum for all benefits of £250;

(e)   it must not be conditional on or associated with, or part of an arrangement involving, the acquisition of property by the charity otherwise than by way of gift, from the donor or a person connected with him; and

(f)   the donor must be resident in the United Kingdom at the time the gift is made, or is in Crown employment as defined in s 28(2)(a) of the Income Tax (Earnings and Pensions) Act 2003 (Crown employees serving overseas) or the grossed up amount of the gift would, if in fact made, be payable out of profits or gains brought into charge to income tax or capital gains tax.

Section 25(1) provides that the donor must make an appropriate declaration. Section 25(6) provides that a qualifying donation has effect as the gift of the grossed up amount of the gift. Thus the charity can recover the amount of tax attributable to the gift. Section 25(6) and (8) provide that the grossed up amount is deductible in calculating the profits or gains of the donor. If the gift is paid out of income or gains not subject to tax, the donor has to account to the Revenue for the tax. If the payment is wholly out of taxed income, the donor will not have to pay any more tax (the income used to pay the charity has already been taxed); the charity will be able to recover the tax attributable to the payment.

Gifts of quoted shares

14.46   There is no charge to IHT or CGT on such a gift. From 2000/2001 such a gift will also qualify for income tax relief. The relief operates by allowing the value of the gift to be deducted from the donor's income.

Gifts to educational establishments

14.47   Section 84 of the Income and Corporation Taxes Act 1988 gives relief to companies carrying on a trade or profession or, if they make gifts of certain types of property for the purposes of a designated educational establishment. Section 84(1) provides that the gift must be of an article manufactured, or of a class or description sold by the donor in the course of his trade which qualifies as machinery or plant in the hands of the educational establishment.

Section 84(2) defines what is meant by 'qualifies as machinery or plant'; in effect the article must be regarded as machinery or plant for the purposes of Part II of the Capital Allowances Act 2001 on the assumption that the educational establishment is carrying on a trade.

If the conditions in s 84 are complied with, the donor does not have to bring into account any amount as a trading receipt, or the disposal value of an article falling within s 84(1)(b). If the donor or any person connected with him receives a benefit as a result of the gift, that benefit is chargeable to income tax (s 84(4)).

Section 108 of the Income Tax (Trading and other Income) Act gives a similar relief to traders on a gift of trading stock.

Income of charities

14.48   Section 505 of the Income and Corporation Taxes Act 1988 exempts from income tax most charitable income, so far as it is applied for charitable purposes. If the income is not applied for charitable purposes, the exemption will not apply, and in addition it may be that the trustees will commit a breach of trust.

Section 505(1)(e) exempts the profits of any trade carried on by a charity if the profits are applied solely to the purposes of the charity and either:

(i) the trade is exercised in the course of the actual carrying out of the primary purpose of the charity; or

(ii) the work in connection with the trade is mainly carried out by beneficiaries of the charity.

Many charities operate shops in prominent high street locations. The income from these shops may not come within the exemption in s 505(1)(e), and in this situation the usual practice is to establish a separate trading company, which then enters into a covenant with the charity to pay all the income to it. In this way the income will not be taxed.

Stamp duty and stamp duty land tax

14.49 Section 129 of Finance Act 1982 provides that stamp duty is not payable on any conveyance, transfer, or lease to a charity. Section 129(2) provides that the instrument must be stamped with a stamp denoting that it is not chargeable with any duty.

Charities do not have to pay stamp duty land tax provided that the charity holds the land for use in the furtherance of the charitable purposes of the purchaser or another charity, or as an investment from which the profits are applied to the charitable purposes of the purchaser. In addition, the transaction must not have been entered into for the purpose of avoiding tax (Finance Act 2003 Schedule 8).

Value added tax

14.50 Charities are liable for VAT, both on goods and services they provide and purchase.

REMUNERATION OF CHARITY TRUSTEES

14.51 Under the Trustee Act 2000 charitable trustees may be entitled to remuneration; for a discussion of these provisions, please see chapter 2 above.

Clause 73A as inserted by the Charities Bill provides that charity trustees or someone connected with such a person are entitled to remuneration out of the funds of the charity provided the following conditions are satisfied:

(A)   The amount or maximum amount of the remuneration:

    (a)   is set out in an agreement in writing between:

        (i)   the charity or its charity trustees (as the case may be), and

        (ii)   the relevant person, under which the relevant person is to provide the services in question to or on behalf of the charity; and

    (b)   does not exceed what is reasonable in the circumstances for the provision by that person of the services in question.

(B)   Before entering into that agreement, the charity trustees decided that they were satisfied that it would be in the best interests of the charity for the services to be provided by the relevant person to or on behalf of the charity for the amount or maximum amount of remuneration set out in the agreement.

(C)   Immediately after the agreement is entered into there is, in the case of the charity, more than one person who is a charity trustee and is:

    (a)   a person in respect of whom an agreement within (A) is in force, or

    (b)   a person who is entitled to receive remuneration out of the funds of the charity otherwise than by virtue of such an agreement, or

    (c)   a person connected with a person falling within paragraphs (a) or (b) above,

the total number of them constitute a minority of the persons for the time being holding office as charity trustees of the charity.

(D)   The trusts of the charity do not contain any express provision that prohibits the relevant person from receiving the remuneration.

INDEMNITY INSURANCE

14.52   Charity trustees are empowered to purchase indemnity insurance, and to pay the premiums out of the funds of the charity (clause 73E as inserted by the Charities Bill). However, this insurance cannot include inter alia indemnities for fines imposed in criminal proceedings, or any liability incurred by him to the charity that arises out of any conduct which he knew or must reasonably be assumed to have known was not in the interests of the charity or in the case of which he did not care whether it was in the best interests of the charity or not.

PUBLIC CHARITABLE COLLECTIONS

14.53   Part 3 of the Charities Bill contains provisions about public charitable collections. It is necessary to obtain a public collections certificate from the

Commission. If the collection is to be made in a public place, it is necessary to obtain a permit form the local authority for the area.

SUMMARY

14.54

- In order to be charitable, a trust must be exclusively for the relief of poverty, the advancement of education, the advancement of religion, or other purposes beneficial to the community.

- Apart from trusts for the relief of poverty, the trust must be for the public benefit.

- If the charitable purpose fails at the outset, the assets can be applied cy-près if there is a general charitable intention; if there is a subsequent failure, no such general charitable intention is required.

- A gift to a charity must vest within the perpetuity period, but thereafter charities are not subject to the rule against perpetuities.

- The Charity Commissioners can make schemes for charities.

- The Charities Act 1993 has provisions to deal with appeals and collections where the charitable purpose fails.

- Most charities must be registered with the Charity Commissioners.

- A charity must usually disclose the fact that it is a registered charity.

- The Charity Commissioners can make schemes for charities dealing *inter alia* with the administration of the charity, establishing common investment funds, etc.

- The Charity Commissioners may permit a charity to make payments in discharge of a moral obligation.

- The costs of solicitors acting for charity trustees can be taxed by the court.

- Charity Commissioners must usually sanction any court proceedings on behalf of the charity.

- Charities can sell charity land as long as they comply with various requirements.

- Charity trustees must keep accounting records.

- Charity trustees can be incorporated.

- The Charities Act 1993 contains provisions dealing with the execution of documents and the protection of purchasers.

- There are various exemptions from taxation for charities.

Chapter 15

Trusts on divorce

THE MATRIMONIAL HOME

15.1   It is believed that most married couples and cohabitees now purchase the matrimonial home in joint names. Of course the correct legal analysis is that the legal estate in the house is transferred to both parties, who then hold it on trust. In equity, the spouses or cohabitees are joint tenants or tenants in common.

The standard Land Registry transfer contains a declaration as to whether the purchasers are joint tenants or tenants in common. If the declaration is that the purchasers are tenant in common, a restriction will be entered by the Land Registry preventing the disposition of the property by a sole trustee.

What is the position if the house is in the name of both parties to a relationship, and they have been registered as joint tenants in equity? It could be argued that the registration as joint tenants was conclusive, and that evidence that one party contributed more was irrelevant. However, in *Stack v Dowden [2005] EWCA 887* S and D cohabited and had four children. They then purchased the family home as joint tenants both at law and in equity, but they were not advised about the difference between joint tenants and tenants in common. The relationship broke down, and there was litigation as to their respective shares in the family home. The evidence was that S had contributed more than D. S limited her claim to 65% of the home, and was awarded this.

It was held that the mere fact that the parties had been registered as if they were joint tenants in equity did not stop a court holding that their beneficial interests were different.

However, in *Clarke v Harlow [2005] WTLR 1473* C and H met in 1977, and cohabited until 2003. H was a successful solicitor, but C had various jobs, some full-time, some part-time.

In 2001 a property, Bank House, was purchased, and it was declared in the transfer that the parties were joint tenants. It was understood that H would pay the mortgage instalments, and the cost of refurbishing the property.

When the relationship broke down, H argued that C was not entitled to one-half of the proceeds on the principle of equitable accounting.

It was held that in the absence of fraud or mistake, the declaration of trust in the transfer was conclusive. It was open to the court to infer an agreement to vary this, but such an inference would only be made in exceptional circumstances. There was no duty to account unless there had been a breach of some duty or obligation owed by one party to the other.

Once the parties separate, then equitable accounting can apply. In this case, all the improvements were carried out before the separation. There was no suggestion that C would contribute to the cost. In addition, it had always been understood that H would pay the mortgage instalments, so there was no room for the doctrine of equitable accounting.

Enforcement of a sale of the property

15.2 Section 14 of the Trusts of Land and Appointment of Trustees Act 1996 authorises any person interested to apply to the court if the trustees refuse to sell. The court may make such order as it thinks fit. The operation of this section has already been examined in chapter 9.

Section 24A, as amended, of the Matrimonial Causes Act 1973 confers wide powers of sale on the court in matrimonial proceedings. It provides that where the court makes a secured periodical payments order, an order for the payment of a lump sum or a property adjustment order, then on making that order, or at any time thereafter, the court may make a further order for the sale of such property as may be specified in the order, being property in which or in the proceeds of sale of which either or both of the parties to the marriage has or have a beneficial interest, either in possession or reversion.

LUMP SUMS FOR THE BENEFIT OF CHILDREN

15.3 The court has power to order the payment of a lump sum for the benefit of a child. If the sum is large, it may be that the court will order that it should be settled. On the other hand, if it is small, the expense involved in a settlement will render one inappropriate in the circumstances. Such orders are rarely made.

PROPERTY ADJUSTMENT ORDERS

15.4 Sections 21 to 24, as amended, of the Matrimonial Causes Act 1973 confer wide powers on the court to make property adjustment orders in connection with divorce proceedings. On granting a decree of divorce, a decree of nullity of marriage or a decree of judicial separation (whether, in the case of a decree of divorce or of nullity of marriage, before or after the decree is made absolute), the court may make any one or more of the following orders:

(a)   an order that a party to a marriage shall transfer such of his or her property as may be specified to the other party, or to a child of the family;

(b)   an order that a settlement of such property of a party, as may be specified, must be made to the satisfaction of the court for the benefit of the other party to the marriage and of the children of the family or either or any of them;

(c)   an order varying, for the benefit of the parties to the marriage and of the children to the family or either or any of them, any ante-nuptial or post-nuptial settlement; or

(d)   an order extinguishing or reducing the interest of either of the parties under any marriage settlement.

It should be noted that 'property' has a broad meaning, and includes income as well as capital. It also includes future interests like reversionary interests.

This book is not intended to deal with the orders which could be made under this section which do not involve trusts; however, it may be that the court will decide that it would be appropriate to vest property, frequently the house, in the parties on trust. If the house is the subject of an order, the order, or any trust instrument required to implement it, should deal with the following aspects:

• who is entitled to live in the property;

• who is to be responsible for the outgoings like insurance;

• when the house can be sold, for example, when a child has attained 18;

• the proportions in which the parties are to be entitled to the proceeds of sale; and

• the circumstances in which the property can be mortgaged to raise money for future major repairs.

VARIATION OF AN EXISTING SETTLEMENT

15.5   Sections 21 to 24, as amended, of the Matrimonial Causes Act 1973 provide that the court may make an order varying for the benefit of parties to the marriage and of the children of the family or either or any of them any marriage settlement. The court may also make an order extinguishing or reducing the interest of either of the parties to the marriage under any such settlement.

It should be noted that the courts have tended to construe the word 'settlement' widely. In *Brown v Brown [1959] P 86* there was a conveyance to spouses as joint tenants. The conveyance contained an express declaration of a trust for sale. It was held that this was a settlement. In *Brooks v Brooks [1993] 3 WLR 548* the husband was a member of a pension scheme established after the date of the marriage. This was held to be a post-nuptial settlement within the Matrimonial Causes Act.

RESETTLEMENT OF PROPERTY

15.6   The court may make an order for the resettlement of property. This will occur when the legal estate is already held upon trust, and the court may vary the trust rather than make an order for the transfer or settlement of property.

FACTORS TO BE TAKEN INTO ACCOUNT BY THE COURT

15.7   Section 25(1), as amended, of the Matrimonial Causes Act 1973 provides that the court must have regard to all the circumstances of the case, first consideration being given to the welfare while a minor of any child of the family who has not attained the age of 18.

Section 25(2) provides that in relation to a party to a marriage, the court shall have regard to the following matters:

(a)   the income, earning capacity, property and other financial resources which each of the parties to the marriage has or is likely to have in the foreseeable future, including in the case of earning capacity any increase in that capacity which it would in the opinion of the court be reasonable to expect a party to the marriage to take steps to acquire;

(b)   the financial needs, obligations and responsibilities which each of the parties to the marriage has or is likely to have in the foreseeable future;

(c)   the standard of living enjoyed by the family before the breakdown of the marriage;

(d)   the age of each party to the marriage, and the duration of the marriage;

(e)   any physical or mental disability of either of the parties to the marriage;

(f)   the contribution which each of the parties has made or is likely in the foreseeable future to make to the welfare of the family, including any contributions by way of looking after the home or caring for the family;

(g)   the conduct of each of the parties, if that conduct is such that it would in the opinion of the court be inequitable to disregard it; and

(h)   the value to each of the parties to the marriage of any benefit which, by reason of the dissolution or annulment of the marriage, that party will lose the chance of acquiring.

In relation to a child of the family, s 25(3) requires the court to have regard to the following matters:

(a)   the financial needs of the child;

(b)   the income, earning capacity (if any), property and other financial resources of the child;

(c)   any physical or mental disability of the child;

(d)   the manner in which he was being and in which the parties to the marriage expected him to be educated or trained; and

(e)   the considerations mentioned in paragraphs (a), (b), (c) and (e) in subsection (2).

The court will thus take into account entitlements under trusts, including discretionary trusts, and pension rights.

LIFE POLICIES

15.8   There are three situations to consider with regard to life policies.

- The policy may still be owned by the policyholder.

- The policy may have been the subject of a declaration of trust in favour of the spouse and the children.

- The policy may have been used to fund the purchase of the matrimonial home.

The policy can of course be surrendered, but it may be that it can be treated as a paid-up policy. If the policy is not surrendered, it is clearly property within s 24 of the Matrimonial Causes Act 1973, and can be made the subject of orders under that section. If the policy is subject to a declaration of trust, this is clearly a settlement for the purpose of s 24, and the settlement can be varied or resettled.

If the policy has been used to fund the purchase of the matrimonial home, the policy may have to be maintained. If the mortgagee agrees, it may be possible to surrender the policy, and treat the mortgage as an instalment mortgage.

PARTNERSHIP INTERESTS

15.9   It is clear that the partnership interest of a party to a marriage is property for the purpose of ss 21–24, as amended, of the Matrimonial Causes Act 1973. However, it may not be possible for the court to make any order regarding the partnership interest as the partnership agreement may prohibit any form of assignment. Furthermore, any order with regard to the partnership interest may be undesirable as it might cause the partner to lose interest in the business to the detriment of the former spouse and the children of the marriage.

SHARES IN PRIVATE COMPANIES

15.10   There is no doubt that shares in small companies may be made the subject of an order under ss 21–24, as amended, but again there may be restrictions in the articles of association of the company prohibiting the transfer of shares.

PENSION BENEFITS

15.11   The Pensions Act 1995 introduced pension 'earmarking'; 'pension sharing' was introduced with effect from 1 December 2000.

Section 21A of the Matrimonial Causes Act 1973, as amended, provides for pension sharing. It applies to:

(i)   shareable rights under a specified pension arrangement; or

(ii)   shareable state scheme rights.

Section 21A(2) provides that the reference to shareable rights under a pension arrangement is to rights in relation to which pension sharing is available under Chapter I of Part IV of the Welfare Reform and Pensions Act 1999. It also provides that the reference to shareable state scheme rights is to rights in relation to which pension sharing is available under Chapter II of Part IV of the Welfare Reform and Pensions Act 1999.

The pension sharing order must specify the percentage value to be transferred.

Section 24B(1) of the Matrimonial Causes Act 1973 provides that on granting a decree of divorce or a decree of nullity of marriage or at any time thereafter, the court may make one or more pension sharing orders in relation to the marriage. These orders can be made either before or after the decree is made absolute, but any pension sharing order under the section is not to take effect unless the decree on or after which it has been made has been made absolute (s 24B(2)).

Section 24B(3) provides that a pension sharing order under s 24B may not be made in relation to a pension arrangement which:

(a)   is the subject of a pension sharing order in relation to the marriage; or

(b)   has been the subject of pension sharing between the parties to the marriage.

There is a similar provision with regard to shareable state scheme rights in s 24B(4).

With regard to earmarking, section 25B(1) provides that the matters to which the court is to have regard under s 25(2) above include:

(a)   in the case of s 25(2)(a) (see **15.7** above), any benefits under a pension arrangement which a party to the marriage has or is likely to have, and

(b)   in the case of s 25(2)(h) (see **15.7** above), any benefits under a pension arrangement which, by reason of the dissolution or annulment of the marriage, a party to the marriage will lose the chance of acquiring.

In relation to benefits under a pension arrangement, s 25(2)(a) is to have effect as if the words 'in the foreseeable future' had been omitted.

If the court determines to make a financial provision order under s 22A or 23 (i.e. in connection with divorce, separation or nullity proceedings), the following provisions apply:

- to the extent to which the order is made having regard to any benefits under a pension arrangement, the order may require the person responsible for the pension arrangement in question, if at any time any payment in respect of any benefits under the arrangement becomes due to the party with pension rights, to make a payment for the benefit of the other party (s 25B(4));

- the order must express the amount of any payment required to be made as a percentage of the payment which becomes due to the party with pension rights (s 25B(5));

- any such payment by the person responsible for the arrangement:

    (i)   shall discharge so much of his liability to the party with pension rights as corresponds to the amount of the payment; and

    (ii) shall be treated for all purposes as a payment made by the party with pension rights in or towards the discharging of his liability under the order (s 25B(6));

- where the party with pension rights has a right of commutation under the arrangement, the order may require him to exercise it to any extent (s 25B(7));

- the section applies to any payment due in consequence of commutation in pursuance of the order as it applies to other payments in respect of benefits under the arrangement (s 25B(7));

- the power conferred by subs (7) above may not be exercised for the purpose of commuting a benefit payable to the party with pension rights to a benefit payable to the other party (s 25B(7A));

- the power to require the person responsible for the pension arrangement to make payments for the benefit of the other party or the power to require a party with pension rights who has a right of commutation under the arrangement to exercise that power may not be exercised in relation to a pension arrangement which:

  (i) is the subject of a pension sharing order in relation to the marriage; or

  (ii) has been the subject of pension sharing between the parties to the marriages (s 25B(7B)).

Section 25C(1) contains provisions dealing with lump sums. It provides that the power of the court to order a party to a marriage to pay a lump sum to the other party includes, where the benefits which the party with pension rights has or is likely to have under a pension arrangement include any lump sum payable in respect of his death, power to make the provisions in the order set out in s 25C(2). Section 25C(2) provides that the court may:

(a) if the person responsible for the pension arrangement in question has power to determine the person to whom the sum, or any part of it, is to be paid, require him to pay the whole or part of that sum, when it becomes due, to the other party;

(b) if the party with pension rights has power to nominate the person to whom the sum, or any part of it, is to be paid, require the party with pension rights to nominate the other party in respect of the whole or part of that sum;

(c) in any other case, require the person responsible for the pension arrangement in question to pay the whole or part of that sum, when it becomes due, for the benefit of the other party instead of to the person to whom, apart from the order, it would be paid.

Section 25C(3) provides that any payment made by the person responsible for the arrangement under an order made under ss 22A or 23 by virtue of s 25C discharges so much of his liability in respect of the party with pension rights as corresponds to the amount of the payment.

265

Section 25C(4) provides that the powers conferred by this section may not be exercised in relation to a pension arrangement which:

(a)   is the subject of a pension sharing order in relation to the marriage; or

(b)   has been the subject of pension sharing between the parties to the marriage.

Section 25D(3) provides that 'a pension arrangement' not only includes an occupational pension scheme or a personal pension scheme but also extends to a retirement annuity contract and an annuity or insurance policy purchased or transferred for the purpose of giving effect to rights under a pension scheme.

TAXATION CONSEQUENCES

Disposals between spouses

Inheritance tax

15.12   Transfers between spouses are exempt. This exemption continues until the divorce is made absolute, even though the parties are living apart (s 18 of the Inheritance Tax Act 1984). If it is not possible to claim this exemption, it may be that it will come within s 11 – dispositions for the maintenance of the family.

Alternatively, it may be that s 10 of the Inheritance Tax Act 1984 will apply. This provides that a disposition not intended to confer gratuitous benefit is not a transfer of value, and s 11 provides that a disposition is not a transfer of value if it is made by one party to a marriage in favour of the other party or of a child of either party. It must also be for the maintenance of the other party, or subject to limitations for the maintenance, education or training of a child. This section also means that a disposition on divorce is not a transfer of value.

Capital gains tax

15.13   Section 58 of the Taxation of Chargeable Gains Act 1992 provides that on disposals between spouses, both are to be treated as if the asset was acquired from the one making the disposal for a consideration of such amount as would secure that on the disposal neither a gain nor a loss would accrue to the one making the disposal. However, this provision applies only if the parties are living together, and so any disposals between spouses must take place in the tax year of separation in order to take advantage of this provision.

EXAMPLE

S1 purchases an asset for £300,000, and spends £50,000 improving it.

S1 gives it to spouse S2 when the asset is worth £500,000.

As long as S1 and S2 are living together, then S2 will be deemed to acquire the asset for £350,000. There will be no charge to capital gains tax as far as S1 is concerned.

If s 58 does not apply, the parties are connected persons until the divorce is made absolute, and so any disposal between them will be deemed to be at market value.

In the above example, if S1 and S2 are not living together, then S2 will be deemed to dispose of the asset at market value, £500,000, and will incur a liability for capital gains tax.

Settlement of the matrimonial home

15.14   This is where one spouse is given the right to live in the matrimonial home, perhaps for life, or alternatively until a child has attained a specific age. Ultimately, the proceeds from the sale of the house are to be divided between the parties.

Inheritance tax

15.15   As a result of the changes to the taxation of trusts, the settlement will be a chargeable disposal, and so IHT will be payable if the assets transferred are in excess of the nil rate band. In addition there will be principal charges to IHT and also proportionate charges. For a fuller discussion of the taxation of trusts created during the lifetime of the settlor, please see chapter 13.

However, for the reasons outlined above, the creation of the settlement will not be a transfer of value, but when the spouse in occupation ceases to be resident there, again there will be an exit or proportionate charge to IHT as far as the interest of that spouse is concerned.

Capital gains tax

15.16   Normally the settlement should not give rise to any liability for CGT because it will come within the private residence exemption. However, for this to apply, the settlement must take place within three years of the dwelling house ceasing to be the only or main residence of the non-occupying spouse (s 223(1) of the Taxation of Chargeable Gains Act 1992). If this provision does not apply, it may be that ESC D6 will operate to exclude liability. It should be noted that this applies only if the occupying spouse has continued to live in the house. In addition, the non-occupying spouse must not have elected that another house should be treated for CGT purposes as his main residence.

As this is not an immediate post death interest, if the right to occupy the house terminates, for example because the occupying spouse remarries, there will be a deemed disposal at market value of the interest the trustees hold, but there will be no charge because of the private residence exemption. If it terminates because of the death of the occupying spouse, again there will be a deemed disposal at market value, but there will be no charge to CGT because of the private residence exemption.

SUMMARY

15.17
* Clients should be advised about the difference between joint tenants and tenants in common.

* On divorce, the courts can order property to be settled, the variation of an existing settlement, or the resettlement of property.

* Normally there will be no charge to IHT on transfer between spouses or ex-spouses.

* If the former matrimonial home is settled, usually there will be no IHT or CGT payable when the settlement is created but there may be when it terminates.

Chapter 16

Passing of property on death

INTESTACY RULES AND THE STATUTORY TRUSTS

Total intestacy

16.1   Section 33(1) of the Administration of Estates Act 1925 imposes a trust in the case of a person who dies intestate. It provides that on the death of a person intestate as to any real or personal estate, such estate shall be held in trust by his personal representatives with the power to sell it – with power to postpone such sale and conversion for such period as the personal representatives, without being liable to account, may think proper.

Section 33(2) provides that out of the ready money of the deceased (so far as not disposed of by his will, if any) and any net money arising from disposing of any other part of his estate (after payment of costs), the personal representatives must pay all such funeral, testamentary and administration expenses, debts and other liabilities as are properly payable thereout having regard to the rules of administration contained in that Part of the Act. Having done that, the personal representatives are then required to set aside a fund sufficient to provide for any pecuniary legacies bequeathed by the will, if any.

Section 33(3) directs that during the minority of any beneficiary, or the subsistence of any life interest, the money, or so much thereof as may not have been distributed, may be invested under the Trustee Act 2000.

Section 33(5) provides that the income of so much of the real and personal estate of the deceased as may not be disposed of by his will, if any, or may not be required for administration purposes, may as from the death of the deceased be treated and applied as income. If necessary, the income must be apportioned between the life tenant and the remainderman. This applies however the estate is invested.

Partial intestacy

16.2   Section 33 clearly contemplates that the section will apply to a partial intestacy, as subsection (2) refers to setting aside a fund for any pecuniary legacies bequeathed by the will. However, s 49(1) of the Act provides that 'where any person dies leaving a will effectively disposing of part of his property, this Part of this Act shall have effect as respects the part of his property not so disposed of ...'. The Part referred to is Part IV, whereas s 33 is in Part III. Notwithstanding the apparent conflict between the two sections, it is considered that a court would impose a trust under s 33(1) in a partial intestacy.

What is the position if the will imposes an express trust? It may be that the terms of the trust imposed by the will are identical to the statutory implied trust, in which event there is no problem. However, the terms may differ, in which event it is probable that the terms of the express trust will prevail.

IS A TRUST FOR SALE NECESSARY IN A WILL?

16.3   It is very common for the draftsman of a will to impose a trust for sale on the residue, thereby causing some lay clients to complain that they do not want all their property to be sold. In what circumstances is it desirable to impose a trust for sale?

If all the beneficiaries are of full age and capacity, there is no need to give the residue to trustees to hold on trust for the beneficiaries, or to impose a trust for sale.

It used to be the case that, if there was a possibility that infants would be entitled, and land would be included in the estate, there would be a Settled Land Act settlement unless a trust for sale was imposed (s 1(1)(ii)(d) of the Settled Land Act 1925). There was also a Settled Land Act settlement if land was given to beneficiaries in succession.

Since Settled Land Act settlements can no longer be created as a result of the Trusts of Land and Appointment of Trustees Act 1996, there would seem to be no point in imposing a trust for sale as far as land is concerned.

However, the 1996 Act only applies to land, so if there are assets other than land, then the trustees have no implied power to postpone sale Therefore it is a good idea to include such a power.

MONUMENT, TOMB AND ANIMAL CASES

16.4   Testators may wish to provide for the maintenance of their tombs after their deaths, or for the care of a much loved pet. There are various objections to these trusts. It is essential that a trust should have a beneficiary. In *Morice v Bishop of Durham (1804) 9 Ves 399* Sir William Grant said at pages 404–405:

'There can be no trust over the exercise of which this court will not assume control; for an uncontrollable power of disposition would be ownership and not trust. If there be a clear trust but for uncertain objects the property, that is the subject of the trust, is undisposed of ... But this doctrine does not hold good with regard to trusts for charity. Every other trust must have a definite object. There must be somebody in whose favour the court can decree performance.'

These trusts may also infringe the perpetuity period, and they may also be void on the ground that the purpose is not defined with sufficient certainty.

Notwithstanding these objections, the courts have been prepared to uphold some of these trusts. It is now accepted that testators can make provision for the maintenance of a tomb or monument. In *Pirbright v Sawley [1896] WN 86* the testator bequeathed some consols to the rector and churchwardens of a church for the maintenance of an inclosure in which the testator wanted to be buried. It was held that the gift was valid for at least a period of 21 years from the death of the testator.

It should be noted that s 1 of the Parish Councils and Burial Authorities (Miscellaneous Provisions) Act 1970 provides that a burial authority or a local authority may agree with any person in consideration of the payment of a sum of money by him, to maintain a monument or other memorial to any person situated in any place within the area of the authority to which the authority has a right of access. However, the agreement may not impose on the authority an obligation with respect to maintenance for a period exceeding 99 years from the date of the agreement.

Gifts for the maintenance of animals have also been upheld. In *Re Dean (1889) 41 Ch D 552* the testator devised his freehold estates to trustees subject to an annuity payable to his trustees for 50 years. The trustees were to use the annuity for the maintenance of his horses and hounds. It was held that the trust was valid.

Other purpose trusts have also been held to be valid, for example for the saying of masses, or the promotion of fox hunting.

As mentioned earlier, an objection to these trusts is that they infringe the rule that there must be certainty of objects. Draftsmen need to be wary of this requirement when drafting such trusts. In *Re Endacott [1960] Ch 232* the testator gave his residuary estate to the North Tawton Parish Council for the purpose of providing some useful memorial to himself. It was held that the gift failed; one of the reasons for the gift failing was that the purpose was of far too wide and uncertain a nature to qualify as an enforceable trust.

FULLY SECRET TRUSTS

16.5   It may be that a testator will wish to benefit a beneficiary without naming that beneficiary. This can be done by means of a fully secret trust. In *Ottaway v Norman [1972] Ch 698* Brightman J said at page 711:

> 'The essential elements which must be proved are: (i) the intention of the testator to subject the primary donee to an obligation in favour of the secondary donee; (ii) communication of that intention to the primary donee; (iii) the acceptance of that obligation by the primary donee either expressly or by acquiescence. It is immaterial whether these elements precede or succeed the will of the donor.'

However, in *Wallgreave v Tebbs (1855) 2 K & J 313* it was held that the trust must be communicated before the death of the testator. Wood V-C said at pages 322 and 326:

> 'Here the devisees knew nothing of the intention of the testator until after his death … the case is reduced to one in which the testator has relied solely on the honour of the devisees, who as far as this court is concerned, are left perfectly at liberty to apply the property to their own purposes … .'

Thus if the trust is not communicated during the lifetime of the testator, the devisees or legatees take the property absolutely. Furthermore, the details of the trust must be communicated before death, even if in a sealed envelope. If trust is communicated during the lifetime of the testator, but the details are not communicated, there will be a resulting trust in favour of the estate of the testator (*Re Boyes (1884) 26 Ch D 531*).

There is some doubt as to whether a trustee himself can take the property. In *Re Tyler [1967] 1 WLR 1269* a secret trust was created *inter vivos*. The trustee prepared a memorandum to the effect that he was entitled to £500. Whilst the memorandum was admissible in evidence, the court was not prepared to rely on it as the trustee stood in a quasi-professional relationship to the donor (he was employed in a solicitor's office). In addition, Pennycuick J thought that the trustee might have been confused.

HALF SECRET TRUSTS

16.6   These occur where there is a gift to a beneficiary, but it is clear from the will that the beneficiary is intended to be a trustee. The beneficiary will be forced to hold the property on trust for those people whom the testator has specified should benefit. In *Blackwell v Blackwell [1929] AC 318* the testator executed a codicil giving a legacy to five persons on trust to invest according to their discretion and 'to apply the income ... for the purposes indicated by me to them'. The testator orally communicated the terms of the trust to the legatees. It was held that they were bound by the trust.

Although there is some doubt about it, it appears that the trust must be communicated before the will is executed (see *Re Keen [1937] Ch 236* at page 246).

If there is a half secret trust, it is doubtful whether the trustee can benefit under the trust. In *Re Rees [1950] 1 Ch 204* the testator created a half secret trust. It was held that the trustees were not entitled to the balance after giving effect to the wishes of the testator. The argument that it was a conditional gift was rejected, the condition being that the beneficiaries should give effect to the wishes of the testator. Evidence that the testator intended the trustees to take was held inadmissible because it conflicted with the express terms of the will. The court also expressed the view that if the testator intended the solicitor who drafted the will to take, that intention should appear plainly on the will.

MUTUAL WILLS

16.7   In *Healey v Brown [2002] WTLR 849* W and H were joint tenants of their matrimonial home. They made mutual wills under which they left their interest in the house to each other, and then to the claimant. The residue of the estate went to B, who was the son of the defendant by a previous marriage. W died first, and H then transferred the house into the joint names of himself and B. On his death, the claimant alleged that he held the house on trust for the claimant and himself. It was held that this was correct.

However, there must be clear evidence of an intention to create mutual wills, and the mere fact that spouses make mirror image wills does not mean that they have made mutual wills. In *Birch v Curtis [2002] 2 F.L.R. 847* H and W had both been married before. They made wills in 1986. W died first, and H remarried. He subsequently made further wills. On his death, W's children alleged that where H and W had agreed to make wills in a certain format, the doctrine of mutual wills applied. It was held that this was not the case.

THE DUTIES AND POWERS OF EXECUTORS AND ADMINISTRATORS

16.8   The authority of executors commences at the moment of death, and so they can dispose of the estate of the deceased immediately after the death. In practice, although there are some assets which the executors can dispose of without a grant, such as personal chattels, it will be necessary to produce the grant in order to sell most assets, for example land.

Administrators do not derive any authority from a will, and so they have no power until authorised by the court to act. Once the personal representatives have been granted letters of administration, their authority may date back to the date of death.

Section 25 of the Administration of Estates Act 1925 provides that the personal representatives of a deceased person are under a duty to:

(a)   collect and get in the real and personal estate of the deceased and administer it according to law;

(b)   when required to do so by the court, exhibit on oath in the court a full inventory of the estate and when so required render an account of the administration of the estate to the court; and

(c)   when required to do so by the High Court, deliver up the grant of probate or administration to that court.

Section 39 of the Administration of Estates Act 1925 provides that personal representatives have wide powers, discretions and duties in dealing with the real and personal estate of the deceased. Section 39(1A) (inserted by the Trustee Act 2000) provides that s 39(1) is without prejudice to the powers conferred on personal representatives by the Trustee Act 2000.

It should be noted that whilst at least two trustees are required to give a valid receipt for capital money arising out of the sale of land (s 14 of the Trustee Act 1925), a sole personal representative can give a valid receipt for capital money (s 27(2) of the Law of Property Act 1925).

TAXATION

Inheritance tax

Death estate

16.9   Section 4(1) of the Inheritance Tax Act 1984 provides that on the death of any person tax shall be charged as if, immediately before his death, he had made a transfer of value and the value transferred by it had been equal to the value of his estate immediately before his death. The rate of tax is determined by cumulating all the PETS and *inter vivos* chargeable transfers in the seven years preceding the date of death. If they amount to more than the nil rate band, the whole of the estate is taxable at 40 per cent; if less, the unused part of the nil rate band can be offset against the death estate, and only the balance will be taxable at 40 per cent.

Potentially exempt transfers

16.10   Since 22 March 2006 a potentially exempt transfer is a transfer of value:

(a)   which is made by an individual on or after 22 March 2006; and

(b)   which, apart from this section, would be a chargeable transfer (or to the extent to which, apart from this section, it would be such a transfer); and

(c)   to the extent that it constitutes either a gift to another individual or a gift into a disabled trust or a gift into a bereaved minor's trust on the coming to an end of an immediate post death interest.

Gifts to individuals and to trustees of a trust for a disabled person are thus PETS. In addition, if a life interest under an immediate post death interest terminates during the lifetime of the life tenant, and a trust for a bereaved minor comes into existence, then the life tenant will make a PET.

If the donor survives for seven years after making a PET, no IHT is payable. If the donor dies within the seven years, IHT is payable. However, tapering relief may operate to reduce the amount of IHT payable (s 7(4)). The amount of relief is:

PET within 0–3 years of death   100% of IHT payable – no reduction.
                3–4   80%
                4–5   60%
                5–6   40%
                6–7   20%

Note that tapering relief only reduces the amount of IHT payable; it does not reduce the value for IHT purposes, nor does it affect the value for cumulation purposes.

In order to determine the rate of tax on death, the PET must be cumulated with:

(a)   all *inter vivos* chargeable transfers made in the seven years preceding the PET; and

(b)   previous PETs provided they are within seven years of death.

16.10 *Passing of property on death*

If a PET was made more than seven years before death, the PET is ignored for all IHT purposes.

Examples

a e = annual exemption

(i)	1997	*inter vivos* chargeable transfer
	1998	PET
	2003	PET
	2006	Death

It will be necessary to calculate the IHT payable on the 2003 PET.

It will have to be cumulated with the 1997 *inter vivos* chargeable transfer, but not the 1998 PET as this was more than seven years before death.

(ii)	2003	*inter vivos* chargeable transfer £106,000
	2005	PET £306,000
	2006	Death

No IHT is payable on the *inter vivos* chargeable transfer as it is within the nil rate band.

How much of nil rate band is left to offset against the 2005 PET?

Assume nil rate band is		£300,000
Deduct 2003 *inter vivos* chargeable transfer	£106,000	
Less a e x 2 (if not used in one year, annual exemption or balance of annual exemption can be carried forward to next year)	£6,000	£100,000
		£2000,000
2005 PET		£306,000
Less a e x 2		£6,000
		£300,000
Less balance of nil rate band		£2000,000
		£100,000
IHT at 40% =		£40,000
(iii) 2001 PET		£506,000
2006 Death		
PET		£506,000
Less a e x 2		£6,000

Assume nil rate band is	£300,000
	£500,000
Less nil rate band	£300,000
	£200,000
IHT at 40% =	£80,000
4–5 years: 60% of tax payable £80,000 =	£48,000

Note that the rates of IHT payable are the rates in force at the date of death, unless they have increased.

The value on which IHT is payable in the case of a PET is the value at the date of the gift; thus the value is frozen. Relief is available if the asset has gone down in value since the date of the gift. Thus, even if the donor is not likely to survive for seven years, it is still a good idea to give away assets which may increase in value.

It may be possible to insure against the donor dying within seven years of the PET.

Gifts with reservation of benefit

16.11   Be careful not to infringe the rules relating to gifts with reservation of benefit – otherwise the PET will be ineffective as far as saving IHT is concerned.

Section 102 of Finance Act 1986 applies where an individual disposes of any property by way of gift and either:

(a)   possession and enjoyment of the property are not bona fide assumed by the donee at or before the beginning of the relevant period; or

(b)   at any time in the relevant period the property is not enjoyed to the entire exclusion, or virtually to the entire exclusion, of the donor and of any benefit to him by contract or otherwise.

The effect of these provisions is that such a gift is ineffective as far as IHT is concerned; at the date of death the donor will still be deemed to own the property. Furthermore, the original gift is still a PET. This means that if the donor dies within seven years of the gift, there is a potential double charge to tax, on the failed PET and the house as part of the estate of the donor. However, tax is not charged twice – the amount payable is the higher of the IHT payable once the IHT has been calculated on the basis that it is a failed PET and on the basis that the house is part of the death estate. Note that the donee still owns the property for other purposes, and so there will be no free uplift to market value for CGT purposes when the donor dies.

If the donor releases the reserved benefit, it will be deemed to be a PET as from the date when the reservation was released.

The Finance Act 1999 inserted special provisions dealing with land. Section 102A(2) provides that at any time in the relevant period when the donor or spouse enjoys a significant right or interest, or is party to a significant arrangement in relation to the land:

(a)   the interest disposed of is referred to (in relation to the gift and the donor) as property subject to a reservation; and

(b)   section 102(3) and (4) above shall apply.

Section 102A(3) provides that subject to subsections (4) and (5), a right, interest or arrangement in relation to land is significant for the purposes of subsection (2) if (and only if) it entitles or enables the donor to occupy all or part of the land, or to enjoy some right in relation to all or part of the land, otherwise than for full consideration in money or money's worth.

Subsection (4) provides that a right, interest or arrangement is not significant for the purposes of subsection (2) if:

(a)   it does not and cannot prevent the enjoyment of the land to the entire exclusion, or virtually to the entire exclusion, of the donor; or

(b)   it does not entitle or enable the donor to occupy all or part of the land immediately after the disposal, but would do so were it not for the interest disposed of.

Subsection (5) provides that a right or interest is not significant for the purposes of subsection (2) if it was granted or acquired before the period of seven years ending with the date of the gift.

These provisions tightened the statutory provisions with regard to houses. It is not now possible for donors to grant themselves a lease at no rent, possibly via a nominee, and then give the freehold to children, and avoid the reservation of benefit. However, if the lease is granted for full consideration, then the reservation of benefit provisions will not apply.

Parents sometimes give a share in a house to a child living with them. The reservation of benefit provisions will not apply if:

(a)   the parents and the children occupy the land; and

(b)   the parents do not receive any benefit, other than a negligible one, which is provided by or at the expense of the children for some reason connected with the gift.

It is beyond the scope of this work to discuss tax planning opportunities with regard to the matrimonial home (for a fuller discussion please see 'Estate Planning for the Middle Income Client' by the author published by Tottel).

Capital gains tax

16.12   After death, it will be necessary for the personal representatives to settle any liability for CGT incurred by the deceased when he was alive. The personal representatives will of course be able to offset the deceased's annual exemption against the liability, and it may be that other exemptions and reliefs will be available.

Any losses incurred by the deceased can be offset against any gains made by the deceased in the tax year of death, but they cannot be carried forward and set off against any losses incurred by the personal representatives. However, s 62(2) of the Taxation of Chargeable Gains Act 1992 permits allowable losses sustained by an individual in the year of assessment in which he dies to be deducted from chargeable gains accruing to the deceased in the three years of assessment preceding the year of assessment in which the death occurs, taking chargeable gains accruing in a later year before those accruing in an earlier year.

The personal representatives are deemed to acquire the assets at market value at the date of death (s 62(1)). Normally the value for IHT purposes will be accepted as being the market value for both IHT and CGT. Frequently the personal representatives will vest the property in the legatees, in which event s 62(4) provides that no chargeable gain shall accrue to the personal representatives, but instead the legatees are treated as acquiring the asset at the market value at the date of death. 'Legatee' is widely defined in s 64(2) as including any person taking under a testamentary disposition or on an intestacy or partial intestacy, whether he takes beneficially or as trustee, and a person taking under a *donatio mortis causa* shall be treated (except for the purposes of s 62) as a legatee and his acquisition as made at the time of the donor's death. Section 64(1) permits the legatee to deduct:

(a)   any expenditure within s 38(2) incurred by him in relation to the transfer of the asset to him by the personal representatives or trustees; and

(b)   any such expenditure incurred in relation to the transfer of the asset by the personal representatives or trustees.

It may be necessary for the personal representatives to sell assets in order to complete the administration of the estate. Any gain will be computed in accordance with normal principles, and the personal representatives are entitled to the annual exemption for the year of death, and the two subsequent tax years; any gain will be subject to tax at 40 per cent. Note that s 64(1) does not apply in this situation, but the Revenue have issued Statements of Practice, SP 2/04, which contain a scale of permitted deductions. In addition, in *IRC v Richards Executors [1971] 1 WLR 571* executors paid fees to solicitors for investigations, valuations, the obtaining of a confirmation in Scotland, and the resealing of the confirmation in England. It was held that the proportion of fees applicable to some stocks and shares was deductible in calculating the capital gains of the executors.

Personal representatives are not allowed to claim the private residence exemption, but they can still claim it if the house is occupied as his only or main residence by the beneficiary entitled to the house under the will or intestacy, and the beneficiary is entitled to at least 75% of the proceeds of sale. The beneficiary must be living in the house before and after death.

Sections 178 and 179 of the Inheritance Tax Act 1984 provide that if shares quoted on the Stock Exchange or the Unlisted Securities Market are sold at a loss within 12 months of death, the lower value can be substituted for IHT purposes. Where this is done, the lower value also becomes the acquisition value of the personal representatives for CGT purposes, so that they cannot claim loss relief as well. There is a similar provision with regard to the sale of land within four years of death, but it is unclear whether the sale price also becomes the acquisition value for CGT purposes as well. Section 187 of the Inheritance Tax Act 1984 provides that the market value for the purposes of CGT of shares for which the relief is claimed shall be their sale value; there is no similar provision with regard to land, and so it could be argued that the lower value did not have to be substituted for CGT purposes. However, s 274 of the Taxation of Chargeable Gains Act 1992 provides that where on the death of any person inheritance tax is chargeable on the value of his estate immediately before his death and the value of an asset has been ascertained (whether in any proceedings or otherwise) for the purposes of that tax, the value so ascertained shall be taken for the purposes of this Act to be the market value of that asset at the date of death. Thus it is probable that personal representatives cannot claim a loss for both CGT and IHT as far as land is concerned. (See Barlow, King & King *Wills Administration and Taxation*, 7th edition, Sweet & Maxwell, page 229.)

Note that losses incurred by personal representatives cannot be transferred to beneficiaries.

Income tax

Income arising before death

16.13   It is the duty of personal representatives to ensure that any income tax due to the date of death is paid or, if a repayment is due, that it is claimed (s 74(1) of the Taxes Management Act 1970). Payment or repayment may affect the amount of IHT due on death.

The personal representatives should report the death to the Inspector of Taxes, and submit a return for the period from 6 April to the date of death. The Revenue can assess personal representatives within three tax years from the end of the tax year in which death occurred; assessments can go back six years from date of assessment.

Personal allowances

16.14 The deceased is entitled to full personal allowances for the year of death.

How do you distinguish between income of the deceased and income of the estate?

16.15 The crucial date is the date when it is due. For succession purposes it may have to be apportioned, but for income tax purposes the crucial date is the date when the payment should be made. For example, if a dividend was declared before death, but not paid until afterwards, it will be part of the income of the deceased.

Shares may be valued on a cum div basis with the result that the dividend may be subject to IHT. When the dividend is paid, it will be subject to income tax. This can result in an element of double taxation. Section 669 of the Income Tax (Trading and other Income) Act 2005 affords some relief, but only to a residuary beneficiary who is absolutely entitled.

The administration period

16.16 This runs from the date of death to the date when the administration of the estate is complete, or in other words, when the residue is ascertained (s 653(1) of the Income Tax (Trading and other Income) Act 2005. The personal representatives are liable only for basic rate tax, but they cannot claim any personal allowances. However, they may be able to offset interest on money borrowed to pay IHT.

If basic rate tax has been deducted at source, it need not be included in any tax return by the personal representatives.

Note that the rule in *Re Earl of Chesterfield's Trusts* does not affect liability for income tax (see 3.3).

Taxation of beneficiaries

General legacies

16.17 General legacies usually do not carry interest or income. However, if interest is payable, it is assessable under Income Tax (Trading and other Income) Act 2005.

Specific legatees

16.18 Specific legatees are entitled to the income from the date of death, but they are not liable for income tax until the asset is vested in them. The income will then be taxed as part of the specific legatee's income in the year in which it arises.

If there is a specific gift of shares in a company, the beneficiary will be entitled to all the income as from the date of death. As the company paying the dividend will have deducted tax at 10% from the gross amount of the dividend, and this satisfies the basic rate liability of a beneficiary, there will be no further tax to pay if the beneficiary is a basic rate taxpayer. However, if the beneficiary is a higher rate taxpayer, then the beneficiary will have to pay additional tax.

Annuities

16.19 Annuities are chargeable under the Income Tax (Trading and other Income) Act 2005. The personal representatives should deduct tax at basic rates when paying.

Annuities may be expressed in different ways. For example:

 (i)   The annuitant is to have such sum as after deduction of basic rate income tax will leave £750.

 (ii) The annuitant is to have £750 free of income tax.

Residuary beneficiaries

16.20 The rules are now contained in Part 5 Chapter 6 of the Income Tax (Trading and other Income) Act 2005.

Residuary beneficiaries with a limited interest

16.21 The personal representatives deduct income tax at basic rate before paying it to a beneficiary, and the beneficiary includes the grossed up amount in his return. All the income paid to a beneficiary in a year of assessment is taxed in that year. Personal representatives should therefore be wary of saving up income, and paying it all in one tax year. It could mean that the beneficiary will have to pay a higher rate tax which he would not have had to pay if the income had been paid regularly.

Residuary beneficiaries with an absolute interest

16.22   Income tax is payable only on the income, not on distributions of capital. Personal representatives must calculate the residuary income each year. They must also calculate the amounts of income paid to the beneficiary in previous tax years and, if this exceeds the total residuary income to which the beneficiary was entitled, the beneficiary is deemed to have an assumed income entitlement of the excess. Any payment in respect of the interest in a tax year will include the assumed income entitlement.

TAX CONSEQUENCES OF DIFFERENT GIFTS

Spouse – absolute or life interest?

Inheritance tax

16.23   It makes no difference, as far as IHT is concerned, whether the spouse has an absolute interest or an immediate post death interest. The spouse exemption applies in both circumstances. (For a discussion of immediate post death interests, see chapter 13 para 13.24)

If the spouse has an absolute interest, the spouse can make use of the *inter vivos* exceptions from IHT and, in addition, can make PETs. A spouse with an immediate post death interest can also do so if the trustees' powers are wide enough so that they can terminate the life interest. Each termination would be a compulsory PET by the life tenant of whatever proportion of the trust assets he or she had to give up.

Capital gains tax

16.24   Where a spouse has an absolute interest, any gain belongs to the spouse.

Where a spouse has a life interest, any gain belongs to the trustees. The trustees will be entitled to a maximum of one half the annual exemption, but the rate of tax on the gains will be 40 %.

The spouse will also be entitled to the annual exemption in his or her own right.

Income tax

16.25   It makes no difference, as far as income tax is concerned, whether the spouse has an absolute interest or only a life interest.

Nil rate band gift

16.26   A very effective method of saving IHT is for the will to contain a legacy up to the nil rate band to the children, with the residue to the spouse.

Note the following points:

- PETs and *inter vivos* chargeable transfers made in the seven years before death will reduce the nil rate band.

- Be careful not to exceed the nil rate band – grossing up may apply if there is a gift free of tax to children or grandchildren with the residue going to the spouse.

- Consider imposing a limit on the legacy in case the nil rate band is substantially increased.

- Be careful also to ensure that a nil rate band legacy does not include agricultural property and business property qualifying for 100 % relief.

Mini or nil rate band discretionary trusts

16.27   This is where an amount not exceeding the nil rate band is settled on a discretionary trust for the benefit of the spouse and children and grandchildren.

Inheritance tax

16.28   No inheritance tax will be payable on creation. However, if the amount given to the trustees exceeds the amount of the nil rate band, or the nil rate band has been exhausted by other gifts in the seven years up to the date of death, or other gifts in the will, IHT will be payable.

There is a possibility of a charge on distributions and on each tenth anniversary. However, the amount of IHT payable should be small.

When a beneficiary dies, the trust property will not form part of the beneficiary's estate for IHT purposes.

It is common for trustees to create nil rate band discretionary trusts in wills, not with the intention that assets to the value of the nil rate band should be transferred to the trustees, but that the trustees should instead take an IOU from the surviving spouse, possibly supported by a charge over the equitable interest of the first spouse to die. When the surviving spouse dies, the IOU is deductible from the estate of the surviving spouse, in effect preserving the nil rate band of the first spouse to die. These trusts are considered in more detail in 'Estate Planning for the Middle Income Client' by the author, published by Tottel.

Capital gains tax

16.29   The trustees will be entitled to a maximum of half of the annual exemption available to an individual. If the trustees dispose of any assets, and become liable to CGT, the rate of tax is 40%. If the trustees distribute the capital in the trust, there will be a deemed disposal of those assets at market value, and if this results in a liability for CGT, the trustees should ensure that they retain enough assets to meet that liability. Hold over relief may be available whatever the nature of the assets.

Death normally wipes out any capital gain, so that a beneficiary acquires the assets at market value as at the date of death. This will not happen with discretionary trusts.

Income tax

16.30   The trustees will pay income tax at 40 % on all income apart from dividend income, when the rate is 32.5%, but if the income is paid to a beneficiary, the beneficiary will receive a tax credit for the tax paid by the trustees. If the beneficiary is not a basic rate taxpayer, that beneficiary will be able to recover at least some of the tax paid. If the beneficiary is a higher rate taxpayer, then the beneficiary will not have to pay any more as the income has already been taxed at higher rates.

For a more detailed discussion, readers are referred to Chapter 13 above.

Two-year discretionary trust

Inheritance tax

16.31   Section 144 of the Inheritance Tax Act 1984 provides that any termination of a discretionary trust within two years of death is not a transfer of value for IHT purposes. Any termination is read back into the will.

IHT may have to be paid on the death of the testator. If there is an appointment in favour of the spouse, the spouse exemption will apply.

Any appointment must not be made within three months of death. The reason for this is that s 65(4) provides that there is no charge when property leaves the settlement if the event in question occurs within a quarter beginning with the day on which the settlement commenced. Section 144(2) provides that the section does not apply in that situation.

However, the appointment can now be made within three months if the appointment would result in an immediate post death interest or a trust for a bereaved minor or an 18 to 25 trust.

Capital gains tax

16.32   There is no special treatment for CGT purposes, so if the trustees hand out any asset other than cash, there will be a deemed disposal at market value of that asset, and if the asset has increased in value, there is a potential liability for capital gains tax. However, holdover relief is available if the assets are business assets which would usually qualify for this relief unless it is a settlor interested trust.

Absolute gifts to children and grandchildren

Inheritance tax

16.33   If the beneficiary dies under the age of 18, the property will still form part of the beneficiary's estate for IHT purposes. However, there will be no charge when the beneficiary attains 18, or if the trustees exercise their power of advancement under s 32 of the Trustee Act 1925, or an express power of advancement.

Capital gains tax

16.34   Any gain made by the trustees will belong to the beneficiary. There will not be a deemed disposal when the beneficiary attains 18.

Income tax

16.35   Trustees pay income tax at basic rate; depending on his or her income, the beneficiary will be able to recover the tax paid, or may be liable to higher rate tax.

Contingent gifts to children

Inheritance tax

16.36   It has been very common for testators to give legacies to children or
grandchildren contingent on attaining a certain age –18, 21, or 25. Strictly they
should have been taxed as if they were trusts without an interest in possession or
discretionary trusts. This meant that inheritance tax would have to be paid on
their creation during someone's lifetime if the assets transferred were in excess
of the nil rate band, or the nil rate band had been absorbed by other discretionary
trusts in the seven years prior to the one you are dealing with. In addition there
would be a charge to inheritance tax every ten years and also whenever any
capital was paid out from the trust by the trustees.

Such trusts usually became accumulation and maintenance settlements, and
received special treatment as far as IHT was concerned. The special treatment
was that if they were created in a lifetime settlement it was not a chargeable
disposal for inheritance tax purposes, but was treated as a PET. If the accumulation and maintenance settlement was created in a will, then the normal rules for
the taxation of an estate on death applied. IHT was payable if the death estate
was large enough, or if the NRB has been absorbed by lifetime gifts. However,
once the accumulation and maintenance trust was going, there was no further
charge to inheritance tax.

This special treatment will now only apply to trusts for bereaved minors.

What is a bereaved minor? A 'bereaved minor' is defined as a person who has
not yet attained the age of 18 and at least one of whose parents has died. A
step-parent and someone with parental responsibility for a child also come
within the definition of parent and so can also create such a settlement.

Various conditions have to be satisfied before a trust will be treated as a trust for
bereaved minors. The most important points are that it is only parents who can
create such a trust. In addition, the trust must be in a will. Furthermore, the
children must become absolutely entitled to everything in the trust on attaining
the age of 18.

So if grandparents create a trust for the benefit of grandchildren, it will be taxed
as if it was a trust without an interest in possession.

If parents create a trust during their lifetime for the benefit of the children
contingent on attaining the age of 18, then again it will be taxed as if it were a
trust without an interest in possession.

What about the statutory trusts which arise on intestacy? Do they qualify for the
special treatment?

The answer is yes, provided the beneficiary is a bereaved minor, which means that one or both of the parents must be dead.

Special treatment is given to 18 to 25 trusts. These are trusts where the contingency is attaining the age not greater than 25. This means that if there is a gift to a bereaved minor contingent on them attaining the age of 25, there will be a charge to IHT when the child attains 25. The rate of tax will be 4.2% in so far as the assets are in excess of the NRB.

This treatment only applies to settlements created by parents for the benefit of their children. In addition, the settlement must be in a will.

Capital gains tax

16.37   The trustees are entitled to a maximum of half the annual exemption available to an individual; the rate of tax is 40 %.

When a beneficiary satisfies the contingency and becomes absolutely entitled, there is a deemed disposal by the trustees at market value. Holdover relief may be available for any assets; this is discussed in more detail in Chapter 13 para 13.33.

Income tax

16.38   Trustees will pay income tax at 40 %. The beneficiary may be able to recover this tax; alternatively, the beneficiary may be liable for more if his income is large enough. Once a beneficiary is entitled to an interest in possession (at the age of 18 if s 31 applies), the trustees will only be liable for basic rate tax.

Free of tax legacies

16.39   The basic rule is that any gift in a will of property in the UK is free of IHT. However, if a legacy is tax-free, and the residue goes to an exempt beneficiary, the legacy will have to be grossed up.

VARIATIONS AND DISCLAIMERS

Inheritance tax

16.40   Section 142(1) of the Inheritance Tax Act 1984 provides that:

'Where within the period of two years after a person's death:

(a) any of the dispositions (whether effected by will, under the law relating to intestacy or otherwise) of the property comprised in his estate immediately before his death are varied, or

(b) the benefit conferred by any of those dispositions is disclaimed,

by an instrument in writing made by the persons or any of the persons who benefit or would benefit under the dispositions, the Act shall apply as if the variation had been effected by the deceased or, as the case may be, the disclaimed benefit had never been conferred.'

Variations

16.41 Note the following points with regard to variations:

- Section 142(1) applies to both intestacies and wills.

- A surviving joint tenant can use s 142(1).

- The variation must be made within two years of the date of death.

- There must be an instrument in writing.

- The section does not apply to a settlement where the deceased was the life tenant.

- The section does not permit the variation of a gift where the deceased reserved a benefit.

- The section does not apply if consideration was given for the variation. An indemnity as regards IHT or income tax might infringe this provision.

- The parties to a variation must be of full age and capacity. If not, the court may be prepared to sanction a variation under the Variation of Trusts Act 1958; to be effective, any order must be made within two years of death.

- If extra IHT is payable, the personal representatives must join in the election.

- Once property has been varied, it cannot be varied again; however, there can be several variations as long as the property is different.

It used to be the case that notice of an election claiming the benefit of s 142 had to be given to the Revenue within six months of the deed of variation. This is not necessary in respect of deeds of variation entered into after 1 August 2002. The election must now be contained in the deed of variation, and notice given to the Capital Taxes Office if more IHT is payable. Presumably those interested will also notify the Capital Taxes Office if a refund is due.

Disclaimers

16.42   Any beneficiary can refuse to accept a gift, unless he has expressly or impliedly accepted the gift, or fails to disclaim within a reasonable time. As long as gifts are not connected in some way, a beneficiary can accept one gift and refuse another. If a non-residuary gift is disclaimed, the gift becomes part of the residue; if a residuary gift is disclaimed, the property passes to those persons entitled under the intestacy rules.

Section 142 applies to disclaimers as well as variations.

Capital gains tax

16.43   Section 62(6) of the Taxation of Chargeable Gains Act 1992 provides that:

> 'Where within the period of two years after a person's death any of the dispositions (whether effected by will, under the law relating to intestacy or otherwise) of the property of which he was competent to dispose are varied, or the benefit conferred by any of those dispositions is disclaimed, by an instrument in writing made by the persons or any of the persons who benefit under the dispositions:
>
> (a)   the variation or disclaimer shall not constitute a disposal for the purposes of this Act; and
>
> (b)   this section shall apply as if the variation had been effected by the deceased or, as the case may be, the disclaimed benefit had never been conferred.'

It should be noted that the section applies to property held by the deceased as a joint tenant.

Section 62(7), as amended by Finance Act 2002, provides that subsection (6) does not apply to a variation unless the instrument contains a statement by the person making the instrument to the effect that they intend the subsection to apply to a variation. The amended s 62(7) applies to all deeds of variation entered into after 1 August 2002.

Income tax

Variations

16.44   Income arising between the date of death and the variation belongs to the original beneficiary. Income arising after variation belongs to the substituted beneficiary.

A variation may be deemed to be a settlement, and the anti-avoidance provisions in the Income and Corporation Taxes Act 1988 may apply.

Disclaimers

16.45   The income belongs to the beneficiary who takes as a result of the disclaimer.

SUMMARY

16.46

- A trust will usually be imposed if a person dies wholly or partially intestate.

- Trusts for the maintenance of tombs or the care of animals may be valid.

- It is possible to have a fully or half secret trust in a will.

- Executors have authority from the moment of death, whereas administrators derive their authority from the grant.

- IHT is payable on the death estate; the rate of tax depends on the *inter vivos* transfers.

- No CGT is payable on death.

- The personal representatives are liable for income tax on all income received during the administration period.

- Beneficiaries are liable for income tax on the income due to them.

- For IHT and CGT purposes variations and disclaimers will be read back into the will if various conditions are satisfied.

Chapter 17

Co-owners of commercial property, personal injury compensation trusts, asset protection trusts, trust deeds and debentures

Trusts often arise in the commercial world. Some of these have already been mentioned – pensions, life insurance and employee share ownership. They also arise in other contexts, which are considered here.

PARTNERS

17.1   If partners in a business purchase an office or factory or other land to be used by the partnership business, then the property may become partnership property, or it may remain the personal property of the partners. In either case the partners will almost certainly be tenants in common in equity.

If the property becomes partnership property, s 20(1) of the Partnership Act 1890 provides that partnership property must be held and applied by the partners exclusively for the purposes of the partnership and in accordance with the partnership agreement.

Whether or not the property has become partnership property, the legal estate will be vested in not more than four partners as joint tenants to hold in trust for themselves and any other partners entitled in equity. If the property is partnership property, then it must be applied solely for the purposes of the partnership and in accordance with s 20(1) of the Partnership Act 1890.

As the partners in whom the legal estate is vested are trustees, they are of course subject to all the duties owed by trustees towards beneficiaries, and must act in the best interests of the beneficiaries.

Disputes between commercial co-owners are governed by the Trusts of Land and Appointment of Trustees Act 1996 (see Chapter 9).

In *Rodway v Landy [2001] Ch 703* R and L were in partnership as medical practitioners. They owned the premises from which they practised as tenants in common in equity. They fell out, and L terminated the partnership. It was held that the premises were not partnership property, and R applied for the sale of the property to her, whereas L applied for an order partitioning the property.

It was held that a sale of the property to R would contravene the prohibition on the sale of goodwill under the National Health Service Act 1977, and it was ordered that the premises be partitioned.

PERSONAL INJURY COMPENSATION TRUSTS

17.2   It may be that a person lacking mental capacity or someone who is under age is entitled to an award of damages for personal injuries. Under s 96(1)(d) of the Mental Health Act 1983 the Court of Protection must approve any compromise agreement about the amount of damages. When the Mental Capacity Act 2005 comes into force the Court or a Deputy appointed by the Court will be able to approve the compromise.

Frequently the damages awarded will be administered by a receiver appointed by the Court of Protection, but in some cases it may be more appropriate for the damages to be made the subject of a discretionary trust.

The person entitled to the award will be treated as the settlor for the purposes of the anti-avoidance provisions contained in the Income Tax (Trading and other Income Act 2005 s 624, and the Taxation of Chargeable Gains Act 1992. This means that any income or capital gains accruing to the trustees will be deemed to belong to the settlor, and taxed as part of his or her income.

Inheritance tax

17.3   As far as inheritance tax is concerned, the settlement will probably come within the definition of trust for disabled persons (see chapter 13 for a full discussion of these trusts), with the consequence that when the person entitled to the damages dies, the whole of the trust property will be subject to IHT.

Although the position is not altogether clear, it seems that the capital of such a settlement will be ignored when considering claims for assistance with residential homes costs, but the income will not be ignored. However, as most trusts for the disabled will give the trustees a discretion as to whether or not the income is applied for the benefit of the person entitled to the damages, only the income actually paid to that person will be considered.

It is usual for the trust deed to allow for there to be at least one professional trustee, to provide for the person entitled to the damages to be able to revoke the trust on regaining capacity, and to describe what is to happen to any of the trust funds left after the person entitled to the damages has died.

Asset protection trusts

17.4   Persons may want to make their property subject to some trust to protect their assets from various unforeseen events – e.g. bankruptcy, protection of spendthrift beneficiaries from themselves, protection of the assets if they have to enter a residential home.

Any person wishing to protect their own assets must have regard to the provisions of the Insolvency Act 1986 providing for the setting aside of transactions at an undervalue. The provisions about intentional deprivation of capital must also be considered if the person applies for assistance from the state, or help with care home fees.

It is not possible for a settlor to create a trust under which he is the life tenant if that life interest is to terminate on the bankruptcy of the settlor, although a provision that the life interest is to terminate if the settlor assigns charges or encumbers his life interest is valid.

Model protective trusts are set out in s 33 of the Trustee Act 1925, and if these trusts are used or express ones to similar effect, the life tenant is deemed to have an interest in possession for IHT purposes. Note that these provisions will not apply if some other trusts are used.

It is possible to protect assets by creating a life interest trust under which the trustees have power to terminate a life interest if the life tenant becomes bankrupt. A discretionary trust will also have the same effect. A member of the class of beneficiaries does not have any rights to any income or capital, so the trustees can decline to hand anything out to a beneficiary if appropriate.

Readers are referred to Chapter 13 for a detailed description of the taxation of trusts.

Trust deeds and debentures

17.5   A debenture is an acknowledgement by a company of indebtedness which may or may not be secured.

A trust deed is frequently used when a company is creating debentures, and in fact it is the only practical way of issuing a debenture if a large number of persons are going to be lenders. If it is intended that the security should be quoted, then it is a requirement of the rules of the Stock Exchange that a trust corporation should be appointed as trustee.

The trustee is subject to all the duties normally imposed on trustees; the main duty is to protect the interests of the lenders. The trustee will also hold any security given for the debenture, usually a fixed charge over the fixed assets, and a floating charge over the other assets.

The trust deed will contain provisions dealing inter alia with the procedure to be followed if there is any default by the company and prescribing what is meant by default by the company.

Index

Index

Index